Above and Beyond

A True Story

Above and Beyond

A true story of
two families,
whose sons
fought heroically
in some of the
bloodiest battles
of World War II

HOLLY SMIRL

The following account is inspired by true events. Some characters have been fictionalized. This book is not connected with or endorsed by any of the depicted characters, descendants or estates in any way.

Printed in the United States of America.

ISBN   978-1-7358696-2-9 (Paperback)
ISBN   978-1-7358696-1-2 (E-Book)
ISBN   978-1-7358696-3-6 (Paper Over Board)

My book may be purchased in bulk for promotional, educational, or business use.
Please contact Amazon sales at 1-888-280-4331

First Edition 2023

For Gary Perkins
who followed the airmen of WWII

Table of Contents

Introduction

$\mathcal{I}$N MAY, 1944, A CROWD waited expectantly while a brass band played the song, "The Stars and Stripes." The press box included reporters from the Seattle Times and Life Magazine. A cool spring breeze blew off the Duwamish River, rippling American flags. The huge airplane hangar doors opened at Boeing Aircraft Plant 2, in Seattle, Washington, as the nose of the new B-17G bomber emerged, pushed by hundreds of shop workers and riveters. The 30,000 pound B-17 heavy bombers were usually towed off the assembly line by tow vehicles, but today the proud men and women who had assembled her, were manually pushing the colorful plane onto the tarmac.

A little boy perched on his father's shoulders said, "It's painted like an Easter egg. Dad." The colorful signatures of 35,000 Seattle workers covered every inch of the bomber's fuselage, from the nose, to the tail section of the airplane.

It had been three arduous years since the war began. Today the Army wanted a celebration to uplift the public, including those tired workers in the aircraft industry. To them it wasn't just a job. They felt they were supporting their men and women fighting overseas. Producing the 5,000th B-17 Flying Fortress was a milestone of the designers, engineers, and the assembly line mechanics. The work at the Boeing aircraft plant was symbolic of

1

the nation's spirit of tenacity. Every propeller, landing gear, and turret was assembled by a worker at the plant. For them, it was personal. It had become a total national effort. It was something they could do for their brothers, husbands and sons who were overseas fighting, while they were on the homefront supplying the men with airplanes, tanks and armaments.

Since 1936 when the plant opened, workers came looking for jobs from all over the country, trying to escape unemployment from remnants of the Great Depression. After the attack on Pearl Harbor, men left to fight while women were left on the homefront. Those wives, mothers and sisters, found jobs in the massive war industry. At this particular Boeing Plant 2, American workers rolled up their sleeves and built airplanes. Banners which hung on the factory walls said, "Let's Get 'em Flying!" Women workers in overalls were called *Rosie the Riveter* in songs and newsreels. They found pride in their work as shown by encouraging notes left by workers inside the airplanes for pilots and crews to find. "GodSpeed" or "Give 'Em Hell," read the messages.

The proud men and women gathered for a photograph with the illustrated bomber, whose image would appear in theater newsreels, newspapers and a feature article in Life Magazine. Aircraft number 337716, so-named "5 Grand" was rolled out onto Boeing Field. A bottle of champagne was broken over her nose. The celebration was a much needed shot-in-the-arm for the American aircraft worker.

The English Prime Minister, Winston Churchill had asked America for help in the summer of 1940, during their desperate eleven-month-long Battle of Britain. The nightly bombing attacks by the Nazi Luftwaffe on the city of London were relentless and devastating. They were the pre-invasion groundwork of Adolph Hitler's campaign to eventually invade the islands of Great Britain. The English people desperately held on and fought back at home, but their soldiers and armaments were dangerously depleted.

5 Grand

U.S. President Roosevelt was in the middle of an election year with his constituents, the majority of whom were isolationists against involvement in the conflicts in Europe. He knew America would eventually be pulled into the war but he needed to win the election first. After his third term victory in 1941, he was able to get Congress to pass the Lend-Lease Program, to lend Great Britain twenty B-17 aircraft and other military equipment. Meanwhile American resources and factories started regularly supplying the Allies as well as building up their own bases and armaments.

The British Royal Air Force used the American B-17s to go on bombing raids into German occupied lands. In those first daytime raids, eight of the twenty planes were frustratingly lost due to engine problems and Nazi fighter attacks. The Boeing bombers were lacking in defensive guns and bomb capacity. With the British Royal Air Force dwindling they were forced to stop all daylight bombing and continue only on night raids.

In 1941, from those terrible losses came knowledge and fore-sight. The British performance feedback on those older B-17s from the Lend-Lease Program, helped Boeing engineers redesign the aircraft. The third generation model B-17G was supplied to the U.S. Army Air Force bases in England after the attack of December 7th, 1941, when Pearl Harbor was bombed by the Japanese. The B-17 had been upgraded with 13 powerful .50 caliber machine guns, a Bendix chin turret and a Cheyenne tail gunner turret for defense against posterior attacks.

Practically overnight U.S. factories converted to production plants, operating 24 hours a day, with streamlined assembly-line production. Many American factories retooled for the needs of their country at war. Auto plants in Detroit, Michigan, built tanks and jeeps instead of Ford and Studebaker automobiles. The B-24 Liberators and P-47 Thunderbolts fighters were built in factories across the country.

For two families, the Perkins from California and the Bouricius from Nebraska, the world would be inexorably changed as millions of young men and women signed up to join the military. Three of the Perkins family of eight, and five of the Bouricius family of nine would find themselves training in the military to go to war.

Lt. Perkins met Dottie Bourcius at a USO dance while he was training at Harvard AirForce Base. They met again at another officer's club dance and shared a few home cooked meals at the Bouricius home in Hastings. During Perk's 51 missions overseas their love grew through letters they wrote to each other.

Above and Beyond is the story of those two families who worked tirelessly on the homefront to support their children fighting in the wars in Europe and the Pacific. You will witness the heartbreak as each family loses one of their own. Their brothers would fight on in grief and against terrible odds, to help win the war. Lt. Perkins and his crew flew their B-17 airplane, *Dead Man's Hand*, out of

Rattlesden, England. They flew their first of 24 bombing missions for the Eighth Air Force and then signed up for a terrifying 27 more, in Foggia, Italy. They were bombing oil refineries and arms factories with enemy jet fighters and flak trying to shoot them down in Eastern Europe and Russia.

Dottie's two brothers worked on the Manhattan Project in New Mexico to produce the first nuclear weapon. She was, by chance, an eyewitness to the first atomic test on July 16th, 1945. That was just two weeks before the bombs were dropped on Hiroshima and Nagasaki, Japan, which would end the war.

World War II was one of the most catastrophic man-made disasters in history. Between 1939-1945, war erupted in Europe and in the Pacific, causing a clash of ideologies and cultures that would change the world forever. The war was fought by men and women around the world and in Germany, Japan, England and the U.S. using new warfare equipment never seen before. Unlike WWI, new designs in aircraft were developed, jet powered planes and nuclear weapons emerged. The Allies and Axis powers competed for natural resources, needed to sustain their arms factories. By January 1942, Hitler controlled 280 million people, over half the population in Europe. The Empire of Japan had conquered 20% of the world population, or 463 million people in the Pacific and China. The two powers seemed unstoppable until the United States entered the war and partnered with the Allied powers offering an endless supply of resources, arms and skilled labor.

Japanese Admiral Isoroku Yamamoto wrote in his diary after planning the December 1941 attack on Pearl Harbor, "I fear all we have done is to awaken a sleeping giant and fill him with a terrible resolve." Both Japan and Germany would soon find that to be true.

By June 1945, the total domestic product, resources and industry of the U.S. had surpassed the Axis and Allied powers combined. Germany and Japan had underestimated the U.S. and her Allies' spiritual and material wherewithal to fight back against the enemy and win.

Prior to 1940, the Army Air Corp had ordered a total aircraft production of less than 3,000 planes. By 1944 the Seattle Boeing Aircraft Plant 2 along with other U.S. factories had built 300,000 aircraft all over the country. In England flying night raids and the U.S. flying missions in the daytime, their combined around-the-clock bombing would defeat the Third Reich. The Japanese would later be stopped by the nuclear bomb.

Like millions of families across the United States, the war took the Perkins and Bouricius young people away to fight. Sadly, it became the youth who must inherit and shoulder the mad destruction of war.

1.

The Early Years—1938

SEVENTEEN YEAR-OLD Clarence Perkins sat on the porch swing of his house and scanned the morning sky, shading his eyes from the hot June sun. He first heard the faint sound of an airplane engine far off in the distance and figured it was somewhere over Muroc dry lake. He tracked the single engine mono wing, holding his breath as it passed over Quartz Hill. His dream of flying airplanes only got stronger from that week in 1927 when he listened to his family's Silvertone radio, mesmerized with the news of Charles Lindbergh's trans-Atlantic flight, New York to Paris. It was a daring undertaking by the little known pilot. Six men had already died attempting the same flight. Perk felt heart-stopping suspense waiting for the moment *Lindy* landed on French soil. After 33 hours in the air, he did land to cheering crowds of Parisians at Le Bourget Field. That single event fueled Perk's interest in aviation for years.

From the time he was eight years old, he devoured books from the library on airplanes and built several models out of scrap wood, including a single-engine aircraft like Lindbergh's Spirit of St. Louis.

Restless at 17, with still a year left at Antelope Valley High School before graduation, he knew somewhere in his future he would learn to fly. Tall with a red shock of unruly hair, Perk, as

Perk, sharing a
tortoise in class

Maurice, Chuck, Perk
and Richard

Perk's high
school photo

his friends called him, was the oldest of five brothers. Lillian and Fred Perkins lived with their boys in a block house they built in Quartz Hill, California.

The hot June desert winds were blowing dust and he squinted skyward as he watched the small plane pass over Muroc and recede toward the horizon. The low hum of the engine became inaudible and the aircraft faded into a faint speck until it disappeared.

He could hear his mom in the kitchen through the screen door. She had been up early rattling around in the kitchen, clanging pans, fixing breakfast for his dad and the brood of boys for which she left cereal and bowls on the table. She had to use the truck to drop his father off at his road construction job before going to work herself at the hospital. She called to his dad, "Fred, we are gonna be late." He said, "Lillian, what's in my lunch today?" Perk didn't hear the answer.

The back door slammed and he could hear the old black 1928 Ford truck back down the gravel driveway creating billows of dust. His dad sat in the passenger seat and his mother called to Perk as he stood on the porch. "Clarence, watch your brothers while we're gone," she enunciated loudly over the noisy thrashing of the engine."

Perk nodded, "Yes, Ma'am."

At the end of the driveway she turned onto Third Ave. Perk watched as the dust clouds followed the disappearing truck. Perk slumped down on the porch steps frustrated that he had to babysit his four younger brothers. He understood, everyone in the family had to help but it didn't make him happy. He was the oldest of the boys and therefore he had that job while his parents were at work. Maurice, his 14-year-old brother, was still asleep. Johnny had polio when he was younger and at 11, wore metal and leather braces on his legs and needed assistance putting them on. Richard was ten and Chuck was the youngest at eight-years-old.

With only three years between them, Maurice was the closest to Perk. The two oldest brothers looked alike with red hair and blue eyes. Maurice had a broad smile and a devilish sense of humor and loved a good practical joke, especially at the expense of his older brother. Perk would find interesting creatures lurking in his bed under the covers, planted there by Maurice. Finally when Perk retaliated by putting a pincher bug in Maurice's bed, that nipped the critter-jokes in the bud and Maurice never did it again.

When they were younger the brothers built forts, and roamed the desert landscape looking for buried treasure. Perk told Maurice the story; "Ancient pirates landed on Quartz Hill when it was an island in a vast ocean in 1542. They buried their wooden trunk of gold coins somewhere near our backyard with a plan to come back to get it later." Perk conveniently found a treasure map in the shed which could lead them to the pirates' treasure. The boys had hours of fun following the map and digging around the desert plateaus, searching behind their house.

Besides treasure adventures, they shared a love of animals and both rode the neighbor's horses in exchange for mucking out their horse stalls. Four years earlier, when Perk was 13 and Maurice was nine, the boys found an abandoned coyote pup in the desert and took it home. Their mom objected but they were determined to raise it, feeding the animal table scraps and walking it on a leash. It never quite became domesticated and eventually their father made them let it go when it bit the back of Maurice's hand. His Dad said, "Wild is wild and coyotes and dogs aren't the same."

On this first day of summer, Maurice resented being told what to do by his 17-year-old brother. He said, "I'm going over to Harry's house to see their new goats."

Perk tried to keep track of his temporary brood saying, "Be home before Mom gets home at five." Maurice grunted, and huffed away.

Perk promised his three younger brothers he would help them build a wooden race car for the Johnson's Drug Store Soap Box Derby, the next weekend. The boys had found some baby carriage wheels and yesterday their dad brought them home two steel axles. Their neighbor with the horse stable gave them some fence boards and a strong rope. With his father's hand saw, a box of rusted nails and an old can of blue paint, Perk and his brothers could make a competitive soap box car.

Louie Massari, Perk's best friend from school, lived a mile up Third Ave. He came over to help with the soap box car and brought some lag bolts. He and Perk had been classmates and buddies since 4th grade. On weekends they built a crystal set radio in Louie's garage. They had most of the parts except they still needed to find a diode or piece of galena or crystal to finish it. Perk loved being at Louie's house because he was from a big Italian family. When Perk came into the Massari kitchen, his mother, Maria, would give Perk a big bear hug and say, "You are too skinny. Come eat." And the aroma of lasagna and homemade bread made him salivate. Meals at the Massari's table were always so boisterous and animated. "What is this thing called a Soap Box Derby?" Donato, Louie's father asked, and then everyone would talk at once explaining what a soap box car was and how they were going to race it.

Perk and Louie could always find something fun and interesting to do like exploring old mines and tinkering on machinery in Louie's garage. He showed Perk how to fix the carburetor and brakes on his brother's old Model "A" Ford Coupe. Louie had a plan to own his own service station and garage someday, fixing cars and selling gas. With his friend's input, Perk thought their soap box car might be the best one in the derby.

Loud screaming came from Perk's back yard. He ran to break up a squabble between Richard and Chuck, who fought over who got to use the paint brush first. Perk found a second brush in the shed and the problem was solved. The desert temperatures had reached 90 degrees and Perk took a break and sat on a rusted porch swing, watching his brothers paint. He was impatient, hot and tired at how slow the day progressed and he picked up a week old local newspaper with headlines, "Nazi Germany Annexed Austria!" He wasn't really sure where Austria was. Probably, somewhere in Europe, he thought. He scanned the inside page, where an advertisement in a box caught his eye for a nearby dude ranch called *Rancho Oro Verdes*. "Raucous rodeos, a tavern, lively barn dances and a luxurious inn with a beautiful swimming pool." What piqued his interest most was a photograph of a waving pilot sitting in a biplane on the Rancho Oro Verdes airstrip. The caption boasted, "Come take a $2.00 airplane ride. Our airport is important to Antelope Valley for mail delivery, crop dusting and passengers. See a real working California dude ranch with cattle, horses and wrangler cowboys."

School was out for the summer and Perk wanted a real job. The dude ranch was by Muroc Air Base, not far from his house in Quartz Hill. He started thinking about a plan to pass off his duties as babysitter, to his 14-year-old brother, Maurice. Perk could work for pay, he thought. "If I offer half of my wages to help the family, my parents might agree." His real reason to work at the dude ranch was to be near the airplanes and airfield. If his parents agreed, he planned to ask his dad for a ride to the ranch this weekend.

Perk's parents were home by sunset and his mother prepared a quick meal of chicken fried steak and mashed potatoes. Dinner always started with a prayer in thanks for "the bountiful meal." His family of seven consumed the dinner plus a gallon of milk and two loaves of bread, standard at each meal. If someone was late for dinner, it was likely they didn't eat. After Perk helped wash the dishes, he sat on the porch with his mother and they listened to the night sounds of the desert.

Tonight it was a warm Friday evening and with the week's work done, his mother looked forward to the weekend and the potluck on Sunday at their Baptist church. After a long silence, out of the blue, she said, "I always regretted not being able to train as a nurse. My family, with six kids, had enough money for only my older sister, Mary, to go to teachers college. There wasn't enough for the rest of us to continue school. Mary had finished teachers college and was the pride of Lillian's family as a school teacher. Perk's mom worked at a hospital as an orderly, changing sheets, bringing food to patients and emptying bedpans. She thought of herself as a nurse but she didn't have the certificate. Perk understood that lament. Consequently, his mother's hopes of college and a prosperous future had transferred to her sons with a desire that they should go to college and do what she wasn't able to do. Perk pondered to himself, "I will go to college but how will that fit into my dreams of becoming a pilot?"

His mother sighed, listening to the cicadas and a distant coyote before she spoke. "When you were a baby, me and your father stayed with relatives in Texas." We had read about cheap land in California under *The Homestead Act* and we packed up and moved west when you were six months old." Perk remembered his mother's stories of his family going west. "Your dad got a good job as a sheriff and he was able to borrow money for a few acres here in Quartz Hill. We lived in a wooden and canvas lean-to on our land, while we built a cinder block house. It was so dusty with the desert winds." She frowned and looked down at her hands wistfully, "Life was hard. We lost your sister to Diptheria and your brother, Johnny, came down with Polio. Still the Lord blessed us with five sons." She was proud that all during those difficult years they had held on to their land with Fred working in the daytime and she working at night. Perk wanted a job, but now wasn't a good time to ask when his mother was talking about the hard times.

Lillian especially harbored a determination that her children wouldn't struggle as she and Fred had. Her sister Mary had married an accountant and they had bought a nice house in Los Angeles. She saw a path of prosperity, through education for her kids. College seemed like a way to better their lives. It had been out of reach for her but she would make sure it was available to her boys. Lillian asked Perk after graduation, next year, to promise that he would sign up for Antelope Valley College and he promised his mother he would.

Aunt Mary and Al were Perk's favorite aunt and uncle. They had moved to LA and came to visit his family often, in the high desert. Mary would describe Oklahoma during those dust bowl

Lillian Perkins   Fred Perkins   Perkins house at Quartz Hill

years of the 1920s. It was a hard life and people had no jobs or food. They got lung problems from the constant wind and dust. She told Perk that Lillian and Fred were the first of their family to go west. After college Mary moved to California with Lillian and Fred, until she found a job teaching. Perk didn't know why Mary never had any children but he figured that was why she adored him and his brothers. "You have taken the best features of both of your parents." She said, "You have Fred's strong angular face of his Blackfoot Indian ancestors and your mother's sweet Irish personality and thick red hair." Jokingly, she winked at him, "And you're smart, like me."

She described her sister, Lillian, as a tall beautiful girl. "She had pretty delicate Irish features and a shock of curly red hair. With that beauty and sweet personality, she captured your father's heart."

His aunt brought books to him and his brothers and Perk loved the stories of the Arabian Nights, Tom Sawyer, and Treasure Island. He read them all a couple of times.

Perk was right. This Saturday morning was a good time to ask his father if he could apply for a job at Rancho Oro Verde. Fred had some errands to do but agreed to drop him off at the dude ranch and come back for him in the afternoon.

Pancho Barnes and the Happy Bottom Riding Club

Fred left Perk at a small sign that said, *Rancho Oro Verde* and under it said Pancho's Fly-Inn. Perk walked down a long dirt road that ran along a field of alfalfa which led to a barn at the end. An older man in dirty ranch clothes and a cowboy hat was working on a fence.

Perk asked, "Excuse me, sir. Are you the owner?"

The man didn't look up from his work but replied, "Son, about all I own are the clothes you see me wearin. Now, hand me a shovel full of gravel and hold this fence post." Perk did what he was told, holding the post until the man could fill the post hole with cement and stabilize it so it wouldn't move.

"Thank you. Now you were sayin?"

Perk stuttered, "Sir, are you the owner of this dude ranch? I'd like a job… sir?" Gene looked him up and down and then looked toward the barn where a figure was walking towards them. Gene yelled, "Hey, Pancho. This boy here is lookin' for a job. You think we can use some help around here?"

Pancho looked Perk up and down while chewing on a cigar, focusing on his red hair. "What kinda work do you do, Red?" Perk immediately knew he had been wrong thinking this was a man. She was a short boxy woman in leather chaps and a wide brimmed hat.

"Yes, ma'am. I can do just about any job you ask me to do… ma'am." I'm a hard worker, and dependable. If you hire me, you won't be sorry."

Pancho looked down at Perk's worn leather high top shoes with a broken shoestring tied in a knot. He towered over her a foot or more but had a sweet, earnest face. She asked, "How old are you?"

"Seventeen, ma'am." he blurted out.

"Are you lookin' for full time work?" she shot back.

Gene leaned against his shovel watching the interrogation. "Red helped me seat this here post." He said, pointing to the half finished gate.

Perk realized Gene was helping him and spoke up, "Well, I will work real hard for you both, this summer. I do have one year left of high school and I am willing to work after school, nights and weekends in the fall."

The lady rancher switched the cigar in her mouth from one side to the other, lifting her chin and staring under her hat brim at the awkward kid standing before her. She nodded her head, turned and walked away speaking over her shoulder, "I guess I can use another pair of hands during the busy season. He's on a trial basis, Gene. Includes room, board and twenty cents an hour for a ten-hour day." Pancho disappeared into the barn.

Perk's eyes opened wide, his jaw dropped and he expelled a little gasp of air. Just like that, he had gotten a job. "Thank you, sir, for speaking up for me." Perk said, grabbing the shovel. Gene nodded.

The ranch hand was a talker, and Perk listened while the old guy in dungarees and worn cowboy boots kicked another post to straighten it. Under his felt hat, his gray hair, pulled back in a ponytail, matched his handlebar mustache and short beard. He noticed Perk watching Pancho in the corral leading a horse on a halter.

Gene pointed to her with his chin, "Pancho Barnes was a famous barnstormer, ya know, setting world speed records. She beat Amelia Earhart's air-land-speed record in 1930." Gene's admiration was evident as he talked about his friend and boss. "During another race, she crash-landed in the Mexican desert and had to hitchhike back to California." Perk listened, half believing the old guy telling him about Pancho's escapades ten years ago.

"You son-of-a-motherless-goat! I'm thinking glue factory if you don't settle down!" Perk could hear Pancho swearing at an uncooperative quarter horse in the corral. As he watched, she struggled to put a bridle on the skittish animal, eventually succeeding. "Whoa, whoa," she soothed the horse, calming him enough to lead him in circles around her.

Perk glanced east toward the airstrip and saw two airplanes and wondered out loud, "Are those her airplanes?" Gene cut him off and continued his story. "She was one of them society ladies, a position which she hated. When Pancho's father passed away she used her inheritance to buy an airplane and this ranch." He added, "To keep it goin' as a dude ranch, she took on extra jobs flying city people to and from Los Angeles, or she did crop dusting jobs up north in Delano."

By the time the second fence post was up and set, Perk had learned a few things about the woman who was now his boss. Gene said, "Red, there's a cot in the bunkhouse. You'll find Pancho's meals aren't great but you won't starve. You gotta be up at six in the morning, mucking out stalls, feeding the horses, mending fences and helping me with other ranch chores. Do you think you can handle it, boy?"

Perk nodded, "Yes sir. I can handle it!" a surprised grin crossed his ruddy face. This was his first job and it was at a ranch with an airport. He couldn't believe his good fortune. What he didn't say was eventually he wanted to trade work for flying lessons, but that conversation would come down the road. For now he would show Gene and Pancho he was a very hard worker.

Rancho Oro Verdes Tavern was a welcoming place where the flyboys from Muroc Air Base met because of their preferential treatment from the aviatrix herself. Pancho embraced them as friends and she had fascinating stories to tell of her flying adventures. She employed the prettiest girls on Wednesday and Satur-

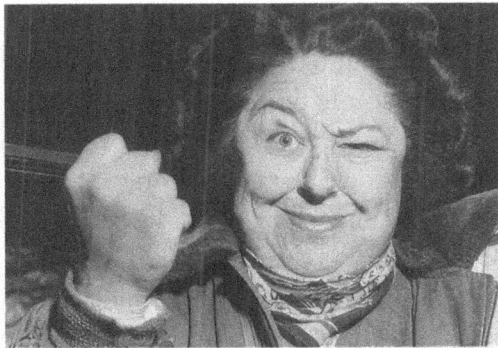

Pancho Barnes—aviator, owner of Rancho Oro Verde,
i.e.. The Happy Bottom Riding Club

Pancho with her aviator friends

Flyer for Pancho's Fly-Inn

day dance nights and she easily could drink any one of the airmen under the table. If the boys got too drunk to get back to their base, she put them up in the inn or in the bunkhouse, discreetly sending them on their way in the morning. Out in the desert the lively tavern was well known in the area. The eccentric hostess never ran out of beer, booze, local girls, ice or jokes.

The scenic desert location, about an hour's drive from Hollywood, was the perfect western movie set location. Hollywood people: movie stars, directors and film crews, shot on location there and then after work, frequented the ranch tavern. Rancho Oro Verde was the only watering hole for miles.

In addition to Pancho's dude ranch in the desert, she ran a rag-tag flying school with a dirt airstrip with two airplanes. One was a Huff-Daland biplane crop duster, currently down for repairs. The Travel Air 4000 biplane was used for Pancho's flying lessons or to transport passengers. Perk thought, "What better flight instructor than a crack ace barnstormer to teach me how to fly an airplane."

One weekend some of Pancho's female flier friends, who called themselves the *Ninety-Nines*, came to the ranch and reminisced about their 1928 Powder Puff Derby. Always the extravert, Pancho unashamedly blurted after a few drinks, "Flying makes me feel like a sex maniac in a whorehouse with a stack of $20 bills!" Perk smirked as he heard her exclamation above the roars of her friends around the piano. There was no doubt she lived life to the fullest. He watched her light a cigar and blow smoke up in the air, bookending her boasts with, "Aww, nothing exceeds like excess." Excessive she was.

Perk was in awe of Pancho, thinking her a true pioneer of aviation. Gene told him Pancho's grandfather had flown balloons in the Great War and he once took his ten-year-old granddaughter, Pancho, to one of the very first air shows. He told her, "Everyone will be flying airplanes when you grow up and you'll be a flier, too." How could he have known that she would be the first woman to get a pilot's license, fly races and become a stunt pilot in Hollywood movies?

"Florence 'Pancho' Lowe was her name and she chose a life on her own terms and not on her wealthy family's expectations." According to Gene, "Pancho wanted more than anything to become a pilot. Her aristocratic parents were against their only daughter's choice. They arranged a hasty marriage to a respectable minister which was a mistake from the beginning. After Pancho's son, Billy was born, Pancho fled the marriage and escaped to Mexico." Gene added, "She never looked back. She was kind of a wild animal that couldn't be tamed, creating a life for herself based on her love of flying."

September

More than once while Perk worked at the ranch, Pancho would reinforce her philosophy. She'd say, "If you have a choice, choose happy." He knew flying airplanes would definitely make him happy. Weekends during the fall and winter of 1938, besides being a ranch hand, Perk cleaned the inside of Pancho's farmhouse. It was a small, two bedroom house with a kitchen and indoor toilet. The frequent desert winds left a layer of dust on everything. Perk swept and dusted the remnants of her past life, a gilded mirror over the hearth, oriental rugs frayed at the corners, a bunch of dusty trophies and faded ribbons she had won at flying races. She built a barn, bunkhouse, air strip, corral, a tavern and swimming pool to make the farm into a dude ranch. After the Stock Market Crash of 1929, Gene said, "She lost the rest of her inheritance and was glad she had sunk most of her money into this 180 acre dude ranch."

October

Perk settled into his senior year at Palmdale High School. He didn't see much of Louie Messari since his friend had tried out for the football team. Practices and games kept Louie pretty busy, plus he had a girlfriend. Perk wasn't interested in sports and anyway he was too skinny, at barely 140 lbs, to take down those 250 pound guys. He wasn't a fast runner, either. He was interested in photography. One of his friends had borrowed a brownie box camera from Mr. Adams who sponsored the Photo Club on campus. Perk was fascinated with the photo process of taking pictures, processing film, and printing images on paper. He joined the Photo Club and was able to sign up for two hours a week in the closet-darkroom at school, run by Mr. Adams.

The Parent Teacher Association had paid for three loaner box cameras for club members, as well as film, chemicals and photo paper for the darkroom. Perk found his favorite photo subjects were people, nature and Pancho's airplanes. From the school library he checked out a book by the photographer, Walker Evans, and another, *An American Exodus: A record of Human Erosion* by Dorothea Lange. He loved how both photographers took pictures of people. His family had struggled during the dust bowl years like the images in the Lange and Evans photographs. Besides photography, Perk's first love was flying. Every Friday after school he took the city bus to Pancho's ranch and worked weekends helping Gene with ranch chores and Pancho with the tavern on Saturday nights.

Pancho with Amelia Earhart

December

While cleaning his boss's ranch house, Perk picked up Pancho's trophies and dusted them carefully. He eyed the photos of female aviators standing arm in arm in front of their derby planes. There was a framed image of Amelia Earhart standing in a group with Pancho and other pilots. There were photos of Pancho with a few Hollywood people who came by the ranch: William Boyd, Gene Autry, Gabby Hayes and Bette Davis were making western movies in the Mojave Desert and after their shoots, they came to Pancho's tavern. The dude ranch and canteen increased in popularity and eventually Pancho hired a cook for the small kitchen that offered thick ranch raised beef steaks and delicious barbecued chicken, a piano player and several pretty hostesses for weekends and Wednesday nights. Perk wondered how a 17-year-old kid like him could be so lucky to get a job like this.

Dottie—April, 1938

Dottie sat in the movie theater between her sister, Lavonne and her friend, Jackie Fowler, who handed her a piece of Dentyne gum. They were all age 15, and soon-to-be sophomores in high school. Her dad had given her and her sister each a quarter to go see the movie, Alexander's Ragtime Band with Tyrone Power and Alice Faye.

"I heard the actress sing the theme song on the radio and it was wonderful," Jackie said. The green curtain parted and the theater faded to darkness and the girls were shushed by the older lady behind them. The cartoon advertising a bag of popcorn, danced across the large screen. Dottie could smell popcorn and salivated. The girls only had enough money for the entrance ticket. She chewed the gum Jackie gave her, which would have to last through the movie.

The blaring newsreel filled the screen, "Hitler takes over Austria on his way to full domination of Europe." There were images of people carrying bundles escaping Vienna. Grainy black and white movies showed the human misery of escaping immigrants. In other news across the world, "Nanking Massacre! The Chinese civil war in Shanghai and Nanking has come under attack by Japanese soldiers."

Dottie whispered to her sister, Lavonne, "This is so dismal. Those poor people. Can you imagine if we lived there?" A Ferdinand the Bull cartoon played next which she enjoyed more than the awful newsreels. The main feature came on and the three girls got lost in the entertaining plot and Tyrone Powers' flawless face. His character abandoned classical music to join a ragtime band. Dottie could relate. She and her sisters played the clarinet in the high school marching band and it was much more fun to play popular tunes like A-Tisket A-Tasket than Mozart.

At the end of the movie, the credits rolled up the screen and the girls sat for a moment longer in the cool theater. "Don't you think Tyrone Power is the most handsome fellow? He has the dreamiest eyes," Jackie said as she looked up at the belt driven

Hastings, Nebraska

Ruth, Dottie, Jackie and Lavonne

23

fans overhead. She continued, "I wish I looked like Alice Faye and could marry Tyrone Power."

The three girls reluctantly left the cool brick theater and stepped out into the summer heat of downtown Hastings. "Jeez Louise, it's hot!" Dottie said as she scanned the street. She spotted her step dad waiting near the corner in his black Ford. He looked like a chauffeur sitting erect behind the wheel as they jumped in and slid across the velvet seats.

"How was the movie, girls?" Guy asked. All the way home they described the scenes, chattering about the singing and dancing in the movie.

Lavonne asked Guy, "Do you think Alexander's Ragtime Band might be out in sheet music, Dad?"

Guy shrugged and said, "Maybe. We can check at the music store." All seven kids in Dottie's family played an instrument in their high school band, and her two older brothers, Bart and Willard, played in their Hastings College orchestra. Guy's father owned a music store in Omaha which sold instruments and sheet music and they could get almost any musical score there.

Fifteen-year-old Dorothy "Dottie" Bouricius was a redhead like her grandmother Keeling and often her hair gave her fits because it was so curly. Sometimes she got compliments about her hair and green eyes, and pretty smile, but she just tolerated her looks and wished she looked like Lana Turner. Ann, her mother, was a good seamstress and made stylish clothes for her three daughters, patterned after clothes for sale in the Sears and Roebucks Catalog.

In 1930, Dottie's real father, Bob Martensen tragically died of heart disease when she was only seven. He had returned from the Great War and had been ill for several years until his death at age 32. He left his wife, Ann, and their four children, Ruth, 9, Dorothy, 7, Robert, 5, and Richard, 2. Her father's devastating illness and death plus the Great Depression, the year before, created an

Bart 20, Willard 18, Lavonne 15, Dottie 15, Ruth 17, Robert, 14, and Dick, 9. All Bouricius

extreme hardship for Ann and her young family. They moved into Dottie's grandmother Keeling's house and Ann became the breadwinner. She had secretarial skills and applied for a job at Guy Bouricius's battery factory in Hastings, Nebraska. The tall handsome entrepreneur was also a single father of three children, after his wife divorced him for another man. Bart, 13, Willard, 12 and Lavonne, 7 were close in age to Dottie and her three siblings. Ann and Guy fell in love and after a year, married and combined her family of four children with his three children.

After a year of nine living in a small house, the couple realized they needed a bigger home for their family. Ann joked, "We need a dormitory." Actually that was close to what Guy found in an old two-story brick school house in Hastings that had room for his expanding business on the main floor and space upstairs for their family of nine to live.

The building needed a new roof and the former school had no indoor toilets when Guy bought it so he hired a plumber to

Bouricius house and battery factory

install two bathrooms, one upstairs and one in the battery factory, downstairs. When the family first moved into what had been the Hastings School, they divided the space into four bedrooms. There was one dormitory-size room for Dottie's four brothers and one for her and her two sisters. They turned a roomy classroom into a bedroom for Ann and Guy and another for a guest room for her grandmothers when they visited. Another area became their large living room with its adjacent kitchen and dining area. They installed lights that ran on Guy's batteries and they used the original coal furnace in the basement for heat that Dottie's older brothers tended. The corner of the basement was Guy's hobby darkroom, used to develop black and white photographs taken with his Kodak box camera. The Bouricius family and their friends often enjoyed developing film and making prints in the old schoolhouse basement. Sometimes they experimented, coloring their photos with photo dyes.

The Hastings Battery Factory and a seven-room house
for their family upstairs

In 1933 Guy officially opened his Hastings Battery Factory, located on Main Street a mile south of the Post Office. They supplied the farmers and businesses with batteries in eastern Nebraska and Council Bluffs, Iowa. It seemed everyone needed batteries and Guy and Ann's business flourished. On rural farms, they provided farm-light batteries where the high wires had not yet been connected. Those batteries lit farmers' homes, were used in farm equipment, and powered some town businesses. In 1936 Guy had orders from the government to supply the Navy batteries for their new submarines and torpedoes. He and his two workers could hardly keep up with the demand. Ann kept the books and ordered supplies. The 1930s Depression and the Dust Bowl years had made it financially difficult for the family of nine, and their farm customers. Businesses like Guy's battery factory in the Farm Belt, often took payment for goods and service with chickens, farm cured hams, fruits, vegetables and eggs instead of cash.

Bouricius cabin, Rocky Mountains   Dottie horseback riding

The warm summers for the large family were filled with camping trips to Colorado where they loved fishing, horseback-riding and hiking. In 1937 Guy and Ann purchased five acres of land at the edge of the US National Park and Guy applied for a permit to build a cabin on the land. He figured he and his boys could build most of it themselves. At first they camped on the wooded property and the family worked on the project part time over several summers. It was a joyful time in their lives and the Peaceful Valley community embraced the Bouricius clan as they enjoyed cookouts, dances and evenings with campfires in the beautiful Colorado Rocky Mountains. Guy bought timber from loggers for their cabin foundation and framing. The boys gathered boulders from the Saint Vrain River for their rock chimney and fireplace. Guy's cabin plans had two-stories with two bedrooms upstairs and one down. They wanted a large living room centered around a rock fireplace, a big kitchen and dining room and an indoor bathroom. They relied on a wooden outhouse for use during construction.

September

During fall and winter the Bouricius family returned to Hastings and their battery business and to the seven kids' schools. The musical siblings in the blended family were close in age and while all but Dick were in high school and college, they found themselves very busy marching in the band during games and doing band competitions. Dottie and her sisters were active in Job's Daughters and other organizations. Guy participated in civic activities as a business owner and his large family often ended up with their pictures in the *Hastings News,* roller skating, ice skating or at football games or other events.

Guy had graduated from college with a degree in engineering and it was expected that all the Bouricius kids would attend the university. The couple encouraged their seven kids to take their education seriously and work hard to get good grades. In the fall of 1938 Bart was a junior at Hastings College, majoring in mathematics and engineering and Willard was taking classes in physics. Their technical discussions around the Bouricius dinner table included Quantum Physics and Einstein's Theory of Relativity. Also attending Hastings College was Dottie's sister Ruth, who was in the teachers' program. Lavonne and Dottie were busy juniors at their high school with classes, music, clubs and friends.

It was tough for Ann juggling her secretarial duties of their battery business with household meals and keeping her large family in clothes which she made herself. She and her mother were always sewing, knitting and patching coats, sweaters and britches. She tailored Guy's suits and made quilts and drapes for the house. Ann organized household chores so all the kids at home had jobs. Guy borrowed from the bank for his four kids' tuition and paid it back in the spring, interest free. The Bouricius kids worked in the battery factory to help with college expenses.

Dottie's sister, Ruth, being the oldest girl and a college freshman, had certain benefits her two younger sisters didn't have. At 18, she went out on dates and attended college organization meetings. Her younger sisters grumbled and complained, "Ruth always has all the fun."

Dottie, Bob, Ruth and Lavonne

Her mother reasoned, "Ruth is two and a half years older than you girls and age has its privileges." Dottie knew she wasn't able to go out with boys until she was in college. However, they had permission to go to mixed dances and parties organized by their different school clubs. Dottie had her 15th birthday in the upstairs living room of the school house and all her friends came. The next day her grandmother gave her a diary which she faithfully wrote in everyday.

November

"I developed pictures of Toad. He really likes Ruth and is always grinning and stammering around her. Tonight we listened to the *Fibber McGee and Molly Show* and I made chocolate candy. Grandma gave me 25 cents. Mom made me a white blouse and is remaking a skirt of Ruth's for me. I listened to *Radio Hit Parade* and I heard my favorite swing song, Benny Goodman's, *Sing, Sing, Sing*. Ruth and I danced the *Lindy Hop* to it, rather badly."

December 21, 1938

"We cut down our Christmas tree this morning. Grandma Martensen, Mom, and we three girls made ornaments, strung popcorn and cranberries while Willard made a star for the tree top. It is probably the prettiest Christmas tree in Hastings, Nebraska."

2.

Graduation and Coming of Age—1939

Perk 1939

January

As 17-year-old Perk stocked the tavern and cleaned Pancho Barnes ranch house and he got to know the eccentric aviator. She encouraged his curiosity about aviation, and told him stories of her racing years and stunt flying. On one of those days in January 1939, Perk mustered up the courage to ask her, "Would you give me flying lessons in exchange for work on the ranch?" She wasn't surprised and said, "I have seen how you look at the airplanes on the field, Red, studying takeoff and landing maneuvers." She paused, "OK, if your parents consent we can work something out." Perk's heart leaped from his chest because this was the closest he had ever come to getting in an airplane.

When he asked his folks, Perk presented it with the added benefit of extra income for his family since his mother could only be able to work three more months due to her surprise pregnancy. She was due in July and her income meant the difference between status quo or tightening their belt. Perk promised to contribute

$5.00 a week to help with the expenses. Perk's mother had her concerns, with a discussion between his parents until his father's final word, "It will be good for the boy." It was settled. He would work off his lessons doing ranch work. Pancho had increased his pay to 40 cents an hour and he felt he was almost getting the lessons for free.

February

On fair-weather weekends during the winter, Perk got a couple of observation rides. He sat in the Travel Air 4000 biplane's rear seat, watching Pancho, in the front seat, take off, maneuver the controls, and land effortlessly on the little airstrip. He was thrilled with air flight and marveled how effortlessly she controlled the airplane.

As Perk logged backseat flight hours in the open cockpit biplane, one day Pancho said, "Hey Red, climb into the front seat this time, and I'll sit in the back." She first asked him to *drive* the aircraft on the ground in circles, using the throttle and the brakes, switching the flaps up and down to increase or decrease

"Happy Bottom Riding Club"

Muroc AFB nearby

Travel Air 4000

speed. "This is like driving my dad's truck," he thought. For the first time behind the controls of the airplane, he found he was having the time of his life. The Travel Air never left the ground but the wind in his face, the smell of fuel, and the controls in his hands was an exhilarating experience for the 17-year-old.

March

Perk was asked to work at the lively Wednesday night tavern dances as they became more popular. Pancho hung a new shingle, renaming the ranch, "The Happy Bottom Riding Club," a nod to the soreness experienced by dude ranch guests after the horseback trail rides. Some patrons implied that it meant something else, and the jokes and rumors of after-hours activities circled through the bunk house, but Perk never saw any of that.

Pancho Barnes seemed to be just another one of the flyboys gathered around the tavern bar. "We touched the top of trees and nearly clipped the chimney of a two story farmhouse," the aviatrix said as everyone roared. She loved being the life of the party, "I flew in the 1929 Women's Transcontinental Air Derby, Santa Monica to Cleveland. Day five of the race, I flew the leg in clear weather to Pecos, Texas. When I got to the airstrip there was dense fog. So, I lowered my landing gear and touched down, realizing too late, in the middle of the airstrip was a damn parked car with the couple necking! I hit it, flipped the plane up over the surprised occupants, and landed upside down in front of them. I fell out of the cockpit on my head and got up and walked away, a little bit smarter." The crowd howled again at her colorful tales and other near-miss stories.

The popularity of those Sunday brunches, Wednesday night dances and Saturday night parties had grown. Perk began to see famous test-pilots from Muroc show up, like General Jimmy Doolittle, Bob Hoover, Chuck Yeager and Hap Arnold. There were a few western movie stars like Loraine Day and George O'Brien who appeared at the ranch after filming, to add to the glamor at the Rancho Oro Verde Pub.

His most favorite days at the ranch were when Pancho had time for Perk's flying lessons. After a few take-offs and landings, she let him take the controls and he piloted the biplane down the runway, lifted off a hundred feet in the air, circle and set it back down, a bit too hard for Pancho's taste. She then showed him how to lift the nose for a smoother landing. "It's all timing, Red." She encouraged him. "You'll get the hang of it."

May

Soon Perk was doing take-off and touch-downs, short flights around the ranch and he worked on perfecting his landings, often buffeted by high desert winds. He was beginning to understand the tail rudder and wing flaps to control the direction and speed.

By the end of May he had 20 flight hours under his belt. He was learning to adapt his flying skills to that fickle desert weather. After a surprise dust tornado on the airstrip as he landed, Perk set the biplane down like a baby and jumped from the cockpit with sand grit in his teeth. Pancho congratulated his expert landing. "You aced that, Red," she said with a mouth full of unlit cigar.

While paying for flight lessons he was still able to give his mother $10 dollars of his winter pay, working after school and weekends at the ranch. Barbara Jean, Perk's baby sister was born a month before and his mom was grateful for the extra money because she still wasn't back working her shift at the hospital. He and his four brothers helped with their new sister and took turns changing diapers and feeding her.

Perk really wanted that Civilian Pilots License but he fretted to Pancho, "I've only completed a third of the 100 hours required. I hope to get it by next year." "Don't be in such a hurry, Red. You are doing well, so don't rush things. I think you are gonna make a damn good pilot. You have a level head on your shoulders and you could find a good career in the expanding aircraft industry. Anyway, you are going to be in college next year and you might set your sights on engineering."

Perk said with a smirk, "What can be more important than flying?

Oh, college. Right. My grades are good enough in math, science and history but I can't spell worth beans and I got a C in English, only with the help of a pocket dictionary." Perk's face brightened when he talked about his drafting class, "My last drawing of the landing gear of a Lockheed 5b Vega, got an A. I do like technical drawing with math equations and tables," he said. "Mr. Simpson, my drafting teacher, encouraged me to become a designer so engineering might be a good major."

June

The high school graduation, Class of '39, came fast and Perk collected his diploma and caught the old town city bus to the dude ranch. It was all a formality, he thought. Getting a pilot's license is a much bigger prize than a high school diploma. Pancho congratulated him and said, "What are you talking about, Red? You need that precious document to get into junior college. I'm proud of you. This country needs good aircraft designers and that takes college, my friend."

Perk gathered used glasses from the bar and washed and dried them while listening to her advice. He wanted to ask, "How would long hours, sitting at a drafting table allow him to fly airplanes?"

Pancho continued, "Pilot jobs are in mail delivery, crop dusting and the military. Stunt pilots, and barnstormers don't live long. Well, Charles Lindbergh was an exception." She mused, "I don't know how much cash backers and dumb luck contributed to Lindy's longevity."

Amelia Earhart's disappearance, two years earlier in July 1937, had deeply affected Pancho. She still held out hope that her friend would be found alive on some remote Pacific island. Earhart and her co-pilot, Fred Noonan, left California on their attempt to circumnavigate the globe. A last cryptic message had been intercepted by the US Navy while Earhart was flying around looking to land on Howland Island. She thought she was about 1600 miles southwest of the Hawaiian Islands. There was more static and then her radio intercepts went silent. The famous aviator and her copilot were never heard from again.

"Too many pilots I've known have flown to their deaths." she said regrettably. Still, Pancho relished Perk's interest and love of aviation and encouraged him, "Hey Red, find a well-paying career like engineering and fly airplanes on the weekends."

Isolationist mothers march

Charles Lindbergh speaking for isolationism

The subject wasn't entirely up to him. Perk's mother made him promise to attend Antelope Valley College in the fall when she realized his flying passion wasn't going away. Dutifully, that August he registered for classes with one elective title closest to aircraft design; mechanical engineering. On weekends he continued flight lessons at Pancho's.

You're Not Our Hero, Ex-Col. Lindbergh!

WE'RE the youth who built models of the "Spirit of St. Louis" . . . we're the youth who named our dogs "Lindy" . . . we're the youth who used to crowd the airports and the streets of the towns you visited to catch a glimpse of you. We were proud to say that we saw "Lindy" . . .

We admired you for your courage as an aviator, as a pioneer in aviation. But now you've disappointed us, Mr. Lindbergh. Now you ask us to follow you—a holder of the Nazi German Cross—an embittered man who would have us make peace with a mad dictator who makes peace only as a prelude to conquest.

Hitler has realized that any revolutionary ideal big enough to gain the support of the people must have the support of enthusiastic youth. Hitler is now employing the might of German youth to enslave the world.

THAT MAKES IT OUR FIGHT!

We're the American youth—do you hear us? We don't have to be goose-stepped into defending our freedom.

But, instead of leading us in our fight against Hitler, as we felt you would, Mr. Lindbergh, you plead with us to accept slavery willingly!

HEROES FIGHT FOR FREEDOM.

You are no longer a hero, Ex-Colonel Lindbergh!

39

Living at the Happy Bottom Riding Club, close to Muroc Air Base, it was hard for Pancho and her military friends to ignore the build-up of conflicts around the world. Japan had been fighting in Manchuria while Germany was continuing their expansive march across Europe. In the U.S. it was hard to ignore the protests by isolationists at President Roosevelt's build-up of soldiers, bases and arms. He knew it was just a matter of time before America was involved in one of the overseas clashes.

World War I had ended three years before Perk was born with 100,000 American boys dead in battlefields in Flanders and Germany. Twenty years later the people of the United States wanted no part of another foreign war. It had cost them too many of their sons. Isolationists marched and ranted against sending the American military off to fight someone else's battle. Across the nation, placards read, "Save our boys." or, "I did not raise my son to die for Britain."

The escalating war in Europe was covered on nightly radio reports. Hitler and Mussolini were steam-rolling their way across Europe and North Africa, taking territory and cities. The Slovak Republic, Austria and Danzig were invaded and annexed by Germany. Hitler and Stalin stormed across the Polish border in September. Great Britain and France regarded the invasion of Poland, their ally, as a bridge too far and declared war on Germany. Winston Churchill cabled Roosevelt saying the British military was in serious trouble. Although the U.S. still did not join the war, Roosevelt struck a deal called "destroyers for bases," exchanging 50 old destroyers for a 99-year lease to place American military bases in British territories of Canada and the Caribbean.

Campaigning to win re-election the next year, the American President continued to reassure his constituents, "The U.S. will not send our boys into Europe's War" A member of the isolationist America First Committee, the prominent and influential aviator, Charles Lindbergh, got his message out through print, radio, and mass rallies. One of their mottos was, "The Yanks Aren't Coming."

He was a powerful spokesperson for not going to war against Germany, coining the phrase, "The independent American destiny." He explained, "American soldiers ought not to have to fight everybody in the world who prefers some other system of life to ours."

In the minority, the Interventionists, who wanted to help Great Britain, favored aid to our ally and made statements of support, "With a significant amount of territory in Europe controlled by the Nazis', the physical buffer of the Atlantic Ocean between us would be useless." Even FDR said on the radio, "It would be like living at the point of a gun." Still most Americans were removed from the war abroad and went about their daily lives.

The U.S. War Department Doctrine did not allow for aircraft to be classified as offensive weapons. It was thought that there was no need for a long-range strategic bomber such as the B-17. They were considered too complex and expensive. But in September of 1939 when Hitler's forces invaded Poland, the U.S. had only thirteen operational Flying Fortresses and Roosevelt set aside $300 million for 30,000 B-17s to be built for the Army Air Corp. The United States would become the only country developing a strategic bomber. Germany put its military Luftwaffe budget mostly into fighter planes.

Dottie—1939

Dottie Bouricius continued writing in her diary with her life centering around her family, friends and school.

April 11

"My family surprised me at home with a sweet sixteen party. I had no idea as they told me they were stopping at our house to pick up my sister before going to a movie. Berdie, Norma, Virginia, Etta,

41

Mickey and Deloris were there as well as my sister, Lavonne. It was the best birthday I have ever had. Mom and Guy gave me a pair of black and white saddle shoes."

June 16

"We saw Jean Harlow wear equestrian jodhpur pants in the movie *Bombshell*, and last year they were in the Sears catalog for $2.59 a pair. My mom made a pair of Jodhpurs each, for me and my sisters, Lavonne and Ruth. There was a late spring snow today and we built a snowman."

Ruth, snowman, Lavonne and Dottie

Boating on Heartwell Lake

June 21

"We left for Colorado and our Peaceful Valley cabin. We almost have the roof finished and we hope we can set up cots in the living room once that happens. We went to the Mountain Guild potluck and Mom brought Chicken Jack Straw and her peanut butter cookies. Guy has big plans for us to work on the cabin and we girls have big plans to go to the barn dance in Estes Park."

September 15

"Today eight of us were initiated into the Hastings chapter of Job's Daughters at the Masonic Temple and there were refreshments afterward. Then we went boating at Hartwell Lake in the boat my brothers built."

November 21

"Grandma Martinsen came for Thanksgiving and she is going to stay with us for a while. Her memory is not very good. At the Job's Daughter Dance, Don Betts filled my dance card. Afterwards we all went to Jones Drug Store's soda fountain and Don bought me a root beer float."

December 21

"Jackie and I went to see the *Babes in Arms* with Mickey Rooney and Judy Garland. The newsreel showed Hitler and Stalin invading Czechoslovakia, Hungary, Ukraine, Lithuania, Finland and

Poland. My brothers think the United States might go to war soon. Mom and Guy are so worried."

Perk—1940

President Franklin D. Roosevelt decided to run for a fourth term, when historically no one had ever served more than eight years as U.S. President. With the tense events unfolding in Europe and the Pacific, with Japan signing a pact with Germany and Italy, were the reasons he gave to the press, why he was running. When asked why he was running for a fourth term he said, "I feel responsible to continue the job we have started." The President was beloved and like a father to the nation, getting them through the depression and these murmurs of impending war. He was looking tired and gaunt. Although the American people were still overwhelmingly isolationists, Roosevelt felt the U.S. involvement in one or both of the conflicts was inevitable. He needed to be President when that occurred.

Churchill, from 3,000 miles away, pressured Roosevelt, "We are entering a somber phase of what must inevitably be a protracted and broadening war." Hitler started bombing British bases and making nightly raids on London. With the U.S. president's campaign pledge to keep out of the foreign wars, Roosevelt did not respond to Churchill's comments but he subtly began preparing the United States for the possibility of an entrance into either conflict. He passed the U.S. Selective Service Act, supported manufacturing of equipment and arms with government programs and opened up new military bases in the US and overseas. Men signed up to be trained in the Army, Navy and Marines as an alternative to unemployment.

After dinner Perk's mother, Lillian, sewed knee patches on her son's pants, the boys worked on model airplanes and Fred listened to the radio news about the wars going on in Europe and China. "Hitler was denied his non-aggression pact with Denmark, Norway and Finland. Hirohito's Japanese armies took advantage of the Chinese civil war to invade Manchuria, Shanghai and Nanking. The Italian dictator, Mussolini, invaded Albania, Libya and Egypt." Perks parents were shocked by what was happening in the world today.

The nightly ritual of listening to the radio brought news of the wars on two fronts. With two boys in the Perkins household now of military age, the reports also brought anxiety. One reporter said, "There are only a third of Americans who believe Roosevelt's government should risk war by helping the British." Perk's parents, like most of the U.S., remained isolationist.

The American journalist, Ernie Pyle, on assignment in England, wrote about the war during the London Blitz, describing it as "savage." He praised the anonymous heroes who raced across rooftops to douse the incendiaries with sand before they could set other buildings on fire." Ernie made Americans feel the Britons' determination and the horrors that the Germans were inflicting on unarmed citizens. He did not pretend to give his readers an account of the battle. Rather he gave his own impressions that London was resilient, and would survive at a time when Americans were still so resistant about joining the war in Europe.

One night in May, Perk's family listened to President Roosevelt's fireside talk, "We have to harness the efficient machinery of America's manufacturers to produce 50,000 combat aircraft over the next 12 months to confront the approaching store for global war. We have fewer than 3,000 warplanes in our U.S. arsenal and most of them are obsolete." It surprised Americans because they felt firm about insulating themselves from the two escalating wars, far from their shores.

Pancho also listened to the nightly news on the radio. "France, Luxembourg, the Netherlands and Belgium have fallen to Hitler's armies." At the Happy Bottom Riding Club, Pancho heard firsthand rumors from her flyboy friends at Muroc Base, the Pentagon was asking the Army to fast track the development of new aircraft, the training of pilots, and development of munition plants. They were convinced that long-range, high-altitude heavy bombers would be the most effective weapon if America should get pulled into the war in Europe or the Pacific. The U.S. needed to industrialize quickly.

The German Luftwaffe had double the number of fighter aircraft and airmen, compared to the British Royal Air Force. The RAF drew airmen from its colonies including New Zealand, Canada, South Africa, and Australia as well as employing the Polish refugee pilots. Even with those colonial airmen, the war in Europe wasn't looking good for Great Britain.

Pancho listened to Edward R. Murrow's descriptive reporting from England. "This is London. The faint red, angry snap of anti-aircraft bursts against the steel-blue sky, the sound of guns off in the distance…" he reported. And always Murrow's salutation, "Good night and good luck."

The Berlin-Rome Axis pact of 1936 was the basis for the mutual ties between Hitler and Mussolini. But the German leader dominated this partnership and by November 1940 Hitler saw Mussolini as an encumbrance and an ineffectual military leader. Besides failing in his attempted invasion of Greece, the Italian dictator lost a quarter of his merchant ships moored in foreign ports. At the outbreak of hostilities those ships were impounded by the Allies. Further disappointment to the German Chancellor came when he saw how unprepared Mussolini's military was for war. "Their lack of raw materials and insufficient supply and production of armaments, as well as their weak economy is of little help to us." Hitler said. He needed everything Mussolini couldn't give him and he needed to turn his losses into victories. With their mutual war against Britain and France, Hitler said, "We can't rely on this Italian dictator for military aid and arms as we fight on three fronts." The arrogant Italian had become a liability and a dependent.

Pancho changed the radio channel to KABC. "The Battle of Britain raged over the cities of Great Britain and the RAF fought with all their might for their islands." The report continued, "Hundreds of German fighter planes had been shot down and their wreckage could be seen all over the beaches of Dover. One German plane crashed into a ship of the Royal Navy at Plymouth and had to be removed in pieces."

Some of the reporting made it sound like Britain was winning the war, but one of Pancho's aviator friends said the RAF had lost half their airforce and without the help of the United States, the country would soon fall to the Nazis like the rest of the countries in Europe. Hitler appeared to be unstoppable.

In fact, the Royal Air Force lost 1250 aircraft, or 45% of its fleet. Over 700 experienced pilots and crews had been killed in July, August and September of 1940." Pancho was dismayed how deadly this war had become for British, Canadian and Polish aviators.

A British pilot, Hugh Dowding, who had flown military planes in WWI, created an early warning network called the "Dowding System," which successfully integrated air defense sectors into one apparatus. The RAF used volunteer ground observers, raid plotting, radio control of aircraft squadrons, and the effective new British early radar stations. With the Dowding System, these early warning radar systems allowed the Royal Air Force to get their planes airborne to engage the Luftwaffe in the skies over Great Britain rather than being attacked while on the ground.

In all of the chaos, there was one reassuring voice broadcast to battered British citizens and eventually to American living room radios. British Prime Minister, Winston Churchill addressed Parliament, "We shall go on to the end, we shall fight in France, we shall fight on the seas and oceans, we shall fight with growing confidence and growing strength in the air, we shall defend our Island, whatever the cost may be, we shall fight on the beaches, we shall fight on the landing grounds, we shall fight in the fields and in the streets, we shall fight in the hills; we shall never surrender..."

During that brutal summer of 1940, nightly bombing raids of five hundred German aircraft, hit the cities of Birmingham, Liverpool, Manchester, Coventry and London. Hermann Goring, head of the German Luftwaffe, in reports to Hitler, overestimated his successes in England. He had actually lost 25% of his Luftwaffe fighter aircraft strength. Equally as devastating to Goring, were the 175 newly trained German pilots who had been killed or taken prisoner. New Luftwaffe recruits and aircraft trainees were thrown into the heat of battle without proper training.

By September the Luftwaffe had lost a total of 775 aircraft to the RAF's 426 fighters destroyed. Although a terrible loss, Great Britain was reaching air superiority over the Luftwaffe simply by attrition. Hermann Goring reported to Hitler, "The Luftwaffe had pushed the British Fighter Command to the edge of defeat." His cavalier boasting created German complacency and a terrible miscalculation of strategy. The Luftwaffe shifted their aerial bombardment targets from air bases to industrial and communication targets because they thought the RAF was defeated.

Meanwhile, the British Air Ministry was overestimating the size of the German Luftwaffe and production of the German aviation industry, exaggerating the perception their air strength was larger and more dangerous than it was. Great Britain worked harder to increase production of aircraft and air personnel from all over the British Empire.

Seeing the devastating news reports of British losses during the fall of 1940, prompted the U.S. Ambassador to England, Joseph P. Kennedy to remark, "Democracy is finished in England. It may be finished here in the United States, too." The war in Europe looked bleak and Churchill continued his pressure on Washington for their assistance.

At his headquarters, Hitler reviewed the greatly inflated numbers of successes and he concluded the Nazi air superiority had not been achieved over Great Britain at all. His plan of invasion, with *Operation Sea Lion*, would have to be postponed indefinitely. The setback of the Fuehrer's goal, of an invasion of the British Isles by October of 1940, was one of his first failures of the war in Europe.

Just before Thanksgiving, 1940, Perk's father turned into the news report on the radio. The Prime Minister, Winston Churchill's inspiring speech about never giving up frightened Fred, enough to warn his family, "I fought in the Great War in Europe and I hate the idea of the United States getting into somebody else's conflict overseas." As he looked at his two eldest sons, Clarence and Maurice, he remembered seeing men dying in the fields of Flanders, and he was afraid for his boys. Lillian had enough war gloom on the radio and switched the channel to music on the *Hit Parade*.

People all over the nation were listening to the same reports about the war. Lieutenant Jack Higgs, an old friend of Pancho's, stationed at Muroc Air Force Base quietly told Pancho, "Our armed services have been steadily preparing for war. We need 100,000 troops. Bases all over the United States have increased recruitment for all branches, but especially for the Army. Small airstrips around the country, like yours, Pancho, offer potential training centers for air cadets for the development of the growing AirCorp. Now men between 21 and 45, through the Selective Service Act will register for the draft."

Perk was just a few flight hours from getting his civilian pilots license. At 18 he could finally see a path to his future, but he couldn't imagine going into the Army unless he were called up. He liked the idea of working in the aircraft industry. I'd like to work for a company like Lockheed or Boeing Aircraft, designing airplane parts. He thought, "I could save money and buy my own airplane." At least that was his day dream when he was sitting in his college English class.

On Sunday, New Year's Eve, the party at Pancho's tavern started in the morning and lasted until well after midnight. Fifty people or more crowded into the smoke filled bar that evening while plenty of liquor flowed. Glenn Miller's orchestra played loudly on the radio and Perk worked as fast as he could to clear tables, wash glasses, and make runs to the ice house. At one point a dark haired beauty sat on the bar and sang, "Rock For Me," and "Boo-Hoo." The next morning there was the mess to clean up and Pancho's hangover would take an extra day of recovery.

Dottie 1940—Wrote in Her Diary

January 1

"I went ice skating at Heartwell Lake where it was six degrees and so cold. The University of Southern California won 14-0 in the Rose Bowl with Tennessee. Yesterday Lavonne and I saw Sonja Henie, Ray Milland and Robert Cummings in the movie, *Everything Happens at Night*. Perfect. My favorite song is *In the Mood*. My brother, Bart, has a date with Bette."

February 2

"I stayed home today with the flu and read Macbeth. Miss Hilton, principal of our high school, died. She was a Christian Scientist and she had surgery on a tumor but it was too late. I practiced *William Tell Overture* on my clarinet for our North Platte Band Contest next week."

March 21

"I played in the band at the game with Columbus, Ohio. We won 23-19. It was an awfully close game. I got a chocolate frosty after the game with Madelaine."

April 11

"I am 17 today and Mom and Guy gave me a blouse she made, Ruth and Lavonne gave me a music box with a mirror inside. After band practice we all went to the drugstore and Jerry Jenkins bought me a soda."

June 7

"Madelaine and I saw a funny movie about Hitler called *The Great Dictator*, starring Charlie Chaplin. I enjoyed *The Philadelphia Story* much more as it featured my favorite actors, Cary Grant, James Stewart and Katherine Hepburn."

July 2

"Bob Hepting, Ruth's new friend, helped the boys and Guy put the finishing touches on the roof of our cabin and it is finally covered and weather proofed, ready for the snows this winter. There is still a lot of finishing work to be done on the inside but it is finally looking like a cabin. We all had a wonderful hike and picnic at Brainard Lake in the afternoon."

Bouricius cabin, Peaceful Valley

Dottie Bouricius senior picture

September 3

"It is my first day of my senior year at Hasting High School. I had my senior picture taken. My classes are Sociology, French, Typing, Art, and Library. I got a locker with Virginia Motley. After school I went downtown with Mom and Ruth mailed a letter to her boyfriend, Bob Hepting. He is adorable. He graduated from Hasting College and is doing an internship nearby as a Park Ranger at a fish and wildlife preserve. He spent some time this summer at the Rocky Mountain National Park and we all had such a good time while we were there. Bob helped my Dad and brothers build a back porch on the cabin."

October 7

"Today was Ruth's 19th birthday and Bob Hepting sent her a dozen roses. His family from Fort Collins is coming to dinner next weekend to meet our family for the first time. Cub Club planned our Sadie Hawkins dance with punch, doughnuts, apple and dogpatch decorations. Ray Belbe was killed in an airplane crash while training to get his pilot's license. I didn't know him well but it must have been terrible for his family."

November 15

"Roosevelt won again and I am so glad. He's so refined and hopefully will keep us out of the war. My dad is getting more worried that my brothers might have to fight. On the radio we heard a program about the Selective Service Act where all men ages 21 to 45 have to register. That means my brother, Bart who is 22, as well as Ruth's boyfriend, Bob Hepting, who's the same age. We are having twenty for Thanksgiving dinner."

December 10

"A new Harvard Air Base is being built near Hastings with runways and lots of Quonset huts. Guy said it might bring business to the area. Mom and Guy delivered batteries to Ogallala. Ruth and I went to a show: *Congo Maisie* with Ann Sothern. Before the movie we watched a newsreel of a London air-raid where Air Raid Wardens guided people down into the subway bomb shelters. It showed people sleeping on the ground in the station. This is looking really desperate for England."

December 25, Christmas

"Nebraska's Cornhuskers have been invited to the Rose Bowl in California, to play Stanford. We are very excited. Demolay is having a Christmas formal and I hope I'll get asked. Ruth got a letter from Bob saying he hoped to be here for Christmas. I got a diary from Lavonne, perfume from Don, a sweater from Mom, lipstick and an apron from Aunt Nell. Everyone went roller skating at the rink."

December 31

"DeMolay Formal Dance tonight and I went with Don Betz and doubled with Mickey and Buzz. I wore Ruth's velvet wrap with white fur hood and my blue formal. Bob Hepting is coming tomorrow. Ruth and Bob are just nuts about each other."

3.

Awakening a Sleeping Giant

January

Two months after FDR's election, he had one of his radio fireside chats about the looming threat of war to Americans. He talked about our *Arsenal of Democracy*. He said, "This is not a fireside chat on war. It is a talk about national security." He posed the disheartening prospect, "If Great Britain goes down, the Axis powers will be in a position to bring enormous military and naval resources against this hemisphere." He knew Americans were opposed to getting involved in the European war, but he tried convincing them that giving aid to Great Britain helped keep the Nazis at bay and away from the United States shores.

Isolationists didn't have the same aversion to conflict with Japan. Relations became increasingly tense with subsequent Japanese military seizure of parts of China in 1937-39. American outrage focused on the Japanese attack on the US gunboat Paney in Chinese waters and the atrocities of the Nanking Massacre. When Japan seized French Indochina the US, along with Australia, Britain and the Dutch government set up a trade embargo, cutting off steel and 90% of Japan's oil supplies.

March

In the Seattle, Washington, Boeing plant, thirty-eight B-17Cs were produced and twenty were delivered to the RAF as Fortress 1 trainers. From the beginning there were defensive armament issues, where the .30 caliber machine guns froze at high altitude. There were bombing accuracy problems from the start and the B-17C's oxygen systems were not reliable. Boeing rectified those system failures with the new design of the B-17D.

In the spring of 1941 Perk accrued 100 flight hours of training with Pancho Barnes and finally was awarded his civilian pilots license. He was excited to take his father up for a ride. Perk sat in the front seat, while his father sat in the rear. The weather conditions were clear and there was a brisk head wind. He took off from Pancho's air strip and guided the plane, soaring over Antelope Valley past his house in Palmdale and over the high school from where

Quartz Hill, CA

he graduated. Fred pointed at familiar buildings. With the open cockpit the air was crisp and it stung their noses and ears. Perk was proud to show his dad his flying skills and Fred enjoyed seeing familiar things from 500 feet in the air. They banked over Quartz Hill and skimmed the top of trees.

Perk listened as a funny sound, like a sputter came from the engine and he was startled for a moment, and thought, "Don't let me crash and kill my dad." Perk kept his wits about him as the sputtering continued and he skillfully maneuvered the plane back to the small airstrip and landed. Pancho checked out the airplane and found the carburetor had some ice buildup, affecting the mix of air and fuel. After landing, his father shook Pancho's hand thanking her for teaching his son to fly.

That afternoon Gene brought Pancho a newsletter from Muroc Air Base and laid it on the bar of the tavern. "Well, I'll be! She said as she read, "No longer a barnstorming, competitive sport, aeronautics in the military was reorganized by President Roosevelt with the strategic plan, Army Regulation 95-5 which created the United States Army Air Force on June 20, 1941, two days before Germany's invasion of the Soviet Union. The article said that Major General 'Hap' Arnold took command of both the Air Corp and the Air Force Combat Command." Pancho knew General Arnold and she thought he was a tough old bird and the best man for the job.

Perk had breezed through the first year of his college classes and felt that most of it was what he had already studied in high school with the exception of his elective drafting class. Besides school, his life was busy working on the weekends at the ranch. When summer came, Pancho offered him work crop dusting up north, picking up supplies or shuttling dude ranch clients in the Travel Air 4000.

Posters on Perk's college campus asked, "Have you registered for your Selective Service yet?" War was coming closer to isolationist America. Perk was committed to signing up when he turned 21 as most of his friends had already done.

While attending Antelope Valley College, Perk heard the liberal arts discussions often centered on the gloom of impending war in Europe especially after Hitler invaded France. Newsreels showed him standing in front of the Eiffel Tower and his troops marching through the Arc de Triomphe in Paris. At the same time, in the Pacific, Japan had been advancing into Manchuria and China and continued throughout Southeast Asia. Japan had signed the Tripartite Pact with Germany and Italy, forming the Axis Powers.

President Roosevelt and Congress sought to curb Japanese aggression, imposing even stiffer sanctions on the small country. They were trying to force a withdrawal of Japan's forces from the region. The Japanese empire suffered under shortages of natural resources of oil, food and the production of armaments of war. These restrictions only pushed Japan to resent the United States and its allies.

When the German Luftwaffe began an all-out brutal bombing campaign against the city of London in September, 1940 and continued for 57 consecutive nights, American sentiment slowly began to change. More Americans now believed the United States should help England in their fight against the Nazis. Charles Lindbergh continued to speak out, this time at Madison Square Garden in New York. Perk was shocked to see newsreels quoting Lindbergh, "America has no business attacking Germany." During one of FDR's fireside chats, the president was quoted as saying Lindbergh was pro-Nazi.

Even Perk's father thought Hitler was a crazy dictator and became resigned to the fact that only the allied powers, working together, could defeat him. With that growing sentiment, the involvement of the United States in the war in Europe seemed imminent.

Japan's conquest of Manchuria created a long border with Russia and though aligned with Germany as members of the Axis powers, Japan signed a nonaggression pact with the Soviet Union in April 1941. But Hitler had his own ideas about his then ally, Russia. In October the Japanese civilian government of Hirohito entered talks with the US about the embargo against them. However, they did not speak for Japan's military leadership who made the ultimate decisions. The Japanese army was determined to continue their war in Manchuria and the United States was committed to defend China. The failure of these negotiations served as a catalyst for the breakdown of Hirohito's government and the total take over by the Army's General Tojo. He took full control of all foreign policy and was determined toward a course of war with the United States.

December

In that precarious atmosphere of the winter of 1941, twenty-year-old Perk successfully passed his final exams and finished his third semester at Antelope Valley College. His pay from the Happy Bottom Riding Club would pay for gifts for his family. While at the ranch, he dutifully cleaned up after the brunch the day before, wiping tables and putting away bar glasses. Among his chores, he carried cases of Coca Cola and beer to stock the bar. Pancho stopped him and asked, "Hey Red, can you bring the boxes of ornaments from the barn and put up the Christmas decorations for the Wednesday dance?"

"No problem." He complied.

Boxes marked Christmas were stacked in the barn and after moving them to the tavern he found a ladder to hang a string of lights high over the bar. The song, *Santa Claus is Coming to Town* was playing on the radio and Gene was fixing a faucet at the sink while Pancho hummed along with the music.

On the KABC radio station, the music was interrupted by a message, "The President of the United States will address the nation about America going to war." Pancho stopped what she was doing and turned up the volume on the radio. Gene and Perk stopped what they were doing and heard FDR's familiar voice as he addressed the U.S. Congress.

"Yesterday, December 7th, 1941, a date which will live in infamy, the United States of America was suddenly and deliberately attacked by naval and air forces of the Empire of Japan." Roosevelt's voice continued, "I ask that the Congress declare that since the unprovoked and dastardly attack by Japan on Sunday, a state of war has existed between the United States and the Japanese empire."

Stunned, Pancho and Gene looked wide-eyed at each other, speechless. The three working in the tavern stared at the radio in disbelief. They listened further to the broadcast to get more details of the devastation to our U.S. Naval Base's in Honolulu, the Philippines, Guam and Midway Islands. Gene and Pancho had lived through WWI but Perk had no idea what a war could mean to him. The news report said, an untold number of military men and civilians had been injured or killed. The President explained the U.S. Pacific fleet of six ships had been sunk. More relevant to Perk, 169 U.S. Navy and Army Air Force planes had been destroyed. Pancho put her hand over her mouth. Gene's eyes teared up and he had no words as he stared at the radio. Perk could see how the enormous shock of so many lost American lives registered on their faces.

When the broadcast was over and resumed playing music, Pancho and Gene talked in low tones about how FDR's announcement might affect the United States. Perk went back to hanging ornaments, sweeping the floor and washing glasses at the bar. Pancho turned off the music as she wasn't in the mood for holiday tunes. Perk heard Gene say, "We have managed to stay out of this awful war in Europe for two years."

Pancho shook her head and recalled, "I was only 16 during the Great War but I had relatives who fought on the front. I don't want another war either."

Gene lamented, "I was 19 when sent to fight in France in 1918. Many of my friends and two of my uncles never came home. At the Armistice the Germans were banned from building up their military. Look at them now!" He spat out the words and continued ranting, "Japan and Germany have thousands of trained troops and well equipped militaries. Both had to have been preparing for years while the U.S. was sleeping." Gene glared at the floor.

A solemn silence fell over the tavern with its three occupants. As Perk hung the last of the Christmas lights he thought the decorations seemed frivolous to the looming storm that faced his country's future. He couldn't imagine, the United States was at war with this tiny country of Japan, somewhere on the other side of the world. He assumed now he would be called up to go to war. If so, he was ready.

That night one of the flyboys from the base brought Pancho a *Herald Examiner Newspaper*, and after reading it she laid

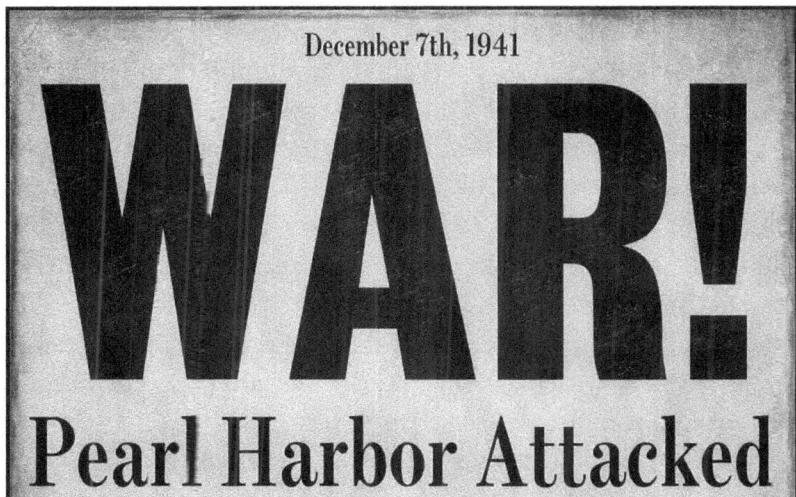

December 7th, 1941

WAR!

Pearl Harbor Attacked

it on the bar. Perk picked it up reading the descriptions of the carnage on that quiet Sunday morning in Honolulu when everyone was asleep. The Japanese had all the advantages during their sneak attack. The newspaper photos showed the extent of the devastation. The ships sunk in the harbor leaned half out of the water, smoke billowing with the hulls still burning. The wreck of airplanes on the runways smoldering. Ambulances at the docks and airfield went around picking up bodies covered by tarps. It made Perk furious. All he wanted to do was sign up and fight immediately.

The subject wasn't far from everyone's mind as the chores continued at the ranch. Perk mucked out the stalls and spread new hay on the floor. Gene muttered while cleaning the dirt from the hooves of a quarter horse, "These allies of Japan will be our enemies now, Red." "Like dominos they will all fall in line, choosing sides as they did in the Great War. It's been 20 years since I was in the trenches. Just enough time for a new generation of cannon fodder to come of age." He said bitterly, "Germany, Russia and Italy are allies of Japan." Shaking his head and pursing his lips, he looked directly at Perk, pointing a hoof pick at him, "I'm too old to serve, but they will be expecting young men like you to sign up, I betcha." Shaking his head, Gene spat on the ground for punctuation.

That week, people in Perk's hometown were indignant and angry that a foreign country, like Japan, could attack U.S. naval bases without warning, sink ships and kill so many service men. Flags were hung at half-staff. Town meetings organized victory funds and people vented in barber shops and bowling alleys. Mrs. Jenkins' boy was stationed in Honolulu and she hadn't been able to reach him. Some women knew their husbands would be called up. Mothers looked anxiously at their sons and knew they would be recruited through the Selective Service System.

As Gene predicted, four days after the attack, Germany and Italy declared war on the United States. America was officially now a country at war on two fronts; in the Pacific and in Europe. There was a call for all able-bodied men to sign up for service. As it was with the young, bravado and boasting promoted their calls for revenge on the *Yellow Peril*. Gene knew the truth. Men died far from home, disillusioned about their heroic intentions to rid the world of a menace. "There was no glory in seeing my friends lying in a trench bleeding and dying alone," said Gene. He pondered to Pancho how fathers would send their sons, their young boys, off to fight wars. Having had WWI experience, Gene felt it was suicide.

The old Victor radio blared, "After the initial shock and grief over the attack at Pearl Harbor, things are happening fast as the country prepares for war." President Roosevelt's measured speech continued, "The U.S. needs to replenish its ships, airplanes and military equipment. We need to strengthen our defenses along the east and west coasts of the country." All able bodied Americans were asked to help by joining the Army, Marines or the Navy.

Pancho and her aviator friends from the base knew this war would be fought on land and sea but also in the skies over Europe and the Pacific. All the west coast flight schools and private air strips like hers might be of interest to the U.S. Army Air Force. Being so close to Muroc Field and March Field, Pancho wasn't too surprised when the brass arrived asking questions. "Tell us about your flight training program? How many instructors do you have? How many men have you trained and how many pilots fly in and out of your airfield? What type of airplanes do they fly? Do you have any airplane mechanics?" They already knew about Pancho Barnes' barnstorming flight record. Her reputation preceded her. At the Wednesday dance and dinner, she talked to her flyboy friends about the encounter and Perk was all ears as he replenished the beer and ice and wiped down the bar at the Happy Bottom Riding Club.

After the attack on Pearl Harbor, Japan achieved a long series of military successes at the beginning of 1942. Guam, Wake Island, and Hong Kong fell to the Japanese, followed in May by the Philippines, the Dutch East Indies (Indonesia), Malaya, Singapore, and Burma. Japanese troops also invaded neutral Thailand and pressured its leaders to declare war on the United States and Great Britain.

Dottie—1941

The U.S. government contracted farmers in Nebraska to supply the military with farm goods. Grain was needed for industrial alcohol and peanuts, soybeans and flaxseed produced needed oil. Prices for crops were stabilized and Uncle Sam provided loans to farmers as well as other assistance. The Bouricius battery factory continued to prosper selling to farmers and businesses.

January

"I started my classes for my second semester. I can't believe I'm graduating, class of 1941! There was a winter formal of Job's Daughters and I asked Don Betz to go with me. We had a great time and ended the evening with sodas at the drugstore."

February 14

"I got a Valentine Day card from Don Betz. It was lovely and very sweet. We had band practice for the Omaha game. The DeMolay formal dance is next weekend. I hope Ruth will lend me her fur muff and cape again."

April 11

"Today is my 18th birthday and I got a skirt and saddle shoes from Mom and Guy. My friends took me to see *The Road to Zanzibar* with Bing Crosby and Bob Hope. On the newsreel we saw Nazis invading country after country in Europe: Poland, France, Yugoslavia and Greece. German soldiers marched toward Russia and the narrator said, 'The world watches as Hitler occupies most of Europe.' While Willard was home from college he taught Ruth to drive. Lavonne and I danced to the song *Jumpin Jive*."

June 23

"We saw the movie, *Citizen Kane* with Orson Welles, who is such a good actor. In the evening Lavonne and I went to our last Tokettes Club meeting. We had a fundraiser and raised $38 for the Red Cross.

Mom and Guy and Grandma Keeling came to my high school graduation. I nearly died of the heat in my black cap and gown. I am excited for the summer and college next fall. I am not sure what courses to take. I am thinking about being a teacher or a secretary."

August 30

"On the way to our cabin in Peaceful Valley, we bought a Navajo rug for the living room which looks great. Bob Hepting came up and helped collect, strip and install 'Y' aspen branches for the banister going up the stairs. We got a lot done on the interior this summer and it looks really nice. I like Bob a lot. Ruth told me she loves him. This afternoon we all took a hike to Brainard Lake and

I found a large Indian arrowhead. It poured rain. On the radio Edward R. Murrow said FDR warned the U.S. might be drawn into the Pacific war against Japan soon. We have to go home to Hastings tomorrow."

September 10

"I began classes at Hastings College on a path toward business and a secretarial career. Lavonne began a teaching program, also at Hastings College. Bart and Willard are graduate students at the University of Wisconsin in Madison studying Mathematics and Physics. Bob Hepting asked Ruth to marry him and she became engaged with no date set for their wedding."

October 22

"I really like my classes at Hastings College. I am taking English, French, History, Algebra, Shorthand and Speed Typing. Our sorority is planning a Halloween Fall Festival and we sold tickets to raise money for the sorority dance. I went on a double date with Madalaine, Jack, and Don Betz. We saw *How Green Was My Valley* with Maureen O'Hara."

December 8

"We heard the shocking news, the Japanese attacked Pearl Harbor in Hawaii! The United States is at War! It was so frightening to hear Roosevelt speak on the radio about all those men killed on board the ships and on the ground. How can such a small country attack a big country like the United States? My brothers and Bob Hepting are already talking about signing up."

Maurice—1942

January

Perk's 16-year-old brother, Maurice, was in his junior year at Palmdale High School when the Japanese bombed Pearl Harbor. President Roosevelt asked for all able-bodied men to join the military to fight our enemies, who had attacked America. Maurice and his friends wanted to sign up that day. "I will be 17 next month but, heck, the war could be over before we're 18." They talked about their 17-year-old friend, Harry Parker, who already had his dad's consent to join the Army and was leaving Saturday.

That night at dinner, after most of his family had finished eating, Maurice declared, "Dad, I plan to enlist in the Navy." Maurice did not expect so much resistance. At first his parents reacted with outrage and forbade their son to go, saying he was two years too young to go into the service.

Fred said, "I served in France and war is bloody, deadly and terrible. I saw my friends die right next to me. You are just too young, son. It's out of the question." Their argument started to fall apart when they were told some of Maurice's 17-year-old classmates had obtained their parents' consent on the enlistment forms and were already on their way to bootcamp.

Lillian and Fred tried pleading with their son not to go. Lillian was in tears. "If you have to go, at least wait until you have finished high school." Fred bargained. He was trying to buy time.

Maurice looked at him defiantly, "In a year and a half the war could be over and I want to serve my country."

His father countered, "At least wait until the end of this school year, please."

Maurice challenged, "And you will sign consent forms if I do wait until June?"

Fred knew his son would find a way to enlist with or without his blessing. Reluctantly Fred agreed, recalling he was only 17 when he joined the infantry. Fred held out hope this conflict would resolve itself within a few months, although he didn't really believe that. Maurice was not happy with the compromise but he agreed to stay four more months and finish the school term.

June

As Maurice's last day of his junior year ended, he went with two friends and enlisted in the Navy at the Palmdale Recruiting office. His parents had tried repeatedly to talk their son out of going, saying he was still too young but Perk's impulsive younger brother had made up his mind and Fred reluctantly signed the consent form. Maurice found his dad's old Army duffle bag in the shed and packed a few things. Fred gave him a razor even though his son hardly had a faint stubble of a few red hairs on his chin. At the bus station, there were tears as Fred consoled Lillian by saying at least he would not be in the infantry fighting in the trenches. He would have several layers of steel hull around him serving on a ship.

Desert winds stirred up small dust tornadoes as Perk's family hugged Maurice and wished him good luck. At Los Angeles he would get a bus transfer south to Liberty Station, San Diego.

Perk put his arm around his mother's shaking shoulders, as the bus turned the corner, and disappeared out of town. Between breaths, Lillian said, "It is the first time he's been away from home. He's so young."

Besides being sad to see his younger brother leave, Perk was a little envious. The thought was always in the back of his mind as he watched the young recruits from his town step on board the same bus that Maurice did. Six hours after Maurice's bus left Palmdale, he arrived at Liberty Station in San Diego for his nine weeks of Naval Recruit Training. He knew there would be another eight weeks of gunnery, and machinery school to follow.

Seaman Apprentice, Maurice Perkins

With training complete, Maurice was given a three day pass to see his family. He took the bus back to his parents house, surprising them by knocking on the front door at dinner. He stood there in his white naval uniform holding flowers for his mom. When she first saw him, she broke down in tears. There were many questions by his brothers and he described the training, marching, gunnery classes and what his quarters were like. "I'm shipping out for Pearl Harbor in four days and probably heading for the South Pacific after that. They don't tell us where. I have to report to San Francisco, the Port of Embarkation, the day after tomorrow." The time with his family went by so fast.

After arriving in the Golden Gate City, Seaman Apprentice Maurice Perkins got his orders to report to the troop ship, Stanton, headed for Hawaii. Two weeks later his mother received a letter, "It has been hard work but I am having the time of my life. I am stationed in the Naval Shipyards at Pearl Harbor, receiving training to fix, assemble and install gun batteries on board naval destroyers. Longer letter to follow." Some of his correspondence was censored out of his letter but his parents were assured their son had arrived safely in Hawaii.

Perk and Louie Messari—1942

They felt it was their duty to fight for their country, so Perk and his best friend, Louie Massari decided to go to a recruiting center downtown and enlist in the Army. Despite his parents, Pancho and Gene's resistance, Perk and Louie thought the wars overseas were passing them by. Louie was on the football team and Perk was in the Photo Club. Both were finishing their third semesters of college but they said they would return to it after they helped defeat the Germans and the Japanese. Many of the eager Palmdale boys had already left for basic training.

Perk and Louie felt both adventurous and apprehensive as they walked into the recruiting office. There were large colorful posters on the storefronts, one for each branch of the service. Once inside

Palmdale, mainstreet

Training poster

Louie Messari

Perk and Louie faced the four cubicles with more posters of the Army, Navy, Marines and the Coast Guard, each hung behind a man in uniform at their desks. The Navy poster asked, "Are You

Good Enough?" The Naval recruiter was talking to a young guy sitting with his father. Behind the Army recruiter was another poster showing the Aviation Cadet Training. Three pilots with leather caps and goggles looked skyward. The Army recruiter stood and shook both their hands and offered them a chair.

"We are here to sign up sir." Louie said as they both handed Sargent Wallace their filled-out applications. The recruiter read through both documents and rubber stamped Louie's papers.

He looked at Louie and told him, "Your basic training is next month." He was told where to report. When the recruiter scanned Perk's application, he saw he had a year and a half of junior college as an engineering major. More importantly, the recruiter was interested that Perk had a civilian pilot's license with over 100 hours in the air. He looked the skinny kid up and down, "So, you have a civilian pilots license?"

"Yes, sir! I have been flying a Travel Air 4000, and trained by Pancho Barnes near Muroc Air Base."

The recruiter's face lit up as he said, "I know her well. I've been to her tavern many times." The recruiter asked Perk if he was interested in being a pilot for the Army.

"Yes, Sir," he blurted a little too enthusiastically.

The man looked down at the college transcripts as Perk fidgeted. "I see you are pretty good at math and physics?" He thumped the recruiter desk with his index finger weighing what he would say, "Well, the only way you are going to be a pilot is to do what I suggest. You need to go home, finish your last semester of school and come back in five months. You can enter the Army as a 2nd Lieutenant, an officer and an aviation cadet. I will hold your application until then."

Perk's disappointment showed on his face. "But I thought... I mean I thought they needed us now? Can't they train me?"

The recruiter was insistent. "Son, the Army has high standards for its air cadets." He said firmly. "Take my advice, Mr. Perkins. Go home. Finish your sophomore year and come back in five months. I will hold your application until then."

The two boys, just 20-years-old, left the recruiting office, and Perk looked at his feet with a scowl. Louie's excitement at enlisting was dampened by his best friend's rejection but he tried to encourage Perk by saying, "Wow! A 2nd Lieutenant! You will already be an officer!" He wrapped his arm around Perk's neck in a choke hold and said, "I will have to salute you, so don't be an ass. Go finish school!"

That last semester went agonizingly slow as Perk watched his friends leave for basic training one after another, including Louie. His classrooms were half empty and filled with mostly girls. Classes were accelerated to finish up in May to get students off campus and into their war training programs. His second mechanical engineering class was studying the 1939 Vultee BT-13 Basic Trainer. Mr. Hadley, his instructor said, "Many pilots were being trained in the Vultee."

Louie wrote to Perk during his nine weeks of boot camp. "Training is pretty tough but we are all committed to fighting the enemy. We are exhausted every night. Meals are *K-rations*. These quonset huts are drafty, with a smudge pot for heating. Don't be too eager to get here, Lieutenant." Louie addressed him by his future Army rank. Louie added, "In aptitude tests I scored high for Radio Operator School. I guess building those crystal sets together panned out. I will come out after the Army Signal Corp training with a rank of Sergeant and if I make it on a bomber crew, I should make Staff Sergeant soon enough." The rest of his letter was about friends he had met and questions about what Perk was doing at college.

To add insult to injury, the news reported there had been an attack by Imperial Japan on the west coast of California. A Japanese submarine fired on a small oil refinery in Santa Barbara, California, doing little damage. By March everyone was on high alert.

The California coast was designated a vulnerable area and the War Department declared all persons of Japanese descent to be interned until the end of the war. Perk read that a hundred thousand Japanese in the US, including women and children were rounded up and taken to prison camps. They left their jobs, homes, farms and businesses across the nation, taking only what they could carry.

Perk listened to LA news radio, "American industry has sprung into action to support the war effort, employing women at jobs usually filled by men who are now overseas in the service." *Life Magazine* did a feature, "Grandparents filled in taking care of children, and volunteering for auxiliary groups and civil defense jobs. Newsreels showed workers and wives helping to transform fireworks and fuel manufacturing into munitions plants. Ford Motor Company began production on armored tanks and trucks. The appliance giant, Westinghouse, produced jet engines and army helmets. Shipyards and steel mills were asked to work three shifts, around the clock. The clothing industry changed almost overnight, into making uniforms and parachutes for the military." Perk saw the world changing around him and he felt stuck at home. Billboards and posters went up asking the public to conserve rubber, metal, wood and any food that might go to feed the troops.

Edward R. Murrow reported on home radios, "The United States has emerged from the longest and worst economic depression in history. After the attack on Pearl Harbor, almost overnight, a giant war industry has developed. Everyone is asked to do their part."

Murrow was eventually sent to London as a war correspondent. He reported on the nightly bombing of that city, known as the German Blitzkrieg. For the first time, the war was brought into the American peoples living rooms.

War bonds would help the government pay for the enormous expense of the war. Signs in downtown Palmdale read, "War Bonds Sold Here." "Keep Them Flying." "Buy a Bond." Organizations like the Elks Club had campaigns to sell war bonds. Families planted Victory Gardens for the troops. A poster at the Palmdale post office said, "Uncle Sam Needs You," with his finger pointing out at the viewer. There were fewer and fewer military men in uniform at the Happy Bottom Riding Club because they had all left for overseas. Pancho kept a can at the end of the tavern bar that was for war bond donations.

BUY A BOND

TO HONOR EVERY MOTHER'S SON IN SERVICE...

BUY AT YOUR LOCAL MOTION PICTURE THEATRE

Buy Bonds Poster at the Post Office

April

It was quiet in the college library with only the loud ticking of the wall clock to break the silence. Perk looked up from his book. There were particles of dust in the light rays from the clerestory windows above him. He returned the copy of *Heart of Darkness* by Joseph Conrad to the shelves and sniffed the pleasant odor of

Antelope Valley College

old books in the aisle. He was studying for his final exams and felt prepared in all his courses except for his English class. It was Friday evening and he grabbed his book bag and ran down the block to catch the five o'clock bus to Pancho's. At the bus stop he saw two men in drab green uniforms and he wished he was going where they were going.

At the desert crossroads, he jumped out of the accordion doors and walked a couple of long blocks to the tavern at Pancho's ranch. Over the bar was a big banner that said, "Happy 21st Birthday!" He had forgotten it was April 10th and his birthday.

Pancho shouted, "There you are!" After his initial blushing, slaps on the back and hand shakes all around he was handed a beer. Perk took a drink of the bitter amber ale and he wasn't used to the carbonation. His eyes smarted and he emerged with a foam mustache. "Tonight you're not working, Red. We're celebrating." Pancho declared. Julie, one of the hostesses, plunked out "Oh Danny Boy" on the up-right piano and Gene brought out a cake with one candle. Perk made a quick wish, blew out the flame and cut pieces of the layer cake for everyone. "Happy Birthday Red!" Pancho toasted again. It was a warm night, in a warm place with warm friends.

May

Perk graduated with a two-year Associate of Arts degree. He was handed a diploma with no fanfare and afterward he and his parents went to Pancho's Tavern for her Wednesday night dinner and dance. Perk showed off his diploma. "Well Hell, Red! I couldn't be prouder than a grizzly bear with its cub!" she exclaimed as she wrapped her arms around him. She had been his mentor in flying and had encouraged him to go to college. Everyone congratulated him and shook his hand. Gene seemed a little emotional as he told him, "Godspeed, son." The next day he returned to his recruiter and received his orders to report to Santa Ana training station.

The War in Europe and the Pacific—1942

Across the country in Washington DC, a top secret meeting, called the Arcadia Conference, between President Roosevelt and Churchill, the two leaders developed a strategy as key leaders in a world war. At the conference both agreed on making a principal military effort to defeat the Third Reich first, because Germany was the predominant member of the Axis powers. They also agreed to a defensive strategy in the Far East, knowing they couldn't give full strength to both theaters of operation at the same time. During the war, neither Germany or Japan could ever know the decision the two Allied leaders had made.

A lot was happening in the European war and in the Pacific theater. In June 1942, a turning point in the Pacific came with the U.S. naval victory at the Battle of Midway. The Japanese fleet sustained heavy losses and was finally turned back. Australian and New Zealander forces in New Guinea and British forces in India were finally able to halt the Japanese advances.

The Luftwaffe's London Blitz bombing of England's capital and other cities, from September 1940 to May 1941 had rattled Great Britain but it hadn't beaten them. With the wreckage of 1700 of Air Marshal Goring's aircraft and a loss of 2600 German airmen, scattered across the beaches of Southampton, Plymouth and Portsmouth, Hitler finally gave up on conquering Great Britain. It was a defeat from which he would never fully recover.

By June the Fuehrer turned his attention to his Russian Ally, Joseph Stalin, whom he had come to despise. He ordered Operation Barbarossa, the Nazi offensive to conquer the vast USSR lands and resources to the east. It was the largest and most powerful invasion force in history with over three million Axis troops, 19 Panzer divisions, 3,000 tanks, 2,500 aircraft, and 7,000 artillery pieces which poured across the thousand-mile-long border. It was a hard fought battle, resulting in 775,000 casualties on the German side and 800,000 soldiers lost from the Soviet Union. Germany successfully advanced and occupied 300 miles inside Russia.

By July 1942, Hitler's all-out offensive to take the industrial city of Stalingrad was successful as they fought bloody battles in the streets, finally occupying the city. But by December, as one of the harshest winters in Russian history closed in on the German troops, the below zero temperatures had settled in and their stores of food, coal and ammunition were running low. The once regal city, named after Stalin, found the occupying soldiers and their captives, starved and frozen.

With ruthless strategy, Stalin sent a counter offensive of his Red Army to the north and one to the south of the city to cut off and surround Stalingrad. The German troops were outflanked, out of food and too weak to put up an effective defense. The German army sustained 500,000 more casualties and 100,000 more starving and injured German troops were taken prisoner. Hitler's campaign to conquer Soviet lands and capture their wealth of resources had been a terrible and costly failure. Historians have said the Battle of Stalingrad was a turning point of the war in Europe.

The British and Americans were bombing cities from the west, Allied armies were moving north from Africa, and the Soviets were attacking from the east. Yet the war would continue for another three years.

Boot Camp and Cadet Training—1942

Perk was 21 and was living away from his home town for the first time. His six week long accelerated bootcamp in Santa Ana, California, was rigorous and exhausting. He gained strength and resolve as he pressed forward over the hurdles and he learned to work as a cooperative team in the newly named US Army Air Force. The training base had a small city of quonset huts, each furnished with 14 cots which included an unnecessary stove because it was 90 degrees in the June heat. Regular and surprise unit inspections of lockers, uniforms, boots and mess kits were a constant worry. No one wanted to be responsible for group push-ups, extra marching, or kitchen duty as punishment for inspection infractions.

A uniform allowance of $150 was given to each recruit. Perk had been fitted for a khaki uniform for work. His olive drab dress wool uniform had brass buttons on the front, pockets and epaulets. His garrison cap had a brown leather hat band and displayed the Army Air Force insignia in the center front. He took pride in his new uniform.

August

His family was not much for writing letters, but his 16-year-old brother, Lloyd had scribbled a cryptic note to Perk at the end of August. "I got all my classes I wanted at school, and afterwards I got a job working at the market for Mr. Phillips. I can't wait to join the Army Air Force too, but dad nixed that saying I was too young. Sending two sons off to war is quite enough for now." Lloyd continued by saying, "We haven't heard from Maurice since he reached Pearl Harbor, Hawaii, so please write to Mom." He closed the letter by saying, "The family is praying for both you and Maurice."

Perk wrote a letter to his mom saying he was doing well in cadet training and he hadn't washed out yet. He hoped to get a pass to come see them by Thanksgiving or Christmas.

September

After boot camp Perk wanted to enter the Army's air cadet program, although nothing was guaranteed. The Army Air Force desperately needed well trained crews to man their ever-increasing fleet of new airplanes. They were still entrusting their $250,000 aircraft to 19 to 23 year-old boys. The two-year college requirement Perk had achieved was dropped from the air cadet requirements soon after Perk joined the Army. The Classification and Replacement Branch of the Army relied solely on a strenuous three-hour written assessment exam, the Army General Classification Test (AGCT). First it measured a recruit's intelligence and eliminated those that were functioning illiterates. There was a series of math tests, chart reading and the visual spatial problems, along with mechanical engineering questions.

Only half of the enlisted personnel passed and entered the air cadet program to become one of the ten man crew on bombers. Ten percent of those cadets would qualify for the pilot training program. Five percent became navigators and five percent bombardiers. The rest became gunners, mechanics and radio operators. The psychological tests and hand-eye coordination assessments would come later during physical training. Perk's college engineering courses and his civilian pilot training had prepared him to do well. He wrote home that he was now an Air Force cadet in training.

As a cadet he was addressed as Mister Perkins by all ranks. He was given an allowance of $225 a month, of which his flight pay of $75 a month he said would be enough for him during his training. The rest he sent home to his mother. The flight pay still continued indefinitely if he were missing in action or became a prisoner of war.

Pilots, Co-Pilots, Navigators and Bombardiers entered the cadet program as 2nd Lieutenants. The Engineer, Radio operator,

Waist Gunners and Tail Gunners were either Sergeants or Staff Sergeants. In addition to classroom work, Perk had to accumulate 60 hours in the air for flight training with each session in the Stearman biplane being just under an hour.

October

In Primary Pilot Training, Perk first sat in the co-pilot seat as his instructor, Lieutenant Frank Dodd, sat in front piloting the plane. Even though he had a civilian pilot's license, he kept silent, watched and learned. He found the controls were a variation to those on the Travel Air 4000. Dodd's training techniques differed from those of Pancho Barnes by scale and size of equipment. He often had to unlearn what he had learned from Pancho.

Stearman

Lancaster, California

November

Perk had accumulated the required 60 hours in the Stearman trainer and was ready to move on. He had made it through the first round of training. From his group of 48 cadets, only five did not pass the required math, physics and engineering tests. They would go on to training in communication, armament, meteorology and radar operations.

Tomorrow was Thanksgiving and Perk asked for and received a week's pass home, considered his "delay-enroute" leave. Aboard the Greyhound bus, the seat next to him had a young sailor asleep, with his mouth open holding his white "dixie cup" hat in his lap. The bus was full of G.I.s and people traveling for the holidays. He was lucky to have gotten a pass because this might be the last he saw his family before leaving for New Mexico and Nebraska. The movement of the Greyhound bus lulled him to sleep as it bumped and swayed around curves going up the Angeles Crest highway to home.

The old truck was waiting at the bus station in Lancaster and Perk waved at his dad, threw his duffle bag in the truck bed and jumped in next to him. It was swell to see him and he wanted to hug his dad but Fred wasn't much for those displays of affection.

"How are you doin, son?" his dad asked fondly.

"I'm good." Perk nodded but added quickly, "Any news from Maurice?"

His dad shrugged and shook his head. Fred's silence was due to the lump in his throat, preventing him from speaking. "Your mother and I got a note in September. He swallowed hard and Perk could hear the worry in his voice. After a few minutes of uncomfortable silence, his father asked, "When do you have to report back?"

Perk explained he had to get himself to Minter field near Shafter, two hours north, by December 5th. His dad offered to drive him there but Perk said he would take the bus, knowing that the old truck might not make the four hour round trip.

While living in drafty tents with smoking stoves and eating cold food, Perk had dreamed of his family's Thanksgiving table. Perk soaked in every sense: the smells, the candlelight on the dining table, the chatter of his mother's voice talking to his brothers and his little sister. He had never appreciated it so much. His brothers put up a Christmas tree early because Perk wouldn't be there for the holidays. There were a few wrapped presents for him under the lit-up decorated tree.

His mom had been preparing the meal all day. Starting at five in the morning she roasted a 25-pound turkey, mashed potatoes and gravy, stuffing, biscuits, homemade cranberry sauce and a pumpkin pie with whip cream. His family, plus his aunt Mary and uncle Earl gathered around the table. The blessing included hopes that both he and his brother Maurice would be returned safely home and the war would end soon. Perk memorized those warm images to take with him.

Perk spent the week at his parents' home, mending fences, putting a new carburetor in the old truck and spending time with his three brothers and three-year-old sister, Barbara. He took the old truck out to see Pancho Barnes and Gene at the ranch. When he drove up, it somehow looked smaller than he remembered.

"Hey there Red! You look like a real officer with your white-wall haircut and spit-shined shoes," she bellowed. "Sit and take a load off and tell us all about your flying adventures."

Perk related stories of the Stearman biplane trainer and how there was a lot more physics and math in his training than he expected. Pancho said she had flown with Frank Dodd, Perk's instructor, and she related a few stories that Perk couldn't repeat.

Seeing Pancho and his family revitalized his spirits and he was ready on Saturday to catch his bus to Minter Field. Everyone posed for pictures and said their goodbyes before Fred drove Perk to the bus station. His father shook his hand and he couldn't conceal his emotions and pride as he looked at his son standing before him.

December

The rural town of Shafter was mostly farms and a small town center with a post office, bank, grocery and coffee shop. The nearby Minter Field was an airbase with a massive tent city and several runways built quickly by the Army six months before the attack on Pearl Harbor. Perk's bus let him off at the commanding officers headquarters where he was assigned his quarters, a lofty term to describe a primitive, drafty eight man tent that made the Santa Ana quonset huts seem like luxury.

With this new round of training and tests, Perk hoped to stay the course and not be one of those cadets to wash out of the program. "I still have skin in the game," he thought optimistically. These courses were very intense and technical. He and his fellow cadets realized the goal of the specialized training was not to wash out trainees but to help them succeed. Many of the lessons he learned had to become automatic, instinctive and the only way they could achieve that was through practical experience in the trainers. Those lessons he learned in cadet training would most likely save his life.

His first meeting with his commanding officer at Minter, laid out the Basic Pilot Training to the room full of cadets. "You men will learn how to fly blind in formation, using only instruments. There are skills you need to know about night and long distance flying." The farthest Perk had ever flown the Travel Air 4000 was for crop dusting jobs in Modesto. He had made a fuel stop at Stockton airport, and the round trip flight only took one hour each way. He had never flown at night.

Vultee BT-13 Basic Trainer

In school, Perk and the group of cadets were introduced to the mono-wing plane, the Vultee BT-13 Basic Trainer which he had studied in his engineering class. Sergeant Hadley showed photos of the Stearman biplane and the BT-13 and explained, "While a biplane wing has a structural advantage it produces more drag than a mono wing aircraft." He pointed at the bi-wing, "Interference between the airflow and the extensive bracing between biplane wings cause substantial drag." In comparison he showed a diagram of the airflow of a mono-plane wing and how it glided over the wing and lifted the aircraft with much less resistance. Besides the wing design, the Vultee had a more powerful engine, the R-985 at 450 horsepower. It was faster and heavier than the primary Stearman trainer. All the cadets were itching to get their hands on the controls. Over the next eight weeks they would learn radio communications, use of landing flaps and how to operate the Hamilton Standard controllable-pitch propeller. On the BT-13, the flaps were operated by a simple crank-and-cable system. He absorbed the information and put it in his notes.

In Europe, besides the B-24 Liberators, the principle heavy bomber used was the B-17 as seen in theater newsreels. The narrator said the Boeing aircraft didn't need fighter escorts because it had 11 defensive Browning M2 .30 caliber guns to defend against enemy fighters. The truth was in 1942 there were no escorts with the range of the B-17. The Flying Fortress bomber flew at speeds up to 260 miles per hour to an altitude of 26,000 feet. The ship's flight range of 2,000 miles, while carrying a 5,000 pound bomb load, was the farthest of any heavy bomber of its time. No fighter plane had that capability. If Perk ended up in the European theater, most likely it would be in a B-17 bomber or in a B-24 Liberator.

On December 12th he was surprised to get a four-day pass to go home to see his parents for Christmas. He caught a Greyhound bus to Lancaster and hitched a ride the rest of the way home with a friend. He knocked on the door of his parents' house at dinner time and his mother answered and was so surprised to see him. Hugs and happy pats on the backs while they set a place for him at the table.

"What have you been doing?" His brothers asked, "Have you flown any bigger Army planes or are you still in trainers? How is the food? Where do you go next? Have you heard anything about the war in the Pacific?" Everyone was talking at once. After all of his answers to their questions, he just wanted to hear their voices and news of home.

The next day Perk borrowed his dad's truck and went to see Pancho. The place was empty of patrons in the tavern with only a few at the dude ranch. Her airfield had been restricted to crop dustering only. The military brass at the base took exception to the flyboys spending so much time with Pancho's girls and there were rumors of security breaches. They weren't making it easy for her to stay in business. Still Pancho was holding on with trail rides and of course the crop dusting. "How the Hell are you, Red? Are they treating you well in flight school?"

Pancho and he listened to a report on the radio about the battle of Guadalcanal to disrupt the airfields and supply chain in the Pacific. The Solomon Islands campaign was one of the most important battles of the Pacific near Australia. In Europe our bombers were taking a beating, losing more aircraft before they or their crews could be replenished.

After his leave, Perk returned to Minter Field and his training schedule and eight weeks passed quickly. He spent mornings in the flight trainer with Sergeant Hadley and afternoons in the classroom and he logged 73 hours in the air. The first month he mastered the pitch propeller and landing flaps lessons as well as the radio communication section. The second month he used those skills in night flying. Unless there was a moon there was little light to see, except for a few house lights from farms and lights on the airstrip. It was mostly instrument flying and landing. The cadets were up early and to bed early studying to stay in the game.

Dottie—1942

January 20

"I did well on all my final exams my first semester at Hastings College. I met Jack in my econ class and he asked me to go out for a coke with him. He seems very nice and polite. Besides Economics, my classes this semester are Business, Industrial Relations. I am in the advanced classes of Dictation, Shorthand and Speed typing."

March 8

"Lavonne's and my sorority are having a spring picnic at Hartwell Park. We have offered our flat bottom boat to float around on the pond. Jimmie Jenkins asked me to the Job's Daughters spring formal. Don Betz signed up for the Navy and is leaving in three weeks. I can't believe how many of my friends are gone. Even Lavonne is thinking of joining the WAVES, a new unit of the Navy. She says she might be stationed in Hawaii or some other South Pacific Island."

Not One, Not Three, But FOUR Bouricii Here This Year To Enliven Campus

One-two-three-four — it's the Bouricius clan counting off as they start for college. Perhaps they don't do it in just that manner, but at least they must make certain that all of them are safely tucked in the grey V-8 before it starts to chug schoolward each morning.

Members of this quartet are Willard, senior; Ruth, junior; and Dorothy and Lavonne, freshmen. Barthold, an older brother, graduated from Hastings college last year; and there are yet two younger boys looking forward to attending the family alma mater. They Saw and See All Summer

The entire group spends the summer in Peaceful Valley, Colo. (which somehow is never quite so peaceful after their arrival), where they are building a cabin. The cabin, a rustic structure with five rooms and a path, is being constructed bit by bit each year. Oftentimes the family becomes more interested in mountain trips than in finishing the cabin—and so the building was without a front door for some time. Each time the family went away for the day they carefully closed the windows—and proceeded through the wide-open space reserved for the door.

The mountains provided Ruth with a hobby—collecting arrowheads and other Indian relics. Her most valued specimen is a large dark arrowhead found in the remains of an Indian camp near Greeley, Colo. She has been offered $200 for this one alone. Ancestral Decorations

The Bouricius home in Hastings is a large stucco-covered structure on south Hastings avenue. Besides a large family and a battery fac-

tory, many things of historical interest are found in their home. Over the fireplace is an assortment of sabers, guns, and other old weapons. These and other items were inherited by Mr. Bouricius from his ancestral estate in the Netherlands.

Photography is the hobby of the entire family—not only picture-taking but also finishing the films. A large collection of colored pictures, most of them taken in Colorado, are displayed to visitors. Those Bouricius Appetites!

Food problems for the family sound similar to those of the campus dining hall. Of course, the family's needs are slightly less than those of the dining hall—but nonetheless whenever Mother Bouricius starts cooking a meal she makes certain that she doubles each of her big recipes, checks to see that she has several loaves of bread, and makes sure that there's at least a gallon of milk.

Sounds like fun, doesn't it? Well it is—unless you're the poppa and have to "pay the freight." Even so, the "Bouricii" figure that the fun and fellowship they have is well worth the pull.

Hastings College news clipping, 1942

April 11

"I am 19 today and my family was there to celebrate. Since Ruth announced her engagement to Bob Hepting, I haven't seen much of her. I got another diary from Grandma Keeling and a plaid skirt and jacket from Mom and Guy. Lavonne gave me perfume and lipstick. After dinner we all went to Heartwell Park and roller skated. We had so much fun."

When the sun comes out from behind a cloud and April weather makes itself too lovely to be ignored, the six lively Bouricii, children of Mr. and Mrs. G. M. Bourlcius try their hands—and feet—at roller skating. Stretching clear across the street in single file, they progress around the winding curves of the Heartwell Park driveway. From left to right, they are LaVonne, Willard, Dorothy, Bob, Ruth and Dick. Dick is an eighth grader; Bob is junior in high school; and the other four are Hastings College students. Another brother, Barthold, is a graduate student at the University of Wisconsin in Madison.

Daily Tribune, 1942

June 16

"President Roosevelt announced we had to switch to a 'wartime economy' which means we all have to conserve gasoline, rubber, metal, silk and sugar. No more making candy, I guess. We have ration cards to buy things. Even shoes and leather are rationed and we are encouraged to save for the troops. Mom and Guy are selling War Bonds to raise money. Our neighbor, Mrs. Peterson, left for Washington state after her husband joined the Navy. Her parents live in Seattle and she plans to get a job there in the aircraft factory. She said they pay well and it will help the war effort."

August 15

"At the cabin we got less done because of all the war shortages and fewer of our family was there to work on the interior floor and upper staircase and landing. My brother Bob joined the Army and went for basic training in July. I will miss him terribly. Bart and Willard joined the Army and are working for the Army Corps of Engineers at Los Alamos, New Mexico. They came to the mountains for a week to help Guy. Bob Hepting is now in Basic Training to become a Naval Pilot. Ruth wants to finish teacher college before they get married. Life sure seems to have accelerated since Pearl Harbor."

November 26

"The newsreels and radio reports of what is happening in Europe are awful, especially to Jewish people. Edward R. Murrow reported on the battle of Stalingrad. The Allies have invaded North Africa bombing Casablanca. We are told those were U.S. victories, but they don't look like it from the newsreels."

December 21

"I did well on all my final exams at Hastings College. I can't believe it has been a year since the attack on Pearl Harbor. A lot of my friends are getting secretarial jobs at the Army base if they have any free weekdays or weekends, making 30 cents an hour. My friend Florence said she could give me a ride from the college to the base and back home after our four hour shift."

4.

The Reality of War

$\mathcal{A}$T A SECRET MEETING IN Casablanca, Morocco, President Roosevelt and Winston Churchill discussed the future of the Eighth Air Force in England. Roosevelt had announced plans for merging the Eighth Air Force with the Royal Air Force in their night bombing raids against the Wehrmacht. When General Hap Arnold found out about the plan, he and Ira Eaker, head of the Eighth Air Force put together a memorandum to present to Winston Churchill. The memo's main point was that the RAF would continue bombing at night and the Eighth would accelerate its daylight bombing raids in Northern Europe. In doing that the German defenses would get no rest with their around-the-clock-bombing campaign. Hitler would then be forced to order his tens of thousands of factory workers to lay down their hammers and pick up helmets to fight in the defense of the Reich. Their vitally important production factories of Luftwaffe aircraft, submarines, and armaments would greatly suffer, ruining the German industry and morale. The Eighth would increase the strength and frequency of the daylight attacks on industry, transportation and oil production, while expanding the thousands of aircraft and armament factories and pilot and crew training facilities in the United States.

Churchill agreed to try their proposal of round-the-clock bombing, but only for a time. Since the D-Day invasion was tentatively scheduled for the spring of 1944, Hap Arnold and Eaker only had a year and a few months to make good on their plan. Their goal was to soften the lands occupied by the Reich with the bombing by the Eighth Air Force and to try to achieve air superiority.

It seemed that everything in Perk's life had been leading up to this month, from the autumn of 1939 while taking flight lessons with Pancho Barnes, to joining the Army and becoming an aviation cadet. Lt. Perkins' part in this plan hatched by Arnold and Eaker and presented to Churchill was a mere grain of sand in the strategy to win the war in Europe. Perk passed all the classroom and flight tests. He got his orders to leave in the morning for Walker AirField, New Mexico, for Advanced Pilot Training. The cadets were trying out for positions in single-engine or multi-engine aircraft and they were supposed to get a total of 75 flight hours before graduating and getting their pilots wings.

He took a Greyhound bus to Los Angeles where he caught an eastbound train to Santa Fe with a transfer to Albuquerque. As he watched the desert landscape pass his window, one of his buddies on the train pointed out some Indian settlements off in the distance. "They must be Acoma or Zuni, I'm not sure," he said. Perk found the desert landscape beautiful having grown up in the California desert. But this was different. There were red and rainbow colored tabletop mountains that rose up out of the large expanses of desert flat lands. Sagebrush and saguaro trees dotted the landscape with the occasional homestead shack. He caught a short bus ride out to Walker AirField. Having traveled for nearly 38 hours, he was starving and stiff from sitting so long. The sprawling Walker AirField had row upon row of quonset hut barracks and multiple airstrips with classroom buildings concentrated in the interior. The base was a couple miles south of the town of Roswell, built by the Army quickly following the attack on Pearl Harbor. Perk walked with his duffle bag straight to the mess hall and wolfed down two bologna sandwiches and a couple of glasses of milk.

At the base headquarters he was assigned a barracks in one of the quonset hut cities adjacent to the PX. Perk put his gear on a bunk and rubbed his frigid hands together muttering.

Another airmen two bunks over commented, "Even the mice in the barracks here, wear thermal underwear."

Perk chuckled, extending his hand, "Hi, I'm Perk from LA." The officer was bundled up in a knit cap and sweater.

"I'm Glenn Halverson, also from Los Angeles."

Perk asked, "Does it ever warm up in here?"

Glenn shook his head, "Nope. It's high desert here at 3,500 feet. The winter temperatures at night drop into the low 20s and it is cold in these drafty barracks." A coal stove in the center belched black smoke from a metal chimney out the roof, but smoke still filtered back into the barracks with a haze in the upper half of the room.

As Perk shoved his gear in his locker they talked. Both cadets seemed to be on the same trajectory to become pilots. Glenn had trained in the same aviation cadet programs in Santa Ana and Oxnard and had earlier gone to LA City college to become an accountant. He too was told by his recruiter to go back and finish up his fourth semester of junior college to enter the service as an officer.

At Walker Field the cadets took instrument training, including twenty hours on the *Link* simulator which recorded and responded to the pilot's controls. It imitated the sensation of flying an aircraft without actually being in the air.

Besides testing in a simulator, wing formations had to be memorized as safety in numbers proved a vital strategy. Perk imagined the layered formation above the cloud layer, of 36 bombers, all assembled before a mission. The possible chaos and accidents at the assembly point is what kept him awake at night. The cadets went over and over the *Buncher* signal instruction where a radion beacon from a signal station shot a light beam five miles into the atmosphere. The pilot ascended in a circle around the Buncher Beacon each taking their designated place in formation. The cadets practiced that exercise over and over in the Cessna Bobcat.

He didn't know where he would be stationed if he passed pilot training. There were locations in Europe, North Africa, French Indochina and the South Pacific. He was being taught skills to deal with those climate hazards of wind, rain, fog or snow in the classroom. He would have to wait to learn how to land on slick runways in the country in which he was assigned.

American boys training for air combat were lucky to be learning to fly in the sunny weather of Texas, Arizona, and New Mexico. At the same time RAF, German and Russian flight trainees had to deal with rain, fog and snow while learning to fly their Lancasters, Heinkels and Messerschmitts. American air cadets flew an average of 300 flight training hours compared to Luftwaffe replacement pilots training for less than 200 flight hours. By 1942 American bomber pilots were flying longer combat sorties than the German Air Force, but RAF and American pilots rarely flew operations

Cessna AT-17 Trainer

more than two or three times a week. German pilots found themselves flying five to six days a week with little sleep.

February

In his Advanced Pilot Training, Perk spent many hours in the Cessna AT-17 Bobcat trainer which was used by the military as a bridge-the-gap between single-engine trainers and twin-engine combat aircraft. The compact four passenger plane had two Jacobs R-755-9 radial piston engines. After six weeks, Perk had logged 37 flight hours in the Cessna.

The flight instructors would ultimately determine who was best for bomber crews and who would fly solo in the fighter aircraft: the P38 Lightnings or the P-47 Thunderbolts. Besides demonstrated skills, it came down to the temperament of the man. Fighter pilots flew alone and their personalities were more that of aggressive fighters. Perk had a cool, level headed, methodical personality and he worked well on a team. He was a leader of men.

March

Perk went up in a B-17 for the first time at Hobbs airfield in the co-pilot seat. During the next month of his training, he logged 35 hours, flying to and from several training bases. He continued in March to fly the co-pilots seat in a B-17 to Wichita Falls, Texas, flying back to Roswell, New Mexico. A few days later he flew Amarillo, Texas, and back to Roswell, logging more flight hours.

Several of the cadets were selected to go for a week-long instruction at Moses Lake, in Washington State, and were trained on B-17D bombers and P-38s. Perk and Glenn had logged an additional 20 hours in night, day, dual and solo flight training in the two types of airships.

At Hobbs-Local, New Mexico, a group of Perk's friends flew a night practice bombing mission. Perk flew as co-pilot to Lt. Robert Williams, the pilot. They were to fly to a target, marked by flare pots, placed in a cross, in which the center was the target. The Williams crew took off at 1800 hours, just at dusk, with fair weather and a few gusts of wind. After two hours Williams navigator Allen Parks still hadn't found the bombing area and they received a message from the base telling them to return because the mission was called off. A weather front was moving in and the pilot was fighting ever increasing high winds. The flares at the target were likely blown out and the winds were far in excess of what Sgt. Sutter, their radio man, had been told. With not enough wind correction, they were further pushed off course and became hopelessly lost. Lt. Williams notified the crew on the interphone he was returning to base and made a 180 degree turn plus a correction for the cross-wind.

The crew did not know they were drifting farther west because of the severe winds and due to their lack of sufficient correction. Allen Parks had flown night training flights before and he and the radio man worked on finding a military beacon or a commercial radio station signal. If they could find them, Parks and Sutter could identify the signal and station to get a bearing. Sutter turned on the radio direction finder (RDF) to get the bearing when they first became lost. If he could locate two stations, the navigator could get a fix. Their approximate location was where the two lines of position crossed when plotted on a map.

Parks continued searching for lights to give them an indication where they were. Sutter said, "Because of the wind, the static on the radio is really bad, making it impossible to find a signal to get a bearing. There were some thunderheads in the area which caused a lot of electrical interference, too. Sutter radioed Perkins and said, "I can't get a response. They must be shut down for the night. No one will answer me and we are well within range."

It was after midnight and they had been in the air for seven hours and Perk could hear the concern in Lt. Williams' voice. They were worried they would run out of fuel before they reached the base. They set up a long range cruise condition with a low manifold pressure and low RPM on the engine to conserve fuel. Finally, Sutter got a code name for a bearing to a radio station. Parks had finally found their location and plotted the route to their base adding a correction factor for the continuing wind drift.

Anxious, Williams and Perkins watched their fuel supply light on engine number two turn red, showing fuel depletion. Perk called the tower and was cleared to land with a straight-in approach luckily because five seconds later number three tank light came on as they lowered their landing gear. Surprisingly, with the wind factor, Williams made a good landing on just two engines. The operations officer was a bit peeved. The crew had left for a three-hour flight and spent nearly 22,000 gallons on an eight hour lost adventure. Lt. Williams had to write a report and take the blame for the late night soiree. His commanding officers warned that there were almost as many aircraft lost in training accidents in the states as there were in combat overseas. That was an experience the crew didn't want to repeat.

April

That evening Perk and Glenn went to the officers canteen and gave a toast to Perk's 22nd birthday with a round of drinks. He thought of home and his mom and dad because he knew they were probably thinking of him, too.

May

Lieutenant Johnson had returned from England after 25 missions and Perk and a few officers joined him at the Officers Club to celebrate. Perk asked what it was like over there. Johnson related a story of 290 B-17 bombers participating in two raids on factories in Schweinfurt, Germany. A devastating loss of 110 airplanes in those two raids with 900 US airmen killed. Perk's first thought was that his friend, Louie Messari was over there and he prayed he was alright. After hearing about that disastrous mission, the air cadets were very sober about what they had ahead of them.

Harvard Air Field, Nebraska

The same month Perk and his friend Glenn were assigned to Harvard Airfield, Nebraska, as part of the 447th bomb group. They were trained on the B-17F Flying Fortress. Having flown the older model, they found there were many new features to this redesigned airplane. The fuselage had been extended ten feet, eight new defensive turrets and machine guns were added. To accommodate the extra weight, an upgraded super-turbo-charged engine was added. The 13 weeks the men were stationed there made it possible for them to finish their duties during the week and get a weekend pass to go by bus to Hastings for R & R.

Maurice—1943

In Palmdale, California, Lillian had roasted a chicken for her family with mashed potatoes and gravy. On April 26, 1943, the Perkins family was gathered for an early Saturday dinner and a telegram arrived by carrier, informing them their son, Pvt. Earl Maurice Perkins was missing-in-action. The brief telegram from the Navy said they regretted that they had no other information at this time. Lillian sat down on a bench by the door and cried as she held the letter to her heart.

A week later the Perkins family received another telegram from James Forrestal, Secretary of the Navy, explaining briefly the circumstances of the USS Aaron Ward, the ship on which their son had served. After all were accounted for, Earl Maurice Perkins was listed as missing in action on April 15, 1943.

Lillian couldn't believe the news about Maurice. She kept busy because she had other sons at home and a baby girl. She told herself Maurice was lost somewhere in the Pacific islands or perhaps in a hospital. She could accept any injury as long as he came home alive. She retreated into her faith and the Baptist church saying, "Whatever happens, it is God's will." Lillian debated whether to write a letter to her son, Clarence while he was away in the Air Force. She decided to wait until she had more information.

B-17G aircrafts were being delivered every day to Harvard Base from factories all over the country. Three days before Christmas a friend of Perk's, Lt. Frank Walters, was landing at Harvard and he brought the plane in too hot. The aircraft exploded on landing, killing everyone on board. Perk was devastated seeing the sobering scene of ten men dying instantly. That woke him up to how easy it was to die in an aircraft.

On hundreds of airfields and training bases around the United States, the U.S. Army Air Force aviation instructors taught men, like 2nd Lt. Clarence Perkins, how to fly fighter planes and heavy bombers. Young students that had been sitting in classrooms or playing on High School baseball teams, a few months before. They were from the industrial areas of Detroit, the sunny beach towns of Southern California and the plains of Montana. The purpose of their intense training was as replacements for those aircrews killed or captured in aerial combat in the skies over Europe or the Pacific. In December 1941 the Army maintained only 340,000 troops. By 1943, those numbers had ballooned to nearly two and a half million soldiers, which they maintained with new recruits until the end of the war.

While Perk was doing his training stateside at Harvard Airfield and getting ready to ship out to England, the first all-American bomber mission took off from Polebrook, Northamptonshire, England. The raid was to attack enemy railroad and marshaling yards at Rouen, France. Previous daylight bombing missions flown by the Royal Air Force had ended with heavy losses as high as 50%. After that the RAF was grounded until they resumed their missions flying only at night.

Fight Back

The U.S. Eighth Army Air Force was being pressured by Washington to fight back against the nightly raids by the Luftwaffe. Brigadier General Ira C. Eaker led the first American daylight raid on board his B-17, *Yankee Doodle*. He was accompanied by Major Paul W. Tibbets, commander of the 97th's 340th Bomb Squadron.

Three years later Tibbets would pilot the B-29, *Enola Gay* on its way to drop the atomic bomb on Hiroshima, Japan. That courageous first raid in August 1942 to Rouen, was a success with no casualties and moderate damage to the eighteen aircraft. Finally the U.S. had aviators in this fight.

Heavy bomber crews got early morning briefings of intelligence reports about the weather, enemy air defense batteries, flak concentration and possible resistance by enemy fighters around the target. The intelligence wasn't always accurate and there were many circumstances where the climate, or number of enemy fighters had changed. General Eaker, head of the Eighth Air Force saw hundreds of bombers in formation who would have to fight their way into the target and get themselves back out without fighter support. The escorts had limited fuel and range capacity compared to the bombers.

One of the largest hazards for bomber aircrews, in the early years of the war, was falling out of the bomber formation to be picked off by Luftwaffe fighter planes. Whether due to flak or other mechanical issues, U.S. heavy bombers who couldn't maintain their airspeed and altitude, for whatever reason, became prime targets for the enemy. The casualty numbers mounted in 1943. They were losing too many airplanes and trained crews. There had been accumulated strategies from past wars, for troops on the ground and at sea, but very little saved experiences using combat aircraft during WWI. No country had ever fought an air war with bombers prior to 1935. This was unproven ground for the military aircraft planners of WWII.

The benefit of safety in numbers in tight bomber formations, proved to be a vital strategy of General Curtis LeMay. He recognized close wing to wing layered boxes of bombers organized in squadrons would save more aircraft and crews on the round trip to the targets. The structure of the combat boxes were called "elements." In the tight "V" formation where there was a lead aircraft and a plane on the left and right of the leader creating a "V." That lead plane was responsible for maintaining its position relative to the squadron's head plane. There were four elements of three aircraft each, forming a 12 plane squadron. Three of those squadrons formed a 36 plane group and three groups formed a 108 plane wing. Each Group occupied a stretch of sky, 600 yards long, a mile wide, and half a mile deep. Huge combat wings would form at five mile intervals to create a Division Column, low and high groups of six planes each. Hundreds, sometimes thousands of aircraft assembled in these boxes before a bomb run. The boxes were designed to take full advantage of the B-17's combined defensive fire power.

In formation, the lowest group of bombers was known to be the most dangerous position and the main target of Nazi fighter attacks. The last plane in the low group was the most vulnerable and nicknamed the "Purple Heart Corner" because of its vulnerable position to be picked off by Luftwaffe fighters.

Perk practiced the formation boxes in the flight training at Walker Air Force Base as well at Harvard Airfield. A radion beacon from a signal station, called the Buncher Signal, shot a

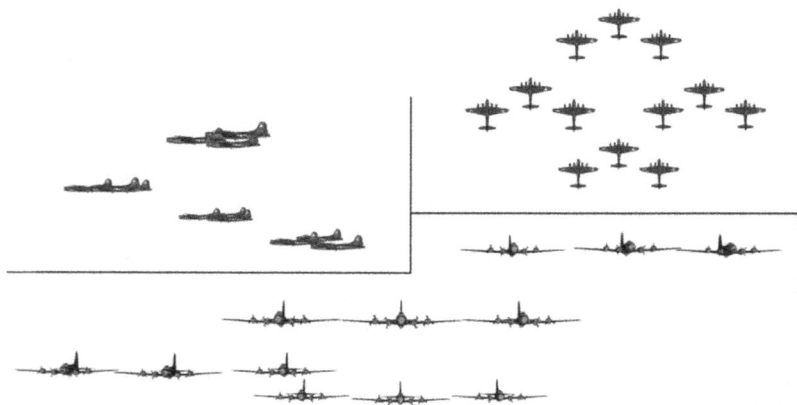

Formation Box

light beam five miles into the atmosphere. The bombers circled around the vertical beacon until every aircraft ascended and took their place in formation. The aviators practiced it over and over in their trainers.

In the spring of 1943, there was only one fighter group in England assigned to provide escort support for the Eighth Air Force. The Army believed their heavy bombers, equipped with thirteen .50 caliber machine guns could adequately defend themselves against the enemy of the Third Reich. The U.S. fighter escorts, the P-47 Thunderbolt and P-38 Lightning lacked the fuel range to escort bombers all the way to their targets and back to their base. They were only able to accompany the formations 1200 miles inside the border of Germany and would have to turn back to refuel. Damaged bombers and vulnerable stragglers who fell out of formation, had to fend for themselves against a pack of Messerschmitt German fighter planes. Many got shot down.

During the autumn of 1943 the casualties in the Eighth Army Air Force had reached such alarming numbers, especially in one seven-day period in October. On the 8th of October, on a raid to Bremen, Germany, the 100th Bomb Group lost nine out of eighteen bombers. The next day, on a mission to Marienburg, Germany, 28 bombers went down with a loss of 280 men. On October 10th, to Munster, Germany, another 30 planes were shot down with many planes disabled resulting in the next mission having fewer planes and less formation defensive power. In three consecutive missions, the Eighth Army Air Force lost almost 900 men who failed to come back to their bases. The 100th Bomb Group was ordered to stand down, not having enough planes or men to mount a raid.

The next disastrous raid to Schweinfurt, on October 14th, the 92nd Bomb Group was short their normal number of 21 aircraft; only able to put up 13 planes. The 306th offered 15 aircraft with many turn backs. Air bases all over England put up what they

Schweinfurt mission

could, with 291 heavy bombers sent out on the mission. Hundreds of German fighter planes were waiting for them, making it the largest and most fierce engagement of bomber and fighter aircraft to date. In the Eighth Army, 60 planes were lost outright and another 17 airplanes that made it back to Allied lines were so heavily damaged they had to be scrapped. In that seven-day period called "Black Week" the Eighth Air Force lost 148 B-17s and 1,480 crews. The men were so beaten and demoralized, returning to their barracks each night, seeing so many empty beds. They were mentally and physically exhausted, needing rest and consolation. So many of their friends were gone. The morale among the airmen was so low because they knew they all were on borrowed time.

This had to be fixed soon or they would run out of airplanes and trained men to fly. Bomber Command first got the idea to retrofit Tokyo Fuel Tanks to the bottom of the wings of the Thunderbolts and Lightning fighter aircraft enabling those escorts to venture farther into enemy territory to protect the bomber formations. It still wasn't sufficient enough range for the fighter escorts.

The P-47 was the largest, heaviest and most expensive aircraft. The P-38 lacked maneuverability and their engines were difficult to maintain. The Lightnings were labeled *Ice Wagons* because their heating systems at higher altitudes were worthless and their windshields froze. The freezing pilots could hardly fly the planes.

P-51 Mustang

The Mustang fighter plane had been developed in 1940 for the RAF with an Allison V-1710 engine which had limited high-altitude and range in England. By 1943 the P-51C Mustang was redesigned with a Packard V-1650-7 engine, a license-built version of the RAF's Rolls-Royce Merlin engine. That change transformed the fighter performance at altitudes above 15,000 feet and with adequate range. It also carried six .50 caliber AN/ M2 Browning machine guns for defense which helped ensure air superiority against the Luftwaffe fighters. Now the favorite escort of the Eighth Army Air crews which they called their "Little Friends." They swooped in, to escort damaged bombers back to England in their daylight raids.

Most hazardous to the U.S. bomber formations were the German ground defensive 88mm Flak guns. They were mobile units that shot up to 57mm shells into the sky. They would explode at the predicted location of the moving target, so that the plane arrived simultaneously at the same point in space as the shell. The Germans used an early computer to do the time, distance and speed calculations. The exploding shells didn't always down a plane but they were able to knock them out of the formation. The enemy fighters would wait for disabled bombers who couldn't keep up, and fly in to pick them off. With the Eighth Air Force's P-51 Mustang escorts, finally it became a balanced fight.

Because of the shortage of planes and qualified crews they were grounded through the end of December 1943 when replacements could arrive and qualified long range escort planes could be used. The Perkins crew were one of those replacements.

Perk was surprised to get a letter from his pal, Louie Massari. His best friend had visited his parents' home in Palmdale and got Perks forwarding address, just prior to shipping overseas. His friend's letter was newsy about first being assigned to training in Spokane, Washington, as a radio operator. The next two lines were blocked by the sensors about where he was stationed but Perk had heard from a friend that he was based in Great Ashfield, Suffolk, England. The rest of the letter related tidbits about mutual friends of theirs. Perk planned to write him back when he had a moment.

Perk opened the parchment-thin V-mail letter from his mother. The first line read, "I hope you are well, son." Then she wrote the terrible news, the US Navy had informed them Maurice, his 17-year-old-brother, was "missing in action in the South Pacific." He read the line again while taking a slow breath of air which caught in his lungs where he held it a moment. His mother said the Navy had no further information about location or dates when he went missing. She said she would write and tell him about any updates and that she was sorry to have to give him this news. Perk took another deep breath and closed his eyes. It couldn't be. His mom said she went to church and prayed for both her sons' safe return from this terrible war. It took him a few days to digest that his brother was missing in the South Pacific, but Perk rationalized Maurice was young and resilient and he figured he would be found. Still that feeling of uncertainty nagged at his conscience that his brother might be gone.

An image of his brother as a little kid flashed in his head. The closest in age to Perk, they played together more than his other brothers. They rode horses at the neighbor's, and built forts and explored their desert home together.

Perk laid back on his cot and looked at the corrugated metal ceiling of their barracks, pushing the idea away that someone in his family might be taken in this war. "Missing doesn't mean dead," he said to himself as he shook that thought out of his head. He wouldn't give up hope and he would write assurances back home in a letter to his mom and dad tomorrow.

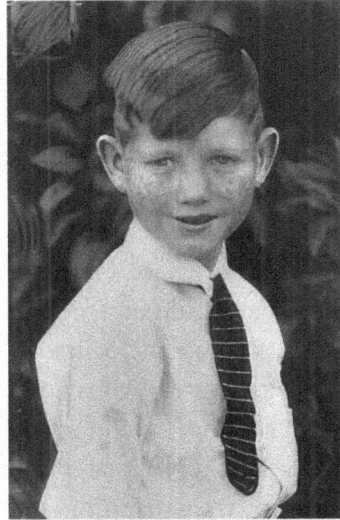

Maurice Perkins—age 7

The next day he wrote an encouraging letter saying there were thousands of islands in the South Pacific and Maurice was most likely hiding or in a prisoner of war camp somewhere." At 17 years old, his brother was athletic and strong, he wrote. "He can survive a prisoner of war camp." That last image of Maurice with his duffle bag stepping onto a Greyhound bus flashed in his head. His brother would turn up somewhere.

The Manhattan Project

August

Another secret conference between President Roosevelt and Winston Churchill took place in Canada and brought about the important *Quebec Agreement.* It was a collaboration between the two leaders to pool each of their scientific research and intelligence, to develop nuclear weapons. The important agreement merged the British *Tube Alloys* project with the American *Manhattan Project.* They further promised in the agreement not to use them against each other or each other's allies without mutual consent, or give secret information about the weapons to other countries.

Army Brig. Gen. Leslie R. Groves was placed in charge of the top secret project of developing a nuclear bomb. At first the research was based at only a few universities, Columbia, Berkeley and University of Chicago. This was a milestone for two countries that would emerge from the war as nuclear superpowers and would change the course of history in the world.

Perk's group of aviation cadets boarded a bus to Oxnard Airfield. They would spend a month in the 14th Flying Training Detachment. In that program, Perk was in concentrated classroom courses, learning about aeronautics, propellers, fuel boost pumps, carburetors and cowl flaps, as well as deflection shooting.

September 28th he was evaluated for ten hours in a flight simulator called a *Blue Box*. He endured a nerve-racking simulated
ride-along evaluation with an aviation instructor. He completed
120 hours of air training in the four engine aircraft including
practice bombing runs with live ordinances.

2nd Lieutenant Perkins passed all the tests and was given the
silver cadet wings and was officially considered an airman. This
small silver pin to be worn on his dress uniform symbolized so
much effort. Without much fanfare Perk simply added to the bottom of a letter to his mother that he had received his wings. Only
his fellow cadets could understand the level of their achievement.

The final Transition Pilot Training began in the fall. The airmen were divided into groups to fly fighters or bombers. Often
it came down to the temperament of the man. Perk was level
headed, methodical, serious, a leader, an ideal bomber pilot's personality. The flight trainers would ultimately determine who was
best for bomber crews and who might fly the P-38 or P-47 Thunderbolt fighters who engaged in dog fights to keep the German
fighters at bay. Many of the cadets had preferences. The fighter
planes were more sexy and "fun" to fly. In the end the need for
fresh bomber pilots and crew took precedence. Instructor Lieutenant Neely said, "Every crew member has an integral role in the
safe operation of the B-17 flying ship." Those who didn't become
pilots became important parts of the ten-man crew team.

Some of the cadets, including Perk were selected to go for
a week-long instruction at Moses Lake, Washington State, and
were trained on B-17, four engine bombers. By mid September
he had logged 20 hours in night, day, dual and solo flight training
in the aircraft.

Glenn and Perk were sent to Harvard Air Field, Nebraska,
as part of the 447th bomb group, for training on the new B-17G
Flying Fortress. Having flown the older model, they found there
were many new features to this airship. The fuselage had been

B-17G Heavy Bomber

extended ten feet. Several new defensive turrets and a total of 13 machine guns were added to its defenses. To accommodate the extra weight of the aircraft, a new super turbo charged Wright engine was installed. Those were some of the several revisions on the B-17 to improve its performance.

A Pretty Redhead from Hastings

Stationed at Harvard for three months, Perk and Glenn were able to finish their duties during the week and obtain passes on the weekends. It was an easy thirty-minute bus ride to Hastings. They stayed at the Hotel Clarke and it was a nice break from base housing and easy to get back to after evenings in town.

Hotel Clark, Hastings, Nebraska

One weekend the 22-year-old air cadets attended a USO dance where Perk met Dottie, a pretty redhead with green eyes and a quick smile. He proceeded to fill her dance card for the evening. They sat drinking Coca Cola and talking. She was 20, taking business classes at Hasting College, working part time as secretary for Colonel Shay at Harvard Airfield. She said she was born and raised in Hastings and she came from a big family of three sisters and four brothers.

Perk told her he grew up in the high desert above Los Angeles, also from a big family of five brothers and one sister. He said he had finished two years of college, majoring in mechanical engineering. When the Japanese attacked Pearl Harbor, he and his friend enlisted. He said he didn't know when he would be deployed to Europe but he thought it would be soon because his training was almost over. They both laughed when they found their birthdays were one day apart on April 10th and 11th. Not wanting the evening to end, Perk asked Dottie to go with him to the next Saturday's officer club dance and she accepted.

"Well, all right then," he said awkwardly. "I'll meet you there." She thought he was really a swell guy. He looked so handsome in his dress uniform and standing next to him in heels she was still a head shorter than he was.

Perk liked that she made him laugh and he was captivated by her intelligence and good sense of humor. He walked her to her bus stop which gave him more time to talk and get to know her.

The next Saturday Perk and Dottie met at the officers club at Harvard Airfield. When the bus stopped Dottie stepped out of the accordion door and walked toward him. They greeted each other with a smile and a kiss on the cheek. She was touched when he brought her a white corsage of gardenias, her favorite. He asked to pin it on her collar. They walked into the officers club where a live band of old WWI vets were playing Tommy Dorsey songs. It was a sparkling evening and they danced to the sounds of Benny Goodman and Glenn Miller. Dottie met a few more of Perk's friends and she introduced some of the girls from her secretarial pool to his friends. After a couple of dances Perk brought them a cup of red punch and they sat on a bench talking about college and their families. When the evening ended, Perk paid for a cab so she wouldn't have to take the bus home.

They met another time at a USO dance and they took a walk across the street to the park among the beautiful fall colors of autumn. Dottie shared with Perk the circumstances for which she was from a combined family after her mother married her stepfather. She explained her dad had died when she was seven years old, leaving her mother with four young children. Her mom became the secretary in her stepfather's battery factory. After they fell in love and got married, they combined their family of seven kids and lived in an old brick schoolhouse.

"We lived upstairs with Dad's battery factory on the first floor." With pride she said, "My dad supplied batteries to all the

Bouricius family 1932—Lavonne, Ruth, Willard, Bart,
Dottie, Ann, Gramma Keeling holding Dick, Robert

farmers in the rural parts of Nebraska, which were needed to power their farm equipment and houses."

Perk asked a lot of questions about her family and her father's factory. He loved hearing stories about her brothers and sisters and he shared a few tales of his growing up in the high California desert with his family. He said he and his brother, Maurice, had a pet coyote, rescued as a cub when its mother was killed by a car. Perk wasn't ready to talk about Maurice missing in the South Pacific yet but only said he was there and had enlisted at 17.

She was fascinated when he told her all about Pancho Barnes, the barn-stormer who knew Amelia Earhart. She was impressed to hear he had his civilian pilots license by the time he was 21. He told her about some of the movie stars and famous test pilots and flyers that came to Pancho's ranch.

Dottie described how "Guy's father owned a music store in Lincoln and all of my brothers and sisters grew up playing various musical instruments in the high school marching band," she said.

She told how their blended family was close. "When my two older brothers, Bart and Willard, went off to Hastings College in 1937, they needed a car to get there. Bart was given an old 1929 Model T Ford which he rebuilt with a Studebaker engine,

113

From left: Guy, Dick, Ruth, Ann, Gramma Keeling, Willard,
Bob, Bart, Lavonne, Dottie in foreground

painted lavender and stenciled animals on the side, calling it *The Ark*. The Ford-a-Baker served as transportation for the five siblings and their friends who often ended up on the running boards on the way to college. Perk chuckled thinking about this hybrid Frankenstein automobile but he was really looking at her pretty face as her eyes twinkled and her mouth formed the words.

Like many American families that found their country at war, both the Bouricius and Perkins families thought of ways to help in the war effort while their own sons and daughters were serving. All six of the Bouricius siblings, except Dottie's 14-year-old brother, Dick, had signed up to join the service or to work for government agencies. Bart and Willard by then had advanced degrees in mathematics and physics. Dottie didn't know at the time that her two brothers were recruited to join the Army Corp of Engineers. They were moved onto an isolated mesa at Los Alamos, New Mexico, in 1943 to help with what was then referred to as the Manhattan

Project under Robert Oppenheimer. The top-secret operation was spread out across the country at several facilities, in an all-out race against the Germans who were also developing a nuclear weapon.

Dottie's younger brother, Robert, joined the Army and was sent to the South Pacific. Ruth married Lt. Bob Hepting on July 26, 1943. While he was away on his first tour in the Pacific, Ruth had moved home and worked for the Red

Dottie's brother, Bob Bouricius

Cross. Lavonne became a WAVE in the Navy, and Dottie was a secretary for Army Colonel Shay at Harvard Air Base, while she continued classes at Hastings College. Guy, her stepdad, built submarine batteries for the Navy. Both her parents sold War Bonds and Ann planted a Victory Garden while conserving things like butter, sugar, metals and nylon which were needed overseas. Perk and Dottie's families were like millions across the country who did their part to support the fighting men in the military. Dottie asked Lieutenant Perkins to dinner with her family on Sunday.

"Sure, I'd love to." Perk replied, surprised. "I never turn down a home cooked meal." He remembered the last homemade dinner he had was at Christmas when he visited his family.

On that brisk September weekend he found himself standing at the front door, nervous to meet her folks. He told himself Dottie was just a good friend and her parents were offering a meal to a lonely G.I. as families often did during the war. The house appeared to be the biggest on the street, and looked like the old two story school house that it once was. Save for a huge vegeta-

The Bouricius house and battery factory

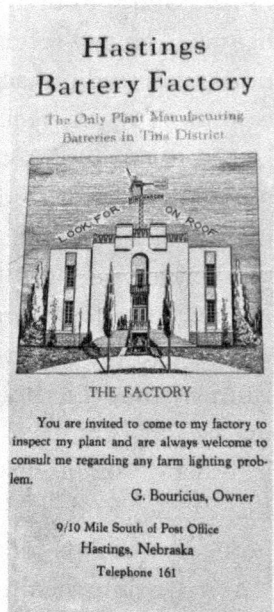

Hastings Battery Factory

The Only Plant Manufacturing Batteries in This District

THE FACTORY

You are invited to come to my factory to inspect my plant and are always welcome to consult me regarding any farm lighting problem.

G. Bouricius, Owner

9/10 Mile South of Post Office
Hastings, Nebraska
Telephone 161

ble garden on the side yard and a porch swing, the old brick building could have still passed as a school.

Dottie invited him into the foyer which had stairs up to their living space and a separate door into their battery business. Dottie asked if he wanted a peek at the machine shop and Perk said, "Yes, I would." She opened the door and the smell of machinery, oil and battery acid hit Perks nose and he saw the rows of farmlight batteries, some in boxes on the floor and some on the production tables. It was a surprisingly small space for the Hastings Battery Factory. The assembly line of production was well organized with glass battery relays, plugs, acid refills and wood crates full of finished batteries ready to ship. They returned to the entrance and closed the shop door.

The couple climbed the pine stairs and entered a large comfortable room on the second floor with high ceilings, wood floors, a large brick fireplace, two couches and a long dining table near an open kitchen. Delicious smells came from the black cast iron stove where Dottie's mother, Ann, turned around to greet Perk.

He extended his hand. "I'm Perk. It's nice to meet you, Mrs. Bouricius. Thank you for having me for dinner," he said smiling.

She was a foot shorter than Perk with kind brown eyes and dark curly hair. She wore a bib apron over a print dress. "Nice to meet you, too, Lieutenant. Dorothy has told us so much about you," she said. "Please, have a seat while I finish getting the dinner on the table." She looked at Dottie, tilting her head, "Can you call your father, Dick and the girls for dinner?" As Dottie left, Ann walked back into the kitchen and spoke over her shoulder to Perk, "We are having stew, mashed potatoes and biscuits, with an apple pie. I hope you brought your appetite, Lieutenant Perkins."

"Please call me Perk. That sounds delicious, Mrs. Bouricius. Can I help you with something?"

"How about I'll call you Perk, if you call me Ann." Answering his question, she said, "Everything is hot and ready to eat."

Guy came in and shook hands with the young officer, saying, "It's nice to meet you, son." The three sisters and their little brother walked into the kitchen and surrounded the table smiling at Perk like Cheshire cats.

Ann said, "Please everyone sit down before it gets cold. Ruth, will you say grace?"

Ruth was brief, ending with, "… and please bring our soldiers home soon. Amen."

Dottie said, "These are my sisters, Ruth and Lavonne. And this is my sweet little brother, Dick," she said sarcastically. He smirked at her and reached for the biscuits and jam. They passed around the potatoes, stew and a bottle of milk.

Guy looked through his spectacles at Perk and asked, "Do you come from a big family, too?"

Perk said, "Yes sir. I have four brothers and a sister."

Dottie's stepsister, Lavonne, was tall and attractive, with light brown hair. She asked Perk, "Are there any others in your family in the military?"

Guy and Ann   Dottie and Ruth   Lavonne

"Yes, my brother is in the Navy somewhere in the South Pacific."

Lavonne said as she passed the potatoes, "I'm supposed to leave for Pearl Harbor next month. I trained as a radar specialist and radio operator in the Signal Corp. I'm looking forward to going to Hawaii."

Dottie said, "Ruth's husband, Bob, is probably somewhere near Hawaii. He's a Naval pilot."

Ruth spoke up and said, "Bob is flying PBYs. They do low altitude reconnaissance, look for submarines, enemy ship convoys, and carry out rescue operations. Bob is supposed to be on his way back to San Diego after his first tour of duty."

Perk asked, "What will he do now in the Navy?'

Ruth answered, "I believe they want him to train other cadets to fly PBYs. He will find out soon."

Dottie, knowing her brother, Dick's partiality to keeping the biscuits closest to him, said, "Dicky, can you please pass *"your"* biscuits around to the rest of us."

Her brother blushed. Dick was short with red hair and freckles and had that awkward manner of a teenager. He passed the

Dottie, Lavonne and Ruth

basket toward Dottie. He was talkative and annoying, saying inappropriate things like, "Do you carry a gun as a pilot?" and "Perk, are you Dorothy's boyfriend?" Dottie's face turned red and she kicked Dick under the table.

Perk judiciously avoided the second question and launched into answering the first. "I will be issued a 45 caliber handgun in case my airplane is shot down over enemy territory and I have to fight Germans," he said, widening his eyes at the captivated boy.

Guy strategically changed the subject, asking the airman questions about the B-17 bomber and Perk asked Guy about the process of building the different types of batteries. Dottie's stepdad explained in intimate detail the parts of the batteries he produced.

Changing the subject, Ann explained that Dottie's brother Bob was in the army in India, but had contracted malaria and was recovering in the base hospital. Guy mentioned his two oldest boys, Bart and Willard who were working in New Mexico for the Army Corp of Engineers.

As dinner turned into dessert and everyone was talking at once, Perk listened to their lively discussions and raucous banter at the Bouricius table and it reminded him of home. He loved it. After dinner Dottie and Perk sat on the porch swing off the garden and watched the fireflies in the moonlight under the constellations. They even spotted a few shooting stars.

They talked about how they both came to be at Harvard Air Force Base. She said she went to work in the secretarial pool and was promoted to Colonel Shay's office because she was fast at typing and dictation. He went through pilot training and Harvard was the last stop before going overseas. It was just luck they had met each other, he thought. He studied her face as she spoke. He looked at her pale green eyes, her freckles, red shoulder length hair and her beautiful smile.

Dottie looked at Perk and remembered the first time she saw him at the Harvard Headquarters of Colonel Shay. He walked up to the receptionist in the office next to hers. He was tall and handsome in his green wool army uniform. He stood with his hat in his hand. Dottie was used to the cocky flyboy types and she heard Perk saying, "Yes, ma'am and thank you." She peeked around the corner at him. Most air cadets had a pick-up line and she knew to stay clear. As they sat on her porch that evening and talked about their families, Dottie knew she liked the handsome lieutenant.

"My sister, Ruth, graduated from Hastings College and was doing clerical work for the Red Cross. We all love Bob and he has become part of their family. Ruth met him by chance during the summer of 42' at barn dances in Estes Park. He was interning as a Park Ranger in the Colorado Rocky Mountain National Park. He became a regular at our cabin, and by the end of the summer Bob gave Ruth his fraternity pin. In the fall, Bob enlisted in the Navy and was trained as a pilot to fly Black Cat PBYs."

Perk remembered that the PBYs were referred to as *flying boats* as they took off and landed on the water around islands without

"Black Cats" PBY Seaplanes

runways. He had heard they were slow aircraft with exterior bomb loads. He thought to himself he preferred flying higher altitude bombers.

After a few USO dances and another dinner at her folk's house, Perk knew he liked Dottie a lot. She made him laugh with her quips that always put him at ease. She was smart and seemed like a really nice girl from a nice family. They both were natural redheads and she joked they might have some distant cousins in their heritage. In truth she had Danish blood and he had Scottish and American Indian ancestors but it was a bantering topic that amused both of them. Dottie's real father's name was Martensen, who was Danish. Her stepfather was Dutch and had a coat of arms showing he was related to Dutch royalty. There was also a family Bible with ancestors going back to the Renaissance. Her mother, Ann, traced her ancestors back to 1776 and the War of Independence between the colonies and Great Britain.

Perk said he was proud that his great-great-grandmother was a full-blooded Cherokee Indian on his dad's side. His mother's family came from Scotland and England which accounted for Perk's red hair and blue eyes. They joked about both their Heinz 57 heritage. Besides his gentile personality, Dottie was attracted to the tall, dashing figure in uniform. He was genuine, intelligent and a bit shy. She liked his quiet, thoughtful demeanor. With his crew getting closer to shipping overseas, Dottie invited him to another Sunday dinner with her family. Ann made roast beef and mashed potatoes, as good as his mom made. Perk thanked Ann again and she said, "My pleasure, Perk."

Dottie wasn't his girlfriend yet and he didn't expect her to wait for him. He told her he thought she and her family were wonderful. Again they sat on the porch swing and Perk reached over and kissed Dottie who was a bit embarrassed but kissed him back. He decided to take a chance and kiss her again. The second kiss was more deliberate and each got lost in the moment. After, they talked and he held her hand and they both didn't want the evening to end. He thanked her for having him for dinner and said he hoped he would see her again before he left. He needed to kiss her one more time and afterward ran for the last bus back to the base. As the whine of the bus bumped its way back to the airfield, he felt like he was floating ten feet in the air.

5.

The Fighting Eighth Air Force

September

One afternoon in the fall, Lieutenant Perkins stood near the tower at Harvard runway watching silver bombers arrive, one after another. It reminded him of the awe he felt some five years before when we watched the airplanes near his house flying out of Muroc Air Force Base. He was 17 then and he had never been in an airplane before, let alone, pilot one. A lot had happened in five years.

Bendix chin turret

Cheyenne tail turret—1943

The earlier B-17 bombers, in which he had been trained, were shorter and lacked defensive power. On these new aircraft there were Bendix chin turrets and Cheyenne tail turrets to better protect the ship from head-on and rear attacks. Dozens of shiny, fresh off the assembly line, bombers flew past the tower and landed at the airbase. They taxied to a hardstand and to his surprise, a number of the pilots and co-pilots were female. He thought of Pancho, and was grateful to her for having taught him to fly. He tipped his hat to those women aviators who had followed in the path of Amelia Earhart and Pancho Barnes, piloting airplanes in spite of limited opportunities for women in the field.

During September 1,200 new B-17 heavy bombers, from Seattle, Washington, and other US factories were delivered to Army Air Force bases across the Midwest. Each airplane cost the government $250,000. By that fall of 1943, Boeing Aircraft had built over 8,000 B-17 heavy bombers. On September 28th and 29th, sixty-four Fortresses landed at Harvard Army Air Force Base in Nebraska. All of them were scheduled to soon leave for the European Theater of Operations or ETO.

He mulled over in his mind his enormous responsibility to his own crew. As their pilot, he needed to keep them safe so they all could do their jobs and get home to their families. It was a huge weight to carry for the 23-year-old lieutenant from Antelope Valley, California.

That same month Lt. Perkins was assigned his nine-man crew. A few days later he was issued a new silver 65,000 pound Boeing B-17G built in Seattle. He had come a long way from the 2400-pound Travel Air bi-plane at Pancho's dude ranch. Perkins stared at the shiny silver fuselage and looked up at the four 1,200-horsepower Wright R-1820 engines. He knew he could push the aircraft to a maximum speed of 287 miles per hour, although cruising speed was 150 mph. He walked under the 104-foot wingspan and looked at the dorsal-fin tail insignia

"K" which signified the plane was part of the 447th bomb group. Under it was the aircraft number 42-31188. He whispered to himself, "What a machine." He would be flying this ship five miles above the earth. The closed bomb bay doors on her under-belly would carry a 5,000-pound bomb load. With its thirteen .50 caliber machine guns defending 360 degrees all around them, it was no wonder the B-17 was called *Fliegendes Stachelschwin* or *Flying Porcupines* by the apprehensive German Luftwaffe. Perk was proud to be flying the most formidable bomber of its time.

The young commander Perkins needed to train his men as a team so they didn't have to think about what they were supposed to do in combat. He had daily drill sessions in their B-17 air-plane. The crew attended first aid lectures, target practice, emer-gency procedure, survival tactics, and geography of Nazi occu-pied territory.

As his first order, Perk asked his nine new crewmen to meet in the mess hall that afternoon at 1600 hours. Some of the air-men already knew one another having shared training locations in California, New Mexico and Texas. They seemed like a nice bunch of fellows and Perk took them out to the hardstand to check out their new bomber. A week of classes and more prac-tice sessions followed until he got to know his crew well. In the evening Perk wrote a letter to Dottie describing each of his crew.

Perk wrote, "Lt. Tom Garrick, my navigator, is from Long Island. He is the old man of the group at age 23 and has a col-lege degree in Optometry. He is the only crew member married with a kid on the way. He had 18 weeks of Navigator School consisting of 500 hours of ground instruction, pilotage, celestial navigation, computed headings, airpeed, radio codes, directional bearings and charting. He knows daytime navigation as well as blind night navigation. Part of his job is to keep our flight log of missions, including time and locations of everything. That will be our only record for intelligence purposes and will be used during our interrogations at HQ. Tom will note when there is or isn't flak, whether we were attacked by enemy fighters, which of our airships go down and if he sees parachutes. He will describe what he sees on the ground and over the English Channel. It is an arduous task and is so important for Army intelligence. He is the executive officer of the waist and his principle duty is to know where the aircraft is and where it is going at all times. He's a quick and intelligent man to have on our team."

"Lt. Tom Foley, is the 22-year-old bombardier assigned to our crew. He is from Denver, Colorado, and studied minerals at the University of Boulder. He is in charge of the bombs from the armorer shack to the IP, or the Initial Point, which is the bomb run, starting from 40 miles from the target. Foley will be the first guy on board our ship in the morning and he gets the bombs into the bomb bay. He is responsible for his two .50 caliber guns in the chin turret and during the mission may have to defend the front of the ship. At higher altitudes he is in charge of checking every 15 minutes to see all crew member's oxygen is operating properly so they aren't oxygen starved which could cause loss of consciousness." His goal is to deliver the bombs to the target for maximum damage to the enemy. He may use the Norden bomb site to take over the plane and drop the bombs on the target.

"Staff Sgt. Harold Overton, 20, is the crew engineer and top turret gunner. He grew up near Phoenix and he and his dad have a gas station and garage in Scottsdale. He knows his way around engines and mechanics. He is a systems specialist on the aircraft and the ranking NCO of the crew. His engineering knowledge of the plane could make the difference between the plane staying in the air or not. He is in charge of every emergency on board from takeoff to landing and he sits in the place of honor just behind and between the co-pilot and pilot to help monitor gauges and keep those systems within limits. When the engineer is not needed as a flight engineer, he becomes top turret gunner and is also free to roam the ship to help those crew that needed it. I like him because he's just a regular Joe and has a great repertoire of jokes that make us all laugh."

"Staff Sgt. Cliff Myers, the radio operator is 21 and a real speed talker, fast like he does code. I'm not sure whether he chews gum faster than his rapid speech. He will take some getting used to. He has the very important job of long-range communication from the Rally Point to the Initial Point. It is Myers who throws out the chaff or aluminum foil strips that are used to confuse and give false readings on enemy radar screens. The German anti-aircraft 88 flak guns track incoming allied bombers according to their radar intelligence. The Christmas tinsel-like chaff gives false readings when dropped out of bombers. Myers is the second ranking NCO supervising the radio room, waist and the bomb bay at drop time. If we have a hung bomb or no-drop, he is responsible for manually discharging our bomb load while hanging six miles above the earth."

"Sgt. Irwin Marcuse is a wisecracking 19-year-old Italian kid from Queens, New York, with a Frank Sinatra face. Besides being the left waist gunner, he is the armorer gunner. He is responsible for firing and maintaining his own guns, he answers to the bombardier for loading, fusing and removal of the safety pins which arm the bombs for the drop. Marcuse has a comprehensive knowledge of the bomb release electrical system and he works closely with Foley, the bombardier for a smooth drop. You can't help but like the guy because he has such a quick wit."

"Sergeant Donald Collier at 19, is the right waist gunner. He was in his first semester of college taking English courses when the Japanese attacked Pearl Harbor. Don has a pretty girlfriend back home in New Mexico and he frequently shows the crew her picture in his wallet. He is a trained assistant to both the radio operator, Myers and Overton, the engineer. When called upon, he can do all three jobs, waist, engineer or radio operator. He is very likable and the most versatile enlisted guy onboard. I have a lot of respect for him."

"Along with Marcuse, Ralph Warren, just 18, my ball turret gunner, scored highest in marksmanship during aerial gunnery training. Besides manning his two guns in the rotating turret, Ralph is the primary observer with the only view under the aircraft if we are attacked from the bottom or on a collision course with another ship. The man in the Sperry Ball Turret needs to be small because he is in a fetal position in that cramped space for most of the mission with his knees up in the air. When doing a normal landing with landing gear down, the ball turret is a few inches from the ground. In the event of an emergency and we have to do a belly landing, the ball turret would be destroyed. There is no room for parachutes, flak vests or May Wests in the ball turret so he has to climb back into the waist, put on his parachute if he has to bail out. Before landing he climbs out of the turret into the waist and makes sure the ball turret guns are facing rear before the landing."

"Bill Moore is 20, short and wiry and can fit in the close quarters of the tailgun position. It is so tight in there as he kneels on an ironing board. Again, flak jackets and parachutes have to be left outside on a hook by the access door. I think the tail, ball and chin turret gunners are the most vulnerable spots on the aircraft and they are pretty brave guys."

"Lt. Glenn Halverson, my co-pilot and a friend from training, has had all the pilot instructions that I have had. He is second in command and coordinates the running of the ship. While we are still in range of the base, he is on the VHF radio and the voice link with other aircraft in the formation. Glenn will call for fighter back up if we are in trouble. He relieves me by flying the aircraft in 15 or 30 minute shifts depending on the situation. I can also send him back to the crew if they need help."

"As the pilot I am responsible for everything that happens onboard the aircraft. If I am incapacitated, the co-pilot takes over my responsibilities. I have been given some navigation, bombardier and engineer and gunnery training, enough to understand those positions if there are problems. The crew counts on me for good judgment and fast reaction in emergencies because there are no second chances. My foremost duty is to fly the airplane to its target, while in formation, drop our bombs and get us home again. Our bombing mission, our aircraft and the crew's lives depended on us working as a team."

October-December 1943

The American Eighth Army Air Force, in Great Britain, was experiencing the bloodiest and most devastating losses of bombers and crews in Europe. The outcome was that the U.S. Army Brig. Gen. Fred Anderson, head of the Eighth Bomber Command shut down all unescorted heavy bomber raids until January 1944. Replacement aircraft and trained crews were badly needed.

At Harvard, Nebraska on October 19th, Perk and Glenn attended a secure briefing with the pilots, co-pilots and navigators of 60 B-17 aircraft. The Commanding Officer mapped-out destination routes to twenty airfields in England. Perk confirmed on the list his crew were assigned to Rattlesden, northeast of London. He had just a few weeks to get his men ready.

The next day Lt. Perkins called for the muster of his crew at 0800 hours and all but Warren showed up. He had spent the previous night on a bender. Lieutenant Perkins sent Glenn to go fetch the hungover staff sergeant and when he showed up disheveled and indignant, his commander told him to climb in the lower ball turret and spin until Perk said he could stop. After doing that exercise for a while, the sergeant would probably never miss a muster again. It was wise for the pilot commander of the aircraft to establish discipline early because a sloppy crew is a dangerous crew.

The men sat in their positions onboard the new aircraft. It could be described as being inside a cigar tube, about 74 feet in length. It was a very tight interior space, especially for the ball turret and tail gunner.

BOEING FLYING FORTRESS
(B-17G)

1. Pilot/Copilot
2. Bombardier (Chin Turret)
3. Navigator (Cheek Turrets)
4. Flight Engineer (Top Turret)
5. Radio Operator
6. Ball Turret Gunner
7. Waist Gunners (2)
8. Tail Gunner

B-17G flight positions

The pilot, co-pilot, bombardier, navigator and engineer were separated from the radio operator, two waist gunners, ball turret gunner and tail gunner by the open bomb bay that had an eight-inch-wide cat walk. The ten bombs would be on floor to ceiling racks, 500 pounds each, five on each side of the interior fuselage. When the bomb bay doors were open you had a spectacular view of the earth five miles below.

As they sat there, Glenn asked, "What shall we call her?" No other branch of the service including the Navy, Marines or Coast Guard were allowed to name their own airplanes. Airmen in the Army never spoke of their aircraft as number 42-31188. It was the nose art and names like *The Fighting Irish* or *Lil' Abner* that playfully identified the American Air Force planes of WWII. They came from popular culture, Disney or comic strip characters like *Tweety Bird*. Names like *Ole Blood and Guts* or *Hitler's Folly*, were directed at their enemy. Most of the nose art images were copied from pin-up girl posters or Vargas calendars. The fetching women were always in various stages of undress proudly adorning the nose fuselage of B-17s, Liberators, Mustangs and Thunderbolts.

Overton finally found a nose artist, on base, who would paint the art and names for $5 bucks. The poker playing gunners recognized the last five numbers on their airplane as cards held by the famous crack shot Wild Bill Hickok at the moment he was shot in the back and killed. It was unanimous among the crew, to name their plane, *Dead Man's Hand*. The artist painted their ships' noses with Wild Bill's last card hand, a graphic of black aces and eights with a red three of diamonds. The unique practice of naming their plane created a close bond between the men and their machine.

Perk's flight team trusted each other with their lives. Still a few crew members carried their religious medals, St. Christopher's or a lucky rabbit's foot. Perk was a realist. None of his job could be left up to good luck charms.

The crew's tour of duty in the Eighth Air Force, in 1942 was complete after 25 missions and then they could go home. What the Army didn't tell them was that the average life expectancy of a B-17 crew that year was 11 missions. There was a 5% average attrition rate or loss of aircraft, with crews shot down or bailing out. Some airmen would be taken prisoner and end up in prisoner-of-war-camps for the duration of the war.

Some of the trainers were pragmatists and tried to toughen up the air men for the task. One such commander in one of Perk's briefings said, "When the U.S. declared war on Germany in December 1941, the Luftwaffe already had three successful

years of experience over the Allies in the aerial war. Their bombers and fighters were superior with better armaments compared
to the Allied planes. Their effective air and ground defenses such
as the mobile land 88 mm flak companies, mounted on railroad
cars, could be quickly moved, according to the intelligence, to
the location of the next Allied bomber attack. German BF109s
and Fw190 fighter aircraft were the best in the world, nearly conquering the British Isles during the eight-month-long Battle of
Britain. The trainer said, "Men, take a look at the guys sitting
on either side of you, because most likely only one of you will be
coming home." The intention of the commander was to toughen
up the men but a few guys wondered what the hell they had done
signing up for the AAF.

The Perkins crew trained in their bomber on day and night
missions over Nebraska and Iowa with some dummy bombing
missions. The first week of November the Perkins' crew was each
issued a forty-five caliber pistol, a hunting knife, a first aid kit,
foreign currency, a silk scarf map of Europe on one side and a few
French and German translation words on the back. Perk's crew
had their final medical checks at the base clinic and in the evening they all went to town but didn't drink a thing as everything
was closed on a Sunday.

At the base mail-call, the next day, Perk received a letter from
his mom, saying there was still no news of Maurice in the weeks
since they received the letter from the War Department. The lack
of information was so very hard for them to bear. His last letter
said he had been assigned to a gunnery unit on board a destroyer,
somewhere in the South Pacific. His mom said she went to church
and prayed for both her sons' safe return. Maurice was young and
resilient and Perk hoped he would be found. He was glad to keep
busy with aircraft training sessions and practice flights.

Perk's thoughts wandered to the pretty redhead, Dottie, with
whom he shared dances at the USO and a few dinners at her

folk's house. He thought of the kiss the last time he saw her and he hoped to see her again. On that last night he asked her if he could write to her while he was overseas and she said she would like that. For now, he had a huge responsibility to his crew, for himself and to the Army. His brother was missing and he vowed to himself, his mother would not get a second letter about another missing son.

In the Army Air Force the crews were identified by their pilot's name. His crew was known as the Perkins crew. In the chain of command, Lt. Perkins had the ultimate responsibility for his men on the ground and in the air. They answered to him, and he in turn answered to his squadron commander. Perk solved disciplinary issues with his airmen in-house, like he did with Sgt Warren. That penance wasn't exactly in the pilot's manual but it did establish Perk's authority. His men respected him and he found he had few problems. A flight commander with poor crew discipline could mean mistakes in battle which could cost all of them their lives.

As their plane commander, Perk tried to instill in his crew how important teamwork was in flying the ship. Every job mattered and they practiced on training missions until the crew members could do their jobs in their sleep. One universal duty was that every man was the eyes and ears of their aircraft as well as an observer for the whole formation. They kept an eye out for collisions, and the general welfare of all planes within their sight range.

Turning Point of Aerial Warfare

A disastrous air bombing mission in Europe changed the course of air combat strategy for the Allies in WWII. Operation Tidal Wave, August 1, 1943, a mission to turn off the oil taps of the Wehrmacht, where 178 B-24 bombers left the Allied air base in Libya, and flew to the oil fields in Ploiesti, Romania. They flew in at 500 feet bombing factories and storage tanks. There were low hanging barrage balloons which were effective land defenses. Sixty of the aircraft were shot down and 600 men were killed or missing. It became known as Black Sunday. The allies knew, at that loss rate, their air war over enemy territory was not sustainable. After that horrific mission, the allies surmised the Luftwaffe was increasing their strength and effectiveness with new technology and weaponry. The British and American Air Forces had to find ways to reduce their losses.

Allied Intelligence, at that time, believed Nazi scientists were developing pilotless bombs, jet engines and nuclear weapons. All three predictions were true. The race between the Allies and German research and development for new weaponry continued throughout the war with Germany leading the way with scientists like Werner von Braun's jet rocketry, early guidance and radar systems on 88 flak shells and buzz bomb rockets. Great Britain's milestones in radar technology and intelligence kept the enemy at bay during the first years of the war while the American development of aircraft design and development as well as the atomic bomb eventually helped end the war. Hitler had underestimated the British and American industries, pilot training and their vast resources from around the globe.

The best offense to defeat the Axis powers was to starve the war supplies to the Nazi Wehrmacht. That overall strategic goal of Churchill and Roosevelt was to choke out those resources and bomb transportation of soldiers and equipment, enemy factories and workers houses, and demoralize the enemy so they could no longer fight. This blueprint for victory would best be achieved by area bombing raids by the RAF at night, while the United States Air Force did precision daylight missions. The around-the-clock bombing gave the enemy no rest.

North Atlantic Air Ferry Route

Perk scribbled out a letter to Dottie to say goodbye and say he was sorry he didn't get to see her again. He wrote eight quick notes to the parents of his crew members. He told them he would do his best to take care of their sons. He said the crew was a great bunch of guys and were well trained and fortunate to be fighting together to end the war. He said he had all the confidence they were prepared for the task they were assigned. He wrote a similar note to Thomas Garrick's wife, Julia. He knew it would mean a lot to families as their loved ones left for combat.

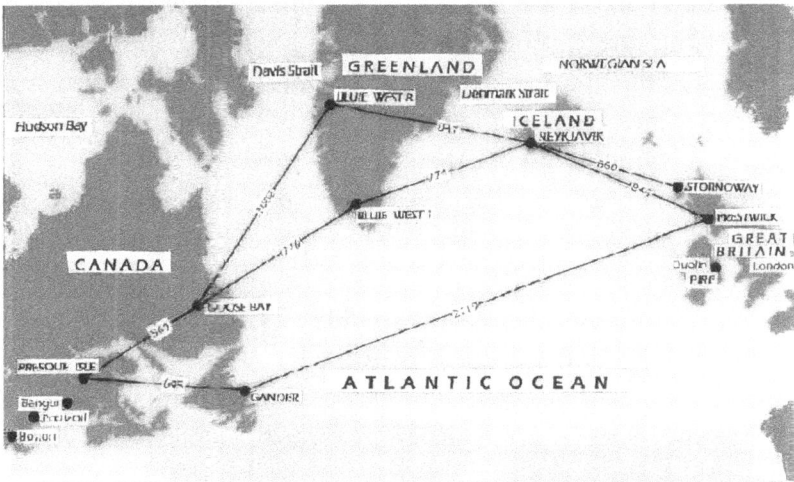

North Atlantic Ferry Route

On November 15, 1943, a squadron of twelve B-17 crews departed Harvard and made the short hop to Kearney, Nebraska. They were on their way to the North Atlantic Air Ferry Route to England. Five months before, the U.S. Army Corp of Engineers with the British had increased their number of bases and maintenance stops. They also established the Middle and South Atlantic routes that were used as alternative transit for aircraft, men and supplies.

On November 16th Perks crew flew to Bear Tower at Fort Wayne, Indiana. He had assigned Collier and Moore each four-hours guard duty on their ship. Collier wrote in his diary, "After guard duty I raided the mess hall and ate eight eggs and drank a quart of milk."

November 17th the squadron left Bear Tower at 0800 and flew to Manchester, New Hampshire. Collier wrote, "That evening we had a hell of a good time at a dance, meeting a couple of pretty nurses."

On November 18th the Perkins crew flew the lead plane from New Hampshire at 1100 to Presque Isles, Maine, staying the night. Each leg of the trip the new aircraft was mechanically checked and refueled. Since this was the squadron's APO, or military address, Perk figured they would be there a couple of days.

November 20, the crew had their medical check, bought things to take with them like candy, gum and toothpaste. They weren't sure how hard it was to get snacks and supplies overseas.

For almost seven hours on November 21, they flew mostly on instruments from Presque Isle to Goose Bay, Labrador, landing at 0200 hours. Garrick proved his excellent navigating skills while mostly over water. Clouds came in for a brief rainstorm and a cold -35 degree weather. The crew was glad to be stopped in a warm place for the night and Perk and Glenn hit the officers' mess before finding their bunks to catch some well-earned sleep.

The Squadron left Goose Bay at 2200 hours, which was 0300 English time. On the way, they encountered some ice but it was mostly a smooth flight. Dead Man's Hand crossed the 979 miles across the Atlantic to the RAF base at Valley, Wales. On the 12-hour trip the crew was told to keep their eyes peeled for ships and subs so there was no getting any shut-eye. As Perk landed at 1000 in the morning, the clouds passed and it was a brilliant cloudless sky.

Perk gave the crew a day off in Wales as they waited for their slot to leave for England. The men hooted like kids and left to ride bikes, dine on rabbit and warm Welsh beer. They made bets on a wrestling match of two locals and in the evening they attended a dance at the wharf, met a few Welsh girls. A couple of the NCO's stayed with the girls until 0500 and barely made it back to the ship before take-off.

On November 23rd the Perkins' crew flew their last two-hour leg, from Wales to Rattlesden, 75 miles northeast of London. Perk was cleared for landing on the main runway and he could see there was a perimeter track and hardstands for fifty aircraft. He and his crew had delivered their aircraft without a hitch and he felt good. They were home for a while as part of the 447th bomb group, 709th squadron in the Mighty Eighth Air Force.

On the northern ferry route from Harvard, Nebraska, to Rattlesden, their squadron hadn't lost any airplanes. Due to bad weather and inexperienced crews, the Army had been losing 10% of their planes on the way to Europe. Last month, a friend of Perks, Jimmy Rockford. and his crew from the 100th got lost, on their flight from Labrador to Wales and they probably never would be found.

Rattlesden, England

The Perkins crew got acquainted with their English base. The two black T-2 hangars and tower were at the northeast end of the air field. The crew was directed to the living and messing sites on the southeast side of the field. The fog had settled on the runways and grassy areas and Perk knew he was going to have to get used to this place.

The Eighth Army had built many air bases in East Anglia, England, for heavy bomber fleets to fly raids against the Nazi occupied territories. The bases were usually about eight miles apart with fifty B-24s or B-17s. When Perk and his crew arrived in England the third week of November 1943, there were 130 British and American air bases concentrated in southeast England. The 40 by 80 mile area was chosen because it had plenty of level open land and it was close to the enemy in mainland Europe, shortening the flights on missions. The towns and hamlets near the bases were transformed into busy communities with American personnel packing the buses, trains, pubs and movie theaters. Over three million G.I.s would pass through the area in 1943-1945.*

The British public were surprised by the often brash behavior of the U.S. soldiers. The English citizens were not used to American GIs approaching the traditionally very formal stuffy Brits. They called them, "Over-sexed, overpaid, and over here." They were chatty, self-assured, generous and girl-crazy. But the English had suffered horrifically during the three years of war, including nightly bombings and food and housing deprivation. The American soldiers became a welcome diversion, to the citizenry of East Anglia and London. Lonely U.S. soldiers and airmen were often welcomed into local homes for dinner and some formed close relationships with the British; even marrying their daughters. Other soldiers and airmen found comfort in the clubs and brothels of Liverpool. Even the children of village families loved the GIs because they seemed to have an endless supply of gum, chocolate and other items, rationed in the British Isles.

---

* Ernie Pyle, the war correspondent, described the men in the bomb groups as if they were Everyman. With a down home way of writing, often mentioning the bomb groups and even specific soldiers in his articles, he noted, "It is sad because the men go, and new ones come and they go, and other ones come until at last only the numbered bomb groups are left." He was resigned to the fact, "As long as we have an army, the bomb group will exist, but my friends in it, may not."

In addition, over half of the military stationed in England were not part of the combat crews. The military support staff; the chaplains, librarians, quartermasters, weather squadrons, military police and those who patched the airplanes after being battered in battle. They fixed the planes, supplied the goods, maintained the facilities, ran the combat operations, fed the men in the mess halls, healed them

2nd Lt. Clarence "Perk" Perkins

in the infirmaries, manned the every-day operations to keep the missions flying against the enemy. They served their country with dedication, contributing to the war effort in jobs much less glamorous than pilots and aircrew, but no less essential to the outcome of World War II.

After eating two hamburgers and drinking three cartons of milk in the officer's mess, Perk was assigned his living quarters. He heard the base had been erected hastily in 1942 for the RAF and then turned into an American base of operations in 1943 for the Yanks.

The Perkins crew had four officers and six NCOs, (non-commissioned officers) making up the ten-man crew. Even though they would eventually fly combat missions together, they lived separate lives on base. They ate separately, their quarters were separate and they socialized separately. There were various sizes of Nissen Huts made of corrugated metal, bent into a half cylinder with a wooden door in front, a couple of windows on either side and a cement foundation. They were cheap to build and useful as offices, libraries, hospitals, theaters, the PX, and weapons storage.

Perk was assigned separate quarters because he was an officer and a pilot. It was a seven by twelve-foot space with a bed,

a locker, a washstand, a table and chair and a couple of dirty windows. There was no running water and he had to transport it from a communal faucet and heat it on the stove for shaving. Perk moved in and put a picture of Dottie up on the wall, with a map of Europe between the door and the wash stand. Inside Perk's locker were his shirts, socks, shaving kit, battle jacket, his .45 caliber gun and some shells, his hunting knife, gas mask, a box that contained military documents and his barracks bag. The three other officers, Glenn, Garrick and Foley, shared a bigger room on the other side of the wall in the same Nissen as his.

The four officers ate in the officer's mess and socialized in the officer's club which had hard liquor. The Red Cross Aero Clubs were for the enlisted men and served only beer. The one exception to these privileges was after a combat strike, all the men, enlisted alike, were allowed in the officer's club for a shot of whiskey and a good meal after a mission. There were different base rules for enlisted men and officers. The NCOs had a curfew of midnight when they went off base on a pass. The officers just had to report to their meetings the next day.

The rest of his NCOs: Overton, Myers, Marcuse, Warren, Moore and Collier were housed in a separate section of Nissen Huts for the enlisted guys. Those huts had six rows of cots, along each wall with a footlocker underneath for a change of clothes, and his personal items. In the middle of the floor was a coal burning pot-bellied stove used for heating the room, heating water or occasionally boiling eggs from the local farmers.

Collier wrote home to his girlfriend, "I have a straw-filled pillow, a wool Army blanket, some communal shelves and a writing desk. There's a map of Europe pinned on the wall showing all the bomb runs of the previous crew. Our hut has a couple of windows on both sides. They are fitted with blackout boards, stacked in the corner, to stop the light from going out and air from coming in, making it stuffy inside. Some of the guys have pin-up girls hung on the sloped walls with posters of Betty Grable and Maureen O'Hara. Hooks around the place held flight jackets, t-shirts and towels. The base regulations were nailed to the inside of the door which nobody read. There was an old radio on the desk left by the last crew which works most of the time."

Although the six enlisted men and the four officers lived, ate and socialized separately on the base, they came together and treated each other like brothers while flying in combat. They worked together for the success of the mission and the safety and well-being of their crew. None of them wanted to fail their buddies.

Rattlesden AirBase was spread out, by design, for safety in case of an enemy attack and it was a long distance to walk to the headquarters or mess hall. Perk saw a lot of the guys riding bikes between buildings or on the farm roads into town. After a month he got tired of walking all over and decided to buy a used bicycle from an airman who was going home. He could ride from his barracks to the showers or mess hall in a lot less time.

Americans, assigned to a base in England, had six weeks of training after their arrival. The first month at Rattlesden brought daily sessions of gunnery school for Marcuse, Warren, Moore and Collier. There was navigational training for Garrick, and Foley who attended classes in the use of the Norden bomb site. Overton, the crew engineer, spent a lot of time in advanced training with the ground crew on base. Perk and Glenn learned about bomb load, weight and lift, what to do if an engine failed and procedures for emergency landings and bailing out.

Perk and Glenn flew on a few training missions as co-pilots in older B-17s, after the airships had seen a lot of duty. The planes smelled of grease, sweat, urine, cigarette smoke and the gunpowder from the spent machine guns. The men practiced bombing missions and flying in tight formations. Perk went on a couple of real missions, sitting in the co-pilot's seat. With the full nerve-racking experience of flying in formation to the IP and on to the target, they dropped their bombs and returned to base while watching for enemy fighters. All rookie pilots needed these live missions before sitting in their own pilot's seat.

Their many briefings emphasized strategic bombing of sites that would weaken enemy forces connected with a planned ground invasion of France in the coming spring or summer. While Perk's crew had ground school, they watched the Rattlesden bombers continue their daily missions attacking ports, missile sites, airfields and marshaling yards in France, Belgium, and Germany. There was bleak news of daily Eighth Air Force combat losses and the Perkins crew knew their intensive training might one day save their lives.

Glenn read in Stars and Stripes News, one of the 447th Bomb Group's B-17 bombers named "Milk Wagon," set the record with 129 missions with no turn-backs. The Army published those successes and downplayed the other heavy losses of bombers.

By November 1943 the aircrew survival rate had become critical with each crew's tour of duty comprising 25 combat missions but with roughly two-thirds of the airmen in combat either dying or captured by the enemy. Those were disturbing odds for any branch of the military. Meanwhile, Perk's crew waited anxiously for news of their first mission.

Major General Curtis LeMay came to the base on a training demonstration to teach how tight formations reduce the loss of planes during combat missions. The German ME109s and the 190s had been known to fly right through the USAAF formations with guns blasting. That had to stop.

LeMay took note of the Schweinfurt and Ploiesti missions that had been a disaster, with a total loss of 120 planes and 1,200 airmen. With that tragic loss, LeMay knew that the attrition rate was not sustainable for the Eighth AirForce. He developed a new strategy of flying in close formation that would save lives and equipment. His training sessions of tight wing to wing boxes would eventually pay off in the cold winter skies over Great Britain.

At the end of November Perk wrote home to his family and a letter to Dottie, giving them his Army Post Office number, at Rattlesden. He told them he and his crew were still training but expected a mission by the first of January.

In the third week of December, and the day before they expected a mission, Perkins and Ralph Warren came down with bronchitis and were in the base hospital.

On Christmas Eve their squadron went on a big mission without the Perkins crew. Fortunately, no planes were lost so their group was still batting a thousand.

Perk's men found the slow start frustrating. It was freezing cold and the crew slept, wrote letters and went to ground school. The extra training at Rattlesden gave the men an advantage. The more training an airman had the better to improve their chances of survival in combat. The weathered airmen of the Luftwaffe had honed their skills in North Africa, Northern Europe and during the Battles of Britain and Stalingrad.

Christmas morning seemed just like any other day. Perkins' crew went to StowMarket and met up with friends from cadet training. The week following Christmas, they attended more ground school and watched training films on the use of the chin and tail turret guns while in formation and how to avoid friendly fire accidents.

While in the base hospital, Perk received a couple of letters from his crew's parents and one from Garrick's wife, Julia. They all thanked him for the encouraging words about their sons. Perk finally wrote Dottie a letter about his brother Maurice missing in action, in the Pacific. He said his family was anxiously waiting for more information but that he hadn't given up hope his brother would be found alive on some island. He didn't mention he and his crew member, Ralph Warren, were in the infirmary with bronchitis.

Perkins and Warren were still in the hospital on December 29th. Garrick and Overton went on missions as replacements for other crews. When they returned to the hut, they grumbled they didn't like flying with other crews because the planes were different and unpredictable and the crews didn't quite work as a team as the Perkins crew did. The next day all missions were scrubbed due to bad weather so they played poker and Collier and Moore lost a few British pounds. When there was a break in the rain, they played football with another hut out in the muddy infield.

Perk received a newsy letter from Dottie that her sister, Ruth, had graduated from college and had left for Jacksonville, Florida, to meet her husband, Lt. Bob Hepting. The couple would continue on to North Island, San Diego, for Bob to receive more training in PBY-2s at North Island Naval base. She said they had found a little apartment on Coronado Island, to rent for a few months until Bob's second deployment back to the South Pacific.

A letter came from Perk's mother saying they still hadn't heard anything new about Maurice. Perk wrote a V-Mail back to her with reassuring words, "The Navy will find him. We both are strong and healthy, Mom. We both can take care of ourselves." The U.S. military now advised using V-mail which put the letters on microfilm for transporting them overseas and then printed them out for the recipient on thinner paper with a self-envelope. It reduced the size and weight of the mail sent overseas. It was so space saving that he was told one bag of V-mail took the space of 37 bags of regular type mail. Army WAC's redacted anything in the letters that might give troop information or ship positions.

6.

Beating the Odds—1944

ON NEW YEAR'S EVE the base commander restricted everyone to base. As Collier described it in his diary, "We felt sorry for ourselves and decided to celebrate New Year's in their own way. Moore and I borrowed the major's jeep to make a beer run. We drove through the MP gate and saluted like we owned the joint. We bought two cases of beer and snacks in town and on the return trip we drove again back through the MP gate and smartly saluted. The major's Jeep was replaced where we found it. Our crew got a little tight, and at twelve o'clock four of us took our forty-fives behind our quarters and fired into the sky at the stroke of midnight. We really knew how to welcome in the new year of 1944."

Perkins and Warren were over their bronchitis after two weeks in the base hospital. The crew were finally intact and ready to fly. After getting out of the hospital, Perk had heard about the New Year's Eve escapade and had a talk with his two gunners. There could have been a black mark on the whole crew. Lt. Perkins was ultimately responsible for his crew's behavior. The boys were lucky their stunt went largely unnoticed, and no one got busted.

In the previous spring of 1943 bomber losses were running 80 per month increasing to 110 losses per month by the summer. Army General Ira Eaker who was in charge of the Eighth Air Force

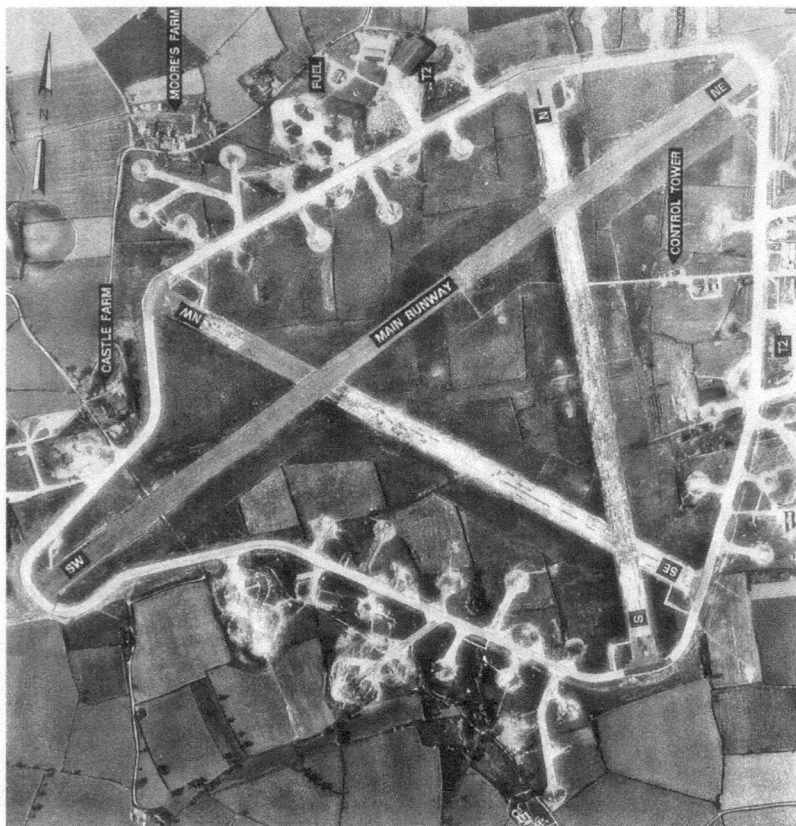

Rattlesden airfield

in England continued to launch bomber raids, without escorts, deep into German held territory. The Army Air Force Generals, Eaker, Hap Arnold and Carl Spaatz held on to the theory that the Flying Fortress, in tight formation, could prevail without escorts to the targets. They were wrong. By September of 1943 the Army bombers and trained crews were getting replaced too slowly to make up for the terrible losses. Then in October "Black Week" saw the loss of 2,030 lost crews and 26% of its aircraft over seven days of torturous raids. The three Generals realized this depletion rate was untenable. Finally the U.S. Army Brig. Gen. Fred Anderson, head of the Eighth Bomber Command, shut down all unescorted bomber raids until January 1944.

Meanwhile, North American Aviation was developing the P-51B Mustang escort for the RAF but it was testing out too slow with their Allison engines. A designer at North American Aviation switched out the Allison for a British Rolls Royce engine and it performed with excellence, surpassing the ME 109 and 190 German fighter planes in ascension rate, speed and altitude performance. U.S. General Jimmy Doolittle took over Eaker's command, fully supporting the fighter escort use of the new P-51s. The Perkins crew flew their first mission in the Eighth Army on January 9th, 1944 with a full fighter escort to the target and back.

Perkins crew

January 9, 1944—Mission: Romilly, France (1)

The Sergeant flipped on the light and yelled, "Lieutenant Perkins, it's 0300. Briefing is at 0400." Perk sat up and put his feet on the cold floor so he wouldn't go back to sleep. He hurriedly washed and dressed and headed to the mess hall and downed bacon, eggs, biscuits and strong coffee. For some airmen the food formed a lump in their throat with some difficulty swallowing due to nerves. Perk, being one of five brothers, knew to eat when it was available because he didn't know when the next meal would come. Their first mission was the culmination of 18 months of training.

In the briefing room the G2 (intelligence officer) stood at the front of the Nissen Hut, holding a long pointer. He pulled the blue cloth aside, uncovering the twelve foot wide map with strips of red yarn crisscrossing it, indicating the route to and from the target. A fat arrow at the end of the yarn pointed precisely where they were to bomb. With a few groans, the other officers stared at the map which revealed Romilly's Airfield, 68 miles east of Paris, France. The marshaling yard near Reims was the secondary target if weather didn't permit the first bomb drop. The G2 officer went over the damage reports from previous runs, the expected German fighter strength, and the heavy flak locations. They got today's weather report along the route and the latest intelligence on enemy defenses: 275 guns north of the target. The CO would "Time Hack" synchronize their watches and conclude by saying, "Make this run count. We don't want to go back there for another visit anytime soon. Dismissed."

The enlisted men attended their own radio, navigation, engineering and gunner briefings. Some information crossed over. The men put on their heated flight suits and parachutes. The gunners grabbed their guns from the gun hut and walked to the truck that would take them out to their planes at least an hour be-

Loading the bombs

fore take-off. The GP (general purpose) bombs had already been loaded in the bomb bay with their nose and tail fuses attached.

The Perkins crew was anxious and full of adrenaline as they climbed aboard. Perk assured his men they were going to put into practice what they knew well. "Everyone do your jobs and be on your toes." They proceeded to check their oxygen lines, electrical and other instruments. They had done this drill many times before. Even though Perk had done the aircraft checks many times on training missions and a couple real ones, today he was the commander and he did everything more deliberately. After all checks, they started their engines and could feel the full throated roar through the fuselage. The lumbering aircrafts, laden with a 5,000 pound bomb load, moved in a line on the taxiways to wait their turn to take off on the main runway. Perk's thought was, "Just make it above the trees with this bomb load."

In the darkness, at full throttle, their aircraft cleared the trees and the landing gear retracted. Perk circled the Buncher Beacon until the rest of the squadrons joined them. He maintained a steady climb, being careful not to collide with the other bombers until the formation was complete.

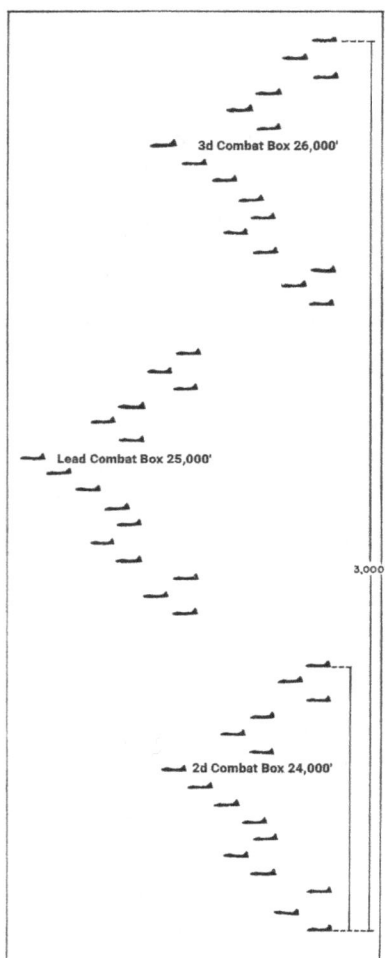

3d Combat Box 26,000'

Lead Combat Box 25,000'

3,000'

2d Combat Box 24,000'

Combat wing—three combat boxes

Perk maneuvered his aircraft, continuing to fly in a wide circle until he reached 10,000 feet. Because of their rookie status their ship was delegated a place back in the formation, number 3 in the high squadron. Colored flares were shot by the lead plane, signaling the entire armada was ready to head toward the target. It was quite a sight to see squadrons of B-17s assemble, directed by the lead-ship and organize themselves into an attack formation and set out on their way across the English Channel. This day there were three squadron formations, lead, high and low for a total of 48 B-17s in the group. The lead fort contained the Group Air Commander, Lt. Gary Allen, flying as the pilot with the Norden Bomb Site on board.

The gunners tested their machine guns over the channel in bursts of four or five rounds.

Dead Man's Hand rose fast to 26,000 feet over occupied France. All crew by then were on oxygen. They put on flak armor suits, all except Moore because it was too tight in the tail. His suit was hung on a knob along with his parachute outside the turret.

Everyone kept an apprehensive lookout for enemy fighters. They encountered heavy prop wash that caused a jousting of the aircraft. It was a wind caused by all the rapidly turning propellers. Their plane's wings, which floated on air to keep the plane airborne, were tossed around causing severe downdraft and instability. The effect dropped one wing which Perk had to counteract with the aileron, used to lift the wing back to level. The quick drop in altitude, caused by prop wash, put the aircraft in danger of a collision in the formation. Perk reacted quickly to correct the drop. The strain on the pilot to keep a 30-ton Flying Fortress in tight formation, was very strenuous and lasted eight hours. He was glad Glenn was there to break him.

It took all of his concentration and physical strength to hold his aircraft steady. With his eyes focused on the lead aircraft, he couldn't deviate even when under enemy attack from fighters and flak. Glenn and his flight engineer, Sgt. Overton helped to monitor the instruments, switches, dials, and gauges, keeping track of fuel pressure, altitude, wind drift, airspeed, and direction of the aircraft.

They were lucky to be in the high position. Perk didn't have to deal with the contrails streaming behind ships in his formation. Those condensation trails, cloud-like water vapor caused by hot airplane engine exhaust mixing with the cold moist air at high altitude, tended to obscure visibility. Those contrails acted as a marker or big arrow pointing to their formation, for the enemy fighters to find.

The necessary 30-pound flak suit made of steel plates weighted his body down but he'd have to get used to it as it protected him against flak fragments and shell splinters, although it wouldn't protect him from a direct hit by cannon fire. His parachute was too bulky to be worn but he had a harness that made it quick to clip on his chute if needed.

Glenn spoke to the crew as they got close to the IP (Initial Point) which was an agreed on landmark that was about 20 miles from the bombing objective. "Keep on the lookout for enemy fighters and make every shot count." At the IP the formation made a 45 degree turn towards the target and began their bomb run. The bombardier on the lead plane used his Norden Bomb-sight and took over that aircraft, factoring in speed, altitude, miles per hour and drift to calculate the bomb release point. His plane would have to be flown straight and level. The other aircraft in the formation would follow the lead and drop their bombs when he issued, "bombs away."

The formations were extremely vulnerable at this point and couldn't deviate from the bomb run. If one took a direct hit they could explode instantly. Some planes would break apart, plunge straight down or make a low descent. Many times an injured aircraft spinning out of control would hit other aircraft in the formation, losing two crews.

As they approached Romilly Airfield, there was flak but no enemy fighters. Lt. Allen's bombardier called bombs away, and the rest of the formation, including Lt. Foley, Perk's bombardier, filed suit, dropping a total of 240,000 pounds of bombs on the airfield. The formation made a wide turn and headed for home.

Southeast of Pas-de-Calais they encountered heavy flak and the crew gritted their teeth as they bounced and jostled toward the channel. They were never so glad to put landing gear down on the Rattlesden airfield. Dead Man's Hand landed with five flak holes in their fuselage, none hitting vital equipment. The trucks picked them up at their revetment parking and shuttled them to headquarters where each was questioned by G2 intelligence officers and offered a double shot of rye whiskey. They had returned alive from their first mission and that was one down, 24 to go.

At dinner they discussed how their training hadn't prepared them for the deafening noise, nonstop vibration of the plane and the heavy weight of the flight clothing. There was the constant threat of oxygen deprivation at 30,000 feet or the bitter cold temperatures of 50 degrees below zero. That stress, plus the underlying fear of being wounded or shot down, caused the men utter fatigue. At the end of a flight, all they wanted to do was eat and go to sleep.

It was a toss-up which part of the army had it worse, the infantry in the trenches, or the airmen doing combat in the skies. Perk's crew had a warm bed and hot food at night where men fighting in the jungles of the Pacific slept in insect and reptile infested trenches with K-rations. Still, most airmen never made it to their 25th mission, being shot down or bailing out behind enemy lines and taken prisoner.

January 11, 1944—Mission: Braunschweig, Germany (2/3)

In the briefing room at 0400 hours, there was a collective groan as the CO showed them on the map their target of Braunschweig. It was known to be heavily fortified, not only with 88 flak guns but with enemy fighters, whose pilots often slept in their airplanes to be ready for take-off.

After the bombers assembled in formation and crossed the English Channel heading for the German border, a nervous banter between Perk's crew began about how Germany looked like Kansas farms. Then someone said, "We're not in Kansas anymore, Toto." Glenn, on edge as much as the rest, told the crew, "Shut up and concentrate on your jobs, men."

Near Braunschweig Ball Bearing Factory, the sky was filled with black clouds of exploding 88s. Jagged fragments of shrapnel came through the fuselage. Flying in formation, wing to wing there was no tactical way to avoid the flak. Warren screamed out he had been hit and Glenn went back to check. He reported to Perkins. a shell fragment hit Warren's flak jacket and he would probably have a bruise. Two inches higher and the shell would have hit Warren in the face and he wouldn't have lived to tell about it.

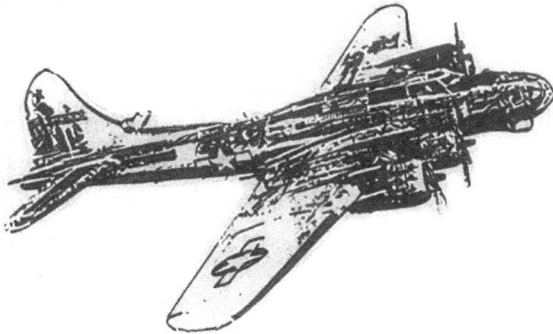

Nine Me 109, German fighters flew in close, attacking the boxes. Glenn muttered, "Damn Jerrys!" A dogfight between German Messerschmitts and American Mustang fighters dove at them head on, often breaking away right before they made contact. The air battle went on for forty-five minutes, all around them. The P-51 fighters were holding their own.

Three 109s tried to get through the formation but failed, thanks to the escort fighters and the Fort's defensive .50 caliber guns. Flak exploded in loud bursts of black smoke through their group, perilous for the German fighters as well as American aircraft. Off their right wing, B-17 number 031 was hit and Perk's crew watched as the wounded aircraft slowly dropped out of formation smoking from one engine. Two 109s went after the fort with a predator's mentality. It was easier to pick off injured prey, than risk the .50 caliber guns of many. Two Mustangs went after the enemy fighters, giving a few crew members on 031 enough time to bail out. Moore saw five chutes as he held his breath watching the wrenching sight of the plane spiraling down.

As they got closer to the target, the lead plane's bombardier finally gave the order, "Bombs away," and the rest of the formation followed, dropping their loads. Foley hooted as the bombs hit the target. Perk made a 45 degree turn and reassembled with the formation. He climbed back up to 26,000 feet and headed for home. The temperature in the aircraft fell to 55 below. Just before the Pas-de-Calais they flew through heavy flak again and watched helplessly as another B-17 from another group got a direct hit and exploded, crashing into the channel with no parachutes. It was so disheartening to watch ten men gone in an instant.

After landing they counted 13 holes in Dead Man's fuselage from flak. Miraculously, no vital parts or the crew were hit. Nine bombers had been reported down with one limping its way to Sweden. A few went down over Germany. One made it as far as the Zuider Zee in Holland and another went down in the North Sea. No one knew anything of their fates. They learned squadron Staff Sergeant John Noble was killed, shot through the neck by a piece of flak. The B-17 that ditched in the English Channel while trying to make it back to base was John Roberts' crew. Nine crews, missing or prisoners of war. After that information, the men gladly took that shot of whiskey.

Back in their quarters, the Perkins crew showered, shaved, and went to the mess hall for supper. No one had much of an appetite but they needed to be near their mates after the disastrous Braunschweig mission.

Two years ago none of Perk's crew had been in an airplane let alone serving in combat inside a heavy bomber. This was the new battlefield at altitudes of 26,000 feet and there were many ways for combat airmen to die. Take-offs were especially dangerous as the B-17s were overloaded with 5000 lbs of bombs in the bomb bay, 17,000 gallons of fuel, 160 gallons of oil in the four engines, plus the gear and crew of ten men. Once the aircraft was five miles up, sub-zero temperatures or lack of oxygen could easily kill airmen in minutes. The bomber crews were exposed to accurate enemy ground 88 Flak defenses and annihilating German fighter planes. Crewmen bled to death if shot on a mission. Parachuting out of a burning plane if they survived, would drop them into enemy territory and they were more likely to be killed by the angry citizenry than by German troops who were bound by the Geneva Convention. If their aircraft made it out of the target area after being shot up on a mission, the landing at allied bases was even more dangerous with damaged equipment. Forty percent of air crashes in WWII occurred during landings.

January 16, 1944—Mission (scrubbed)

With the lead-up to D-Day in the spring of 1944, there was round-the-clock relentless night blanket bombing by the RAF, targeting cities and general industrial areas. The USAAF took over all daylight precision bombing, hitting factories, submarine pens, oil manufacturers, industrial districts, marshaling yards and military bases. Their goal was to starve the German Wehrmacht of ball bearings, fuel, lubricants, munitions, soldiers and equipment. In addition, the raids hit enemy civilian targets, affecting morale, reducing housing for civilian workers who manned munition factories. The major enemy cities in Europe hit by fire bombs were Hamburg, Dresden and Berlin. Tokyo was a recipient of this strategy in the Pacific war. This collaboration started turning the tide in favor of the Allies, creating a war production deficit for the Axis powers.

With Allied successes, at the beginning of 1944 the air crews were further encouraged when told their bomb runs were preparing for the coming invasion of Europe, somewhere on the Italian or French coasts. Still, the enemy targets were heavily fortified with accurate 88 flak ground forces and fierce fighter plane attacks. To the USAAF airmen, some missions felt like suicide runs.

Flak, or the German Aircraft Defense Cannon they called *Flugabwehrkanone* was one of the most effective causes of death or disabler of airplanes. The 34 pound shell was shot from a cannon that exploded like a grenade. It contained a *proximity fuse* with miniature radar that detonated if an aircraft passed within range. Close formations of 500 aircraft at different altitudes were easy targets for the exploding flak shells. The shells would burst through the thin skin of the aircraft. With limited first aid onboard, a crew member who was hit with Flak shrapnel, in the head or a vital organ would certainly bleed to death, before they got back to base.

A couple of crippled British Lancaster bombers had landed at Rattlesden and Perk noticed the RAF crew members wearing infantry helmets over their leather caps to protect them from Flak shrapnel. Perk's crew and those in the USAAF were still wearing the leather aviator caps.

Before his next mission, Lieutenant Perkins pulled some strings and got ten US army helmets for his crew. The only problem with

Perk in his leather cap in 1943

USAAF patch for the Eighth AirForce

the infantry helmets was the aviator earphones that protruded, making the helmets too uncomfortable. He enlisted the base machine shop to do cutouts for the earphones and soon other pilots in his squadron were procuring helmets for their aircrews. Along with the flak vest, Mae West flotation vests and Perk's "Army helmet," Perk's crew felt more protected while on missions.

January 17 and 18

Perk and some of his crew took a bus to London on a 48-hour pass. It was a welcome break from the mess hall food and military housing on base. His bus drove down narrow carriage roads with high hedge rows on both sides. He enjoyed the scenes of British life along the route with views of the countryside, quaint half-timbered cottages with thatched roofs and short entrance doors. Small farms with pump wells, hand plows, free roaming chickens and tethered milk cows. Herds of sheep with long tails, and dairy cows roamed along the main roads. It was in East Anglia's farmers' fields where Rattlesden and other air bases were hurriedly built for the RAF in the late 1930s.

He found the countryside beautiful but as they entered the outskirts of London he could see the battle damaged buildings and piles of rubble from bombings by the Luftwaffe. The British had taken a beating and were still standing. The streets were full of Londoners walking about their city on their way to office jobs and shops.

Glenn, Garrick and Perk got off the bus in the West End and walk near the Thames River. They turned up Shaftesbury Ave. and ended up at Covent Garden's Vegetable Market. Perk bought a couple of apples and they continued walking, looking for a pub. They passed an alley where children were playing and a shop displaying a sign with a British flag and the words, "Keep Calm and Carry On." Perk knew he was going to like London.

Most Brits got around on foot or, the more fortunate, on bicycles. There were few cars because petrol was expensive and rationed like it was in the states. A few Fiats and Austin motor cars were parked along the cobblestone streets. In London the reliable underground subway system served their transportation needs as well as being used as a bomb shelter during air raids. Some underground subway lines were closed due to Londoners taking up residence on the tracks.

The three airmen took the *Tube* to the East End and came up several flights of stairs into the London streets. They blinked from the glare of the sunlight above ground. Glenn said, "I hope there are no buzz bomb attacks while we're here." Those pilotless rocket planes had been so destructive in East London. The three lieutenants looked around to see brick tenements, churches and shells of office buildings reduced to skeletal structures. Poor Westminster Abbey had been bombed in 1941, but it was slowly being restored. Workers went about the damaged buildings cleaning up with shovels and wheelbarrows; some workers using bare hands. Shopkeepers stocked their sparse shelves, factories were still operating and businesses continued while their men in the military were somewhere fighting for the survival of the British Isles. Most Londoners would say the British spirit and tenacity was thanks to the encouragement and leadership of their Prime Minister, Winston Churchill, who fearlessly confronted the Nazis that threatened their islands.

Perk, his co-pilot and navigator walked to the White Horse Hotel where they got a cheap room on the upper floor of the building. Some said those rooms were cheapest because they were the most vulnerable in a Nazi buzz bomb attack.

It was cold as they left the hotel to find a cabaret with a review of torch singers that had been recommended to them. After a couple of songs and a beer, they moved on to a pub called the Captain's Cabin where Yanks were warmly welcomed. They ran into the rest of their crew there and all of them went across the street to a Chinese restaurant where the special was chop suey with beef. Some of the guys were sure the beef was horse meat but Perk couldn't tell. An hour later Perk's tail gunner, Bill Moore, got sick. He had been drinking scotch and chasing it with boiler makers, gin and beer, so it might not have been the Chinese food that disagreed with him. On Perk's first weekend pass in Europe, he, Glenn and Garrick watched over their 19-23-year-old crew like brood hens with their chicks. They survived the night on the top floor of the White Horse Hotel with no buzz bombs disturbing their sleep.

With the build-up of the Army, Navy and Marines before the coming invasion, the Red Cross set up USO Clubs which occupied buildings in London. The Red Cross also operated Aero Clubs for

American Red Cross Club Mobile

the Eighth Air Force bases and Clubmobles that were converted buses that made the rounds to bases with similar services. The clubs never closed and provided meals, recreation, barber shops and laundry facilities for the soldiers overseas. They served snacks, donuts, and coffee by pretty American Red Cross workers. There were games, pool tables and dances often entertained by celebrities like Bob Hope and Glenn Miller.

During the war, English girls found the young American servicemen charming, handsome, humorous, outgoing and plentiful. At least three million GIs would pass through London, arriving in preparation for the Normandy invasion. There were eighty thousand young women filling the void of male workers in farms and offices and armament factories. The Yanks were sharply dressed and were paid five times what the British soldiers were paid, while wearing their wrinkled British tunics. The GIs were very generous and spoiled the ladies with food they couldn't get and nylon stockings and other goods they couldn't buy. Mostly the British women were bowled over by American men, who paid them more attention, gave them compliments and made them feel special. The result was that 70,000 British girls married American servicemen during the war.

January 19

The crew returned to base from London and found, while they were gone, George Hopkins, one of the boys in their hut, went down over France. Poor devil. It was a reminder of how vulnerable they were in combat and why they had to take breaks in London whenever they had the chance.

January 21, 1944—Mission: Noball, France (4)

After a couple of days of bad weather the crew tried out their new helmets on their fourth mission to bomb V-1 bomb factories in Noball, France. It was a short three-hour trip; "In and out," were Perk's words.

Not many people knew the U.S. had bombed France during the war but anywhere the Axis were entrenched, the RAF and USAAF bombed those enemy targets. Foley's bombs hit the Noball target and on their return to England they encountered moderate flak near Calais. They also picked up some big band music over the port city, which was pretty surreal. After landing at Rattlesden, Glenn counted four flak holes in the wing and tail section. Bill Moore had a near miss with a few pieces of shrapnel coming through the fuselage not far from his head. He was happy to have Perk's infantry helmet for protection.

At their debriefing Overton and Moore reported several things of interest to the intelligence officer. They had very clear weather and they observed several flak gun installations not on railroad cars, a long truck convoy near Calais and what looked like an airfield or bunker near the port. That information was noted.

January 22-29

The airmen were frustrated with eight days of snotty weather including fog and rain with no missions. Everyday they couldn't fly, they were that much farther away from going home. The sentiment of most airmen was, "they just wanted to get on with it."

Perk wired money to his mother. His base pay was $165.00 dollars. His flying pay was $82.00, subsistence for the month was $43.00. After Insurance, rations and allotment costs, "I am sending you $40, Mom, since I know I can get by on $50 this month."

Ruth and Bob Hepting in La Jolla, California

Mail came and there was a letter from Dottie who said Ruth's husband, Bob Hepting, was in training in Jacksonville, Florida, and they were leaving for North Island, San Diego. He had signed up for a second tour. She didn't know where he would be stationed. Another letter arrived from Perk's mother saying there was still no word on Maurice and she wasn't giving up hope he would be found. She reported that Perk's brother, Richard, had joined the Merchant Marines and would be ferrying supplies in the war effort. Perk immediately thought of the U-Boat submarines that were taking out Merchant Marine ships. He read in the *Stars and Stripes* newsletter, all Naval and Merchant ships now traveled in large convoys for protection from the enemy subs.

January 30, 1944—Mission: Braunschweig, Germany (5/6)

The men were roused out of their cots at 0400 and after breakfast went to their fifth mission briefing. A collective groan was heard in the room when the map revealed Braunschweig, Germany. Garrick, the navigator, said a little too loud, "Oh hell, not again!" Tensions were high as the crew realized they had to go back to that heavily fortified city. The targets this time were the aircraft

Flak over Germany

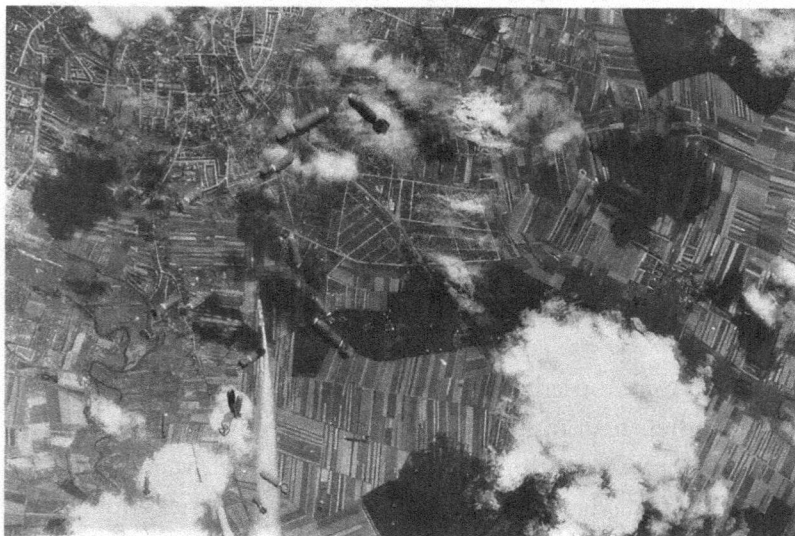

Bombs drop through flak
Braunschweig, Germany

plant and marshaling yards. They were told the flak would be thick. Perk wondered if the Germans somehow knew they were coming. The last mission to Braunschweig flak was thick enough to walk on.

They were in the lead box with their plane, *Big Stoop* equipped with the Norden Bombsight. They were briefed on the precision instrument with an analog calculator that could pin-point a target at 30,000 feet. The secret navigational tool adjusted for air density, the bombers airspeed, wind drift and ground speed in order to hit its mark. Prior to its use, the accuracy at hitting targets was dismal.

Thirty minutes from the IP they encountered heavy flak, in addition to four ME109s that came at their ship head on. Their waist gunner, Ralph Warren knew he hit one of the German fighters because he saw its engine smoking and he watched as it went down out of sight. The remaining three 109s disappeared to safety beneath the cloud cover.

Even though the fighters were gone, the flak didn't let up and Perk continued on the bomb run with bursts of black acrid smoke and shells exploding all around him. The noise was deafening and the violent bouncing of the ship from the explosions was unnerving. Foley, with his face down in the bombsight, took over autopilot control of the aircraft, to level it out on the final run to the target. They continued bouncing for what seemed like hours, not minutes until he called, "Bombs away." Load after load of bombs fell to the earth, releasing the planes of their lethal burden.

Perk led the formation on a wide left turn toward their home base. The formation skirted around the heavily fortified cities of Essen, Dusseldorf and Cologne. Myers picked up more symphony music on his radio from some German station. As he listened, he thought, "It's a damn, strange way to fight a war."

There was nothing like the sight of the white cliffs of Dover for the crew, after a mission like that. Their bomber, *The Big*

Stoop, had 19 flak holes in its fuselage and starboard wing tip. At their debriefing, Warren got credit for shooting down a 109 and Garrick reported to the G2, "Braunschweig Aircraft Factory was lit up like a damn chimney."

January 31—February 2

Four more days of bad weather scrubbed three missions. Perk got a newsy letter from Dottie which told of college classes and her family's activities including ice skating and a Job's Daughter dance. It was comforting to hear about regular everyday activities at home. She told Perk to look out for a box of fudge and cookies she made him for Valentine's day, but she didn't know how well the tin would survive in transit. Aware that the censors would have edited anything about rumors of the coming invasion of the continent, implied in newsreels at the local movie theater, she avoided those topics. Her inquiries of news about Maurice were kind and left a lump in his throat. She signed off with a hope the war would end soon so he could come home. Perk received a letter from his aunt Mary expressing how hard the waiting for information of his brother was for his family. Perk and his crew tried to adjust to those mission-less days by writing letters, playing cards, grumbling and sleeping.

February 3, 1944—Mission: Wilhelmshaven, Germany (7/8)

Back flying *Dead Man's Hand* on their seventh mission to Germany, the Perkins crew's assignment was to bomb the submarine pens and docks at Wilhelmshaven. The secondary target was Bremerhaven. Dead Man's Hand had been a new aircraft when they flew it across the Atlantic to Rattlesden in November. Now it had battle scars, flak patches and one engine replacement. Their bombing altitude was supposed to be twenty-two thousand feet but there was thick overcast at the target. Perk was forced to ascend to twenty-eight thousand feet and head to the secondary target, where they dropped their bombs on the docks, one of the most important harbors for the Kreigsmarine. They couldn't tell whether they hit their mark. The temperature inside the aircraft was sixty-five below zero and Myers got some frostbite on his ears.

Port of Bremerhaven, Germany

There were plenty of flak shells and 15 German fighter planes. The Messerschmits flew head-on directly at them, out of the sun, and at one point came so close that Perk turned his head and winced, waiting for the impact. The fighter missed him by a few feet. Another time an Me 109 ace fighter came so close and they both stared at each other's anxious faces. In those tight spots there was a difference between panic and fear. Panic was paralyzing and fear made the crew sit up and do their jobs earnestly as they were taught, as if their life depended on it.

Back at HQ they heard two B-17s were lost from each of the first and third divisions; none from the 447th. The P-51 fighters downed five German fighters with a loss of three fighters of our own. They were glad to hear two of those Mustang pilots were able to bail out.

Often Perk and his crew felt alone at 25,000 feet. Of course at briefings they took instructions from the commander who plotted the targets, gave them the weather and enemy defense maps. But once in the air he and his crew were on their own. The most perfectly planned mission couldn't succeed if they failed at their tasks. They learned by experience and by experiment. Every mission became a learning exercise with maximum effort. Over the target the crew was alone, in the chaotic scene of air combat. There were a hundred things that could go wrong where they had to make quick life and death decisions, far beyond their age, rank and experience. Still, they carried on from mission to mission.

That afternoon Colonel Hunter Harris presented the crew with the Oak Leaf Cluster medals. After dinner they made a toast to those boys who went down on the last raid, with hopes that there were survivors who could make it back to allied lines. Perk's crew were so exhausted they hit the sack early.

February 4, 1944—Mission: Frankfurt, Germany (9/10)

At the 05:30 briefing for Frankfurt, the airmen were told there were 240 flak gun defenses around the target. At least the squadron would have damn good fighter protection. The mission was a maximum effort with 748 heavy bombers loaded with 5000 pounds GP and some incendiary bombs. Accompanying the formation were 190 fighter planes. Take off was at 0815 hours.

After the London Blitz, Winston Churchill didn't mince words about targeting the factories of the Wehrmacht as well as the workers and their homes. Without housing for the workers, in the icy winter, the lack of labor would be a bigger hindrance to Hitler in the operation of his factories.

During the mission assembly, three planes aborted and while on the mission, another turned back due to mechanical problems. When crossing the border into Germany, a few Me109s breached the formation with one fort lost. Garrick counted three chutes. Flak was heavy over the target and very accurate, particularly on their return over the well fortified Ruhr Valley. Dead Man's Hand sustained fifteen flak hits and had number three engine shot out. Perk feathered it after seeing oil flowing back on the hot supercharger. When he reached the English Channel he was flying two thousand feet above the water, escorted by two Mustangs. Bill had a piece of flak hit him in the leg and Marcuse quickly administered first aid. All that and Thomas Garrick wrote in his log, "We are the lucky ones." There were five ships missing from our group. Major Shepard, our squadron CO, went down over the Ruhr Valley. Of the 748 aircraft 633 were effective. Twenty of the planes were downed. Our escorts shot down eight German fighters at the cost of one of our P-51s. The 447th started landing at 1500 hours. It was absolutely a hellish mission. Thanks to God, only nineteen more to go.

As information of downed planes and lost crews came in after a raid, Perk realized the odds were stacked against them. There was no such thing as an easy combat mission. To fly a B-17 for nine hours in close formation was tough. On board the crew was weighed down with protective equipment. All the while facing flak, fighters and possible mid-air collisions due to the sheer numbers of aircraft flying around you. The airmen sought solace in the base Chaplain and their buddies. Part of Perk's job as pilot was to inspire his men to get up in the morning and get back in the airplane for the next assignment and fight on. They trusted in their team's skills and their brotherhood of men to watch out for each other. Still, most airmen knew there wasn't a lot they could do if their number came up. Perk's men continued to be superstitious and abhorred flying missions with other crews as fill-ins. They figured if they stuck together, their good luck would continue.

February 5, 1944—Mission: Orly, France (11/12)

The next day the boys were up at 0430 hours, briefing at 0600. Bill's leg was bandaged. They weren't flying Dead Man's Hand, but Pistol Packin Mama, which had seen over twenty missions.

The intrepid Perkins crew left on their mission to bomb an air depot in Romilly-sur-Seine, France, a seemingly easy raid. Their group was assigned to fly in the high position of the Fourth Combat Wing at an altitude of 21,900 feet. Take off started at 0825 hours. At assembly something went wrong in the formation. In their squadron, they could not find three of the wings. They visually searched but eventually they fell in with the rest of the wing, crossed the English Channel, continuing on toward the secondary target at Villacoublay.

Thirty miles inside France at 22,000 feet, their plane developed mechanical problems with the number three engine and Perk had to feather the prop. A few minutes later Overton discovered the aircraft's oxygen system went out and Perk quickly reduced the altitude to 12,000 feet where they could operate without oxygen. They found themselves alone, with three quarter power, a full bomb load and no oxygen. All Perk could do was abort the mission. Luckily, one of the Mustangs came to his starboard wing as an escort. Their ship was losing altitude and in order to reduce weight, Perk made the decision to drop their bomb load in a French farmer's field before crossing the Channel. At 10,000 feet they hit some flak over the Pas-de-Calais with a few hits in the fuselage. They flew low across the water and finally made it back to base.

At the post flight interrogation, Perk's crew learned the lead navigator had been off course and flew over the Paris defenses. Two of those three ships were lost. It was also confirmed that Major Shepard went down yesterday over the Ruhr Valley. Perk had been flying next to their ship and a burst of flak hit an engine on Shepard's starboard wing. His fort, *The Lucky Lady*, caught fire and they were last seen going through the cloud under cast. Don Collier said, "We have to believe that some of the fellows were able to bail out."

The cold foggy weather of England matched their blue mood and Perk doubted there would be a mission the next day. After three missions in three days, the Perkins' crew was shaken, discouraged and exhausted. Perk addressed his men and said, "The British RAF have been in this fight since mid-1939. The only alternative for them is to learn to speak German. They can't afford to be discouraged and neither can we. The old British saying, 'Keep calm, and carry on,' applies to the 447th Bomb Group."

Signs of Allied Gains Against the Enemy

The previous year, on January 27, 1943, the United States made their first aerial bombing raid on the submarine pens at Wilhelmshaven, Germany. The RAF and the USAAF struggled with the terrible losses imposed by the seasoned Luftwaffe. Victory in the European war was leaning in favor of the Axis powers.

The strategy of around-the-clock aerial bombing of German factories, oil fields and transportation systems, during the spring, summer and fall of 1943, was beginning to take effect on the Wehrmacht, but at a terrible price to our aircraft and their crews.

In North Africa under the Supreme Command of General Dwight D. Eisenhower, the Axis forces surrendered in May to the Allies. Two months later US General Patton, and Field Marshal George Montgomery took the Italian Island of Sicily. One month later, Montgomery's Eighth Army invaded the mainland of Italy and the Italian Government signed an armistice with the Allies. German troops retreated further up the Italian peninsula toward Rome.

On November 1, 1943, General James Doolittle, the hero of the first raid on Tokyo, established the Fifteenth Air Force headquarters on the Adriatic coast at Foggia, which became a secondary theater of Allied operations.

On the Eastern Front, after the Soviet victory at Stalingrad, the Red Army remained on the offensive, pushing west, liberating Ukraine and Eastern Byelorussia from the Germans. Hitler's armies were on a long retreat toward Berlin with Stalin's armies at their heels. Now the Allies in Great Britain, under the command of U.S. General Eisenhower, were preparing for the coming invasion of Normandy. Hitler was still a formidable enemy but there were cracks showing in his *Thousand Year Reich*.

February 6

With no missions the crew caught up on much needed sleep and some contemplated their vulnerability. They wrote letters home to loved ones. It was too cold to play baseball but they played cards in their hut and Perk lost a few British pounds at poker.

February 7

Another day with no mission but they were called to the HQ because awards were given. Bill Moore, their tail gunner, got the Air Medal from the base commander for downing two 109s. He was such a crack shot. Perk was told they would have a mission tomorrow if the weather was better. There was some talk about the brass counting each mission as only half. The reasoning was the replenishment crews were not coming as expected and those "seasoned" airmen would have to do double. That would mean Perk's crew would have to do 28 more missions instead of 18. It made the war that much rougher. Everyone in the group was very peeved. They were changing the game rules, mid game.

The airmen's diet on base was pretty bland. During downtime, some soldiers had their own chicken pens, others bought fresh eggs from the farmers. Some crews had built their own primitive meat roasting spit and when it was operating men could smell the barbeque all over the camp. All of these presented a welcome change from regular base rations.

February 8, 1944—Mission: Braunschweig, Germany (scrubbed)

Up at 0300 hours, briefing at 0430 hours. The target area was an aircraft plant. The planes were loaded with GP (general purpose) and incendiary bombs. Take off was at 0710 hours. The wing was called back to base because of bad weather. That was always a tough target and the men were glad not to be going.

The rest of the day there was not much going on because of the snotty weather. Perk's NCO's boiled some eggs on their stove which took over an hour to cook. Perk stopped playing cards with the boys because Garrick and Foley were too good and he didn't like always losing.

February 10, 1944—Mission: Braunschweig, Germany (13/14)

It was Ralph Warren's birthday and the Eighth Air Force gave him a hell of a present: a round trip ticket back to Braunschweig. Briefing was at 0430 hours. They were to bomb the same aircraft plant in Braunschweig, Germany, with GP and incendiary bombs. They took off at 0710 hours. In *Dead Man's Hand* they flew the high position in the 4th Combat Wing. When they were twenty minutes from the IP, their fort ran into a barrage of thunderous flak. Their ship bounced and number two engine was hit in the oil line. Perk tried feathering the prop by rotating the propeller to turn-edge first into the airstream to reduce drag. Before Perk had time to do that, all the oil was gone. Immediately their airspeed started lagging and they slipped out of formation.

There was little chance they could make the IP with 5,000 pounds of bombs, and he had to turn back. They would be lucky to bring the ship home safe that far into occupied territory. They made a wide U-turn and headed west alone. There were no fighters tailing them and no escorts in sight.

After a few minutes number two prop ran away and Perk thought it was going to burn so the crew was given the order to get ready to bail out. Just as Moore and Myer, the tail and ball turret gunners, pulled his emergency door handle and climbed into the waist, number two prop froze, eliminating the fire hazard. With only three engines, the ship couldn't maintain the altitude with the bomb load. While precariously low at ten thousand feet, they had no choice but to salvo their bomb load in a Dutch farmer's field.

Thankfully, two escorts, a P-38 and a P-47 joined their ailing ship and the crew cheered, seeing their little friends nearby. Then after fifteen minutes, over the German-Dutch border, five Focke-Wulf 190s attacked the three aircraft from all directions. The dog fight went on for a half hour as Perk flew *Dead Man's Hand* toward the North Sea. They were hit with flak a couple of times and their ship shuttered and bounced but didn't explode. Finally two 190s were hit by their escorts and the wounded planes retreated east. Perk immediately called for a damage check and the crew discovered their hydraulic and electrical system had been shot out and disabled. Marcuse and Collier scrambled to put out a small electrical fire of sparks in the waist caused by a short.

They had flown over 200 miles and when they reached the North Sea they flew at low altitude looking for ships and landmarks. As bum luck would have it, when they reached the English coast they ran into a heavy snowstorm with low visibility. Garrick tried to get a signal. The crew was cold without electricity for their heated suits, but that was the least of their worries. Perk wanted to make it back to their base but he was barely holding the ship in the air, flying at 1000 feet above trees and buildings. Glenn and Garrick had tried to find the nearest airfield in which to land. The 95th Bomb Group's airstrip was pinpointed and they hoped they could make it. Their luck was holding, when in the cockpit the red light on number three engine came on indicating depleted fuel. Perk was out of options.

Without hydraulics or landing gear Perk told the tower he had to do a crash belly landing. As he approached the runway another fuel light came on the number four engine. There was nothing left to keep them in the air. Perk balanced the plane, lifted the nose slightly as the lights guided them down to the white ground as it rose up to meet their belly. They touched down in the heavy snow which helped to cushion their landing. Perk, Glenn and the crew held their breath and held on, sliding sideways off the tarmac and into a snowbank. Their ship came to a stop, silent and tilting like a wounded animal. The snow and lack of fuel likely prevented a fire.

The crew scrambled off the aircraft, so thankful to be alive. They had miraculously survived a crash landing without a scratch and once clear from their aircraft the airmen hugged each other, slapping Perk, Glenn and each other on the back. The runway lights illuminated the plane's engine props, bent from the belly landing like curled fingers. The ball turret sunk into the pock marked fuselage. Perk felt the silence and the freezing night air as snowflakes hit his face. They were alive. The emergency trucks arrived and took the crew to the base headquarters and then to the mess hall for hot drinks and sandwiches. Perk arranged for a transport back to Rattlesden.

Dead Man's Hand had been listed as missing in action, along with 29 airplanes shot down on that mission to Braunschweig; a terrible loss of men. For the Perkins' crew, while on the raid everything that could go wrong, went wrong. The men were thankful they lived through that day. They were grateful to the

Belly Landing

fighter escorts that got them across the North Sea. They walked into their base at 2200 hours to all their friends' great surprise and relief. Just before midnight the crew toasted Ralph Warren with a shot of rye whiskey on his 19th birthday. To their surprise they got credit for that mission to Braunschweig. Five days later the aircraft was repaired at the 95th's airbase and back in service.

All anyone could say about the B-17 was, it was an airplane you could trust. No other long range heavy bomber could have taken the damage their ship had sustained and still brought them home in one piece. There were other airplanes that were larger, faster, flew farther and carried heavier bomb loads. What was exceptional about the B-17, besides its defensive armaments, was its ability to absorb heavy amounts of battle damage and still fly. With well trained airmen, the Army was convinced the dependable Flying Fortress would help win the air war in Europe.

February 11-12

The next two days the men did little else but sleep. It was the kind of exhaustion that overtakes the mind and body like a coma. They were lucky, bad weather had canceled all missions so they

Dead Man's Hand at Rattlesden, England*

had time to recover from the Braunschweig mission. At noon they got up, ate and then went back to bed. Their pass to London had been canceled and the men were peeved. They needed a break. Glenn checked to see if the crew's Air Medals were at headquarters but they weren't ready. That evening the weather

---

* *Dead Man's Hand,* number 42-31188, was the B-17G Perk and his crew ferried from Harvard Airbase in Nebraska to Rattlesden, England. Braunschweig would be the last mission Perk's crew would fly aboard *Dead Man's Hand.* That fortress would be patched, repaired and would go on to become one of the few "Century Ships" to escape destruction on 105 missions over enemy territory. Sadly, her luck ran out on April 19th, 1945, five weeks before Germany surrendered, *Dead Man's Hand* was hit by a single pass through her formation by a German Messerschmitt Me 262 Jet fighter. Her engine #1 caught fire and parts of it and the wing were disintegrating before she went down in Germany. Pilot Lt. Robert Glazener and his crew parachuted out and were captured, becoming POWs until they were liberated in the middle of May. Sadly, her co-pilot, Lt. Harold Cramer did not survive. *Dead Man's Hand* was the last B-17 to be shot down, of the 447th Bomb Group in England.

was starting to improve because there were stars in the night sky and they knew they might have a mission the next day.

After dinner they went to see the movie, *Mr. Lucky,* and after, they had some beers with the guys and sat around telling a few jokes. Marcuse told the one about an exhausted American pilot on his way to R & R in London. The tired airmen had just flown 25 missions over the Reich. As he walked the aisle of a crowded train, he only saw one unoccupied seat next to a well-dressed middle-aged English lady who was using it for her little dog.

The weary pilot asked, "Please, ma'am, may I sit in that seat?"

The woman locked down her nose at the pilot, sniffed and said, "You Americans are such a rude class of people. Can't you see my little dog, Fifi, is using that seat?" The pilot walked away determined to find a place to rest. But on another trip down to the end of the train and back, found himself again facing the woman with the dog.

Again he asked, "Please, lady, may I sit there? I'm very tired." The English woman wrinkled her nose and snorted, "You Americans are not only rude but arrogant. Now leave me alone!"

The pilot didn't say anything else. He leaned over, picked up the dog and tossed it out the window of the train, and he sat down in the empty seat.

The woman shrieked and railed, and demanded that someone defend her against the pilot.

An English gentleman sitting across the aisle spoke up, "You know sir, you Americans do seem to have a penchant for doing the wrong thing. You eat holding the fork in the wrong hand. You drive your automobiles on the wrong side of the road, and now, sir, you've thrown the wrong bitch out the window!"

Everyone roared and a few more jokes were told before Perk left and went to his quarters where he wrote a letter to Dottie. He couldn't talk much about what had happened, where they went or what they were doing, so he talked about their activities on base.

He decided to describe their movie theater. "You love going to the movies and I wanted to describe our quonset hut theater. They throw in a few benches and boxes for us to sit on. The old projector is suspended from the ceiling with loudspeakers placed on tables or benches around the hut. The lights are turned off while they turn on the projector. An image from one of the four reels is projected on the white bedsheet for a screen. At least a couple minutes are spent trying to widen the image and focus, while we miss the introduction. Then the projector bulb goes out and we only hear the audio part with no picture. With groans from the guys, the projectionist replaces the bulb and the picture comes back up. Then the sound track stops and we just see Cary Grant and Laraine Day mouthing the words. Finally, the projectionist gets that fixed and it is time to change to the second reel and we start the process all over again. Sitting on the hard benches and stretching your neck to see around the guy in front, makes for an uncomfortable two hours. Although we welcome the chance to get up and leave, we always seem to come back for more movies."

February 13, 1944—Mission: Noball, France (15/16)

The crews next mission was one of the five factories (#78) south of Paris, which produced the V-1, winged bombs that were terrorizing London. The crews take off started late at 1330 hours and was just 90 minutes across the channel. The factory produced jet engine powered flying rockets which were also called "doodlebugs." They made a buzzing sound just before hitting their target and exploding. The destruction and lives lost had been terrible for Londoners.

It was frustrating to Perk how fast the Jerries were up and running airfields and factories after being bombed. His crew had been on this raid to the Noball V-1 factory just three weeks before. Their recovery was uncanny and he figured either their General purpose bombs weren't very accurate or Germans were using French slave labor to rebuild their production lines quickly.

Perk flew the fort named Scheherazade, which took off late because of a sluggish engine. Late getting to the formation, another ship took their place in #3 position in the first element of the low squadron. They finally were airborne and had to tag on at the rear end. With no more engine problems they crossed the channel and continued on to the target with some flak here and there. As they approached the IP and started their bomb run, the ship that took their place in position #3 was hit by flak and went down in a long flaming smear of wreckage with its parts disintegrating around it. They wondered whose plane it was and felt guilt, dread, and relief all at the same time. Glenn couldn't help but think they had been spared that fate by a sluggish engine. Flak continued to be heavy all around them and their ship bounced and shuttered until the lead bomber called out "bombs away." The bombs fell from 22,000 feet and Garrick reported he saw black smoke rise in the air, a sure sign of a hit and maybe an oil tank explosion.

Perk steered the ship in a slow right turn to head home, always a dicey maneuver because of the possibility of midair collision in the formation. Perk and Glenn watched their starboard and port wings as well as altitude. After they landed back at Rattlesden, more than one of the Perkins' crew thought of the fort that took their place in #3 position.

February 16-17

Finally, a two day pass to London came through. The afternoon train took them into Piccadilly where they got rooms at the Brighton Hall Hotel. It was a swanky place with velvet seats and chandeliers. After an evening at the pub the men looked forward to real beds with comfortable quilts at the hotel. During the night a loud explosion shook the building and the men ran to the window to see the building next door had sustained heavy damage to the top two floors with stray bricks from the blast hitting their hotel and breaking windows. The buzz bomb raid gave all the airmen a good scare. After surviving dangerous missions over Europe they might have been taken out while asleep in their beds in London.

Foley, Glenn and Perk walked around the city, looking at the damage. They ended up having a few beers and eating meat pies at a surviving pub. Because of the city's damaged buildings and food shortages, few pubs were still open. The next day the three lieutenants met four Canadians who took them to a private club where they drank until supper. They actually got a pretty good steak and then took in a show and returned to the pub. They got back to the hotel at four AM.

The three hung-over lieutenants took the early train back to the base. The rest of the crew were supposed to be back in camp at 1300. By 1700 they were still drinking and finally got back to base at 2300. Technically they were AWOL but when they got back to their hut late, nothing happened. They had no mission the next day and the crew stayed close to their bunks trying to get rid of their hangover.

The Big Week

Operation Argument was a series of intensive daylight and night-time raids from February 20-25th, 1944, by the USAAF and the RAF, against the enemy. From the US 8th Air Force in England, 3,300 aircraft participated in the daylight raids while 300 bombers were dispatched from the 15th Air Force at Foggia, Italy. The mission was to hit dozens of targets; aircraft factories, supply lines, oil production and air bases, deep inside Germany, to decimate the Luftwaffe.

February 20, 1944—Mission: Tutow (Rostock), Germany (17/18)

Perk's crew were called up at 0430 hours to be briefed on their eleven-hour-long mission to Rostock, Germany. The target was northeast of Berlin to bomb an airfield near the Baltic coast. The 36 aircraft carried GP and incendiary bombs to be dropped at an altitude of only 12,000 feet. Perk figured this mission was going to be a rough one with strong anti-aircraft defenses. He knew to avoid the Helgoland Island flak tower just off the German coast at the North Sea. He turned toward the Tutow target soon after crossing the Danish peninsula. Besides being a bombing raid, they were sent as decoys to draw the German fighters away from the allied target of Frankfurt, Germany. The formation got to the IP and started the bomb run. They encountered heavy flak and fighters as expected and the target was partially obscured by clouds, 6/10. (meaning the overcast was more than 50% obstructed). The PFF radar ship in their formation led the way and marked the drop spot with smoke flares. Garrick and Collier watched two forts go down and anxiously counted four parachutes. They dropped their incendiaries and turned for home. On their return to the base at Rattlesden at 1715 hours, they found they had a dozen flak holes. They heard from Sgt. Wilson, their friend Frank Henry, was on one of the lost forts on today's mission. It was so unnerving and sad sleeping in a Nissen next to empty beds of missing airmen.

Fallen ships weren't always due to flak or fighters. Equipment malfunction or human error. Mid-air collisions were common. With hundreds of aircraft in tight formations, friendly fire or bombs dropped by Allied planes on the airships beneath them, were a common cause of casualties. Cloud covers were as much the enemy as the Germans, with many missions aborted because of the dangers of flying blind. Not all Air Force fatalities could be explained. The much admired band leader, Glenn Miller, who flew to Allied bases, entertaining troops during the war, took off on a foggy day in December 1944, leaving from England, heading for France. His plane vanished over the English Channel and was never found.

Mission over Diepholz, Germany

February 21, 1944—Mission: Diepholz, Germany (19/20)

At 0630 hours the Perkins crew learned they were going to Diepholz, a target southwest of Bremen to bomb another Luftwaffe air base. At 0850 hours they flew on the left wing in #4 slot and Colonel Swartz was flying the lead bomber. The attacking force had 21 B-17 groups and eight B-24 groups. On the way there they encountered lots of flak and six German fighters. Before the drop they had trouble with the electrical release on the bomb bay doors and Sgt. Overton tried the manual lever which was also jammed. He had to get on the catwalk in the bomb bay and physically dislodge the jammed bomb while looking down into open space four miles above the Earth. At 22,000 feet they dropped their bombs and a few minutes later they caught hellish flak. After they returned to their base they saw a lot of flak damage to other aircraft but to everyone's surprise, all made it back. Someone was looking out for us on that mission.

February 22, 1944—Mission: Schweinfurt, Germany (aborted)

The crew was up at 0400 again for their briefing; the target was Schweinfurt, Germany. Just after crossing the channel the squadron was called back because of bad weather. They were not disappointed due to that target being one of the roughest. In the afternoon, Perk went back into the MTF clinic, "Military Treatment Facility," for a bad lung. The Perkins' crew were spared the next few days' raids as Perk recuperated in the base hospital.

News of the successes of "The Big Week" were discussed in briefings. The Luftwaffe was greatly diminished but the toll on the allies was enormous. The Eighth Air Force lost 137 aircraft and the 15th Air Force lost 89 planes shot down by the defenses of the Third Reich. Over 2200 airmen were either lost or imprisoned. The week of raids had been a strategy to prepare for the coming invasion of France. It marked a critical turning point in favor of Allied Forces in Europe. Germany lost twenty percent or 434 experienced pilots in its Luftwaffe. More importantly 75 percent of the buildings that made up the Luftwaffe aircraft industry were severely damaged.

The crew gathered around the one radio in Perk's hut to listen to the BBC broadcast, John Shags reporting on the war. "The Nazis have had sufficient replacement resources that move about on railroads and truck transports keeping Hitler's war machine fighting. Our courageous RAF, the 15th Air Force and the mighty

Eighth continue to bomb factories, ports and railroads." Shags continued, "In January and February our airmen struck back with fury at the German supply chain of the Third Reich." The boys cheered because he was speaking about their successes in January and during The Big Week. They had flown those bomber missions and had survived.

Bournemouth Rest and Recuperation

February 25-29

The first thing Lieutenant Perkins did when released from the hospital was to give his crew the good news, they were to start a seven-day furlough of rest leave. Overton, Myers, Marcuse, Warren, Moore and Collier took the morning train to London for two days. Perkins, Halverson, Garrick and Foley took a later train directly to Bournemouth because they wanted to spend their whole R & R there. They were staying at a large country mansion by the sea. Many country estates in England were converted to hospitals or rest and recuperation centers for the "friendly invasion" of US servicemen during the war. At any one time there were a half a million personnel, airmen, flight crews and ground crews at 200 airfields in Great Britain. The need for places to escape the rigors of war and the stresses of aerial combat, bolstered morale enormously.

The elegant Canford Cliffs Estate, by the sea, was surrounded by a beautiful garden of meandering paths, flowers, streams and bridges. The luxurious rooms were nothing airmen had ever seen. They rested, dined, rented bikes and explored the boardwalk by the beach. Without the severe food shortages of London and supplemented by the US Army, the crew ate well, frequented the pubs and slept in luxurious beds. They had a great time horseback riding and playing cricket on vast lawns. The ocean air and the outdoors was like a tonic and it took their minds off what they had ahead of them. Garrick and Foley shot pool in the afternoon. That evening they all met up and went to a USO dance. Foley brought a flask of scotch from London and they had a few drinks while they did a little dancing. Seeing the pretty girls, all the guys got pretty homesick for their girlfriends at home.

The four lieutenants had an Irish maid for their two rooms and she was crazy about airmen. Halverson and Foley teased her all the time. Lt. Foley kept asking her for her phone number and she wouldn't give it to him. He said, "Betty, you must be exhausted. You keep running through my head all day and all night." She came back with, "Your head is way too big to contain the likes of me, running through it." They all laughed. The guys went down to play pool in the great hall and listened to music of Benny Goodman on the radio.

They spent the last day at Bournemouth Beach laying in lawn chairs with blankets over them. In the evening they put on their dress uniforms and hit the colorful night spots along the promenade with plenty of great band music and lively dancing. All but Perkins got pretty well stinko. On the walk back to Canford Cliffs, the Lieutenants encountered a group of burly Navy guys. A few things were said, a few boasts were made; comments about their mothers. Things started to get out of hand. Although the two groups were even in numbers, the Navy guys were bigger and older. Perkins was the only one with his head on straight. He said, "Look fellas, we are here, just like you to have a good time. Sorry, we meant no disrespect." They moved away after his fast talking and he was credited with his buddies getting out of there in one piece.

The next morning the ten-man crew took the train to London for one night in the city, to experience the last remnants of their leave. Halvorsen, Perk, Garrick and Foley listened to the radio in the hotel bar trying to hear some news of the rumored allied invasion but there was no news. The airmen stayed on for a last drink, reminiscing about home until Perk left at midnight to go get some shut eye.

A few of the NCOs met a couple of English girls who were out for a good time. The men took them out to eat and drink at a pub in the Soho district and saw a risqué revue of singers and dancers. They boasted that after the show they went to a private party one of the girls knew about.

In the morning Perk and his other officers boarded the train and continued on to their base at Rattlesden. While on the train, Perk read a magazine article about the Memphis Belle, a bomber based in Britain which became the first B-17 crew in May 1943 to complete 25 missions over Europe and return to the United States. The crew toured the country on a victory tour selling War Bonds.

In early 1942 and 1943, it was statistically impossible for bomber crews to complete a 25-mission tour in Europe because their loss rate was 16 percent. However, the Luftwaffe losses were worse at 25 percent of aircrews and about 40 planes a month. In the Japanese squadrons in 1943, the average Japanese pilot flew less than 200 hours before being shot down. Now in the spring of 1944, American crew survival rate had gone up a little because of their increased escort support. The Perkins' crew saw a better chance of completing their missions protected by their *little friends*. As the blur of the green English countryside passed his window, he closed his eyes and fell asleep on the way back to Rattlesden.

Thirty-Five Missions Now to Complete a Tour

March 4, 1944—Mission: Berlin, Germany (recalled) (21/22)

At 0530 hours the intelligence officer revealed the infamous destination to a collective groan in the briefing hut. It was not the first time the Eighth Air Force had been called to bomb the target known as the Big "B." Most of the crew barely had any sleep except for Peck and Glenn who hadn't missed the earlier London train the day before. They flew #2 in the lead box at 25,000 feet, carrying demolition bombs while other ships carried incendiary bombs to hit the business district. An hour before the IP the formation flew into tall thunderheads and had to ascend to 30,000 feet. Garrick watched with alarm as the lowest squadron appeared to be moving up into theirs. Fearful of a collision he quickly radioed Halverson. Glenn radioed Lt. Hanford, lead on the low squadron. Visibility was 10/10, and with relief, the mission was scrubbed and they were recalled back to England. On their return they had to fight their way through the Calais defenses to the channel with a full load of bombs. There were no enemy fighters but a heck of a lot of flak.

March 5

Colonel Harris gave out awards and several of the Perkins' crew received the Air Medal. At the briefing he discussed the 25 combat mission credit for completed bomb runs. The good news was the new system had been revised by the Army Air Force so that particularly dangerous or long missions would be given double credit. Most of Perk's missions were in that category, putting them with credit for 22 missions. The bad news: he confirmed each crew now needed 35 missions to complete their tour. That meant they needed 13 more missions to finish. Don Collier half-heartedly joked, "The brass are trying to confuse us to death with numbers. Our missions are worth double but we need twice as many?" The guys were peeved and grumbled a lot but became resigned to move forward to get the job done.

March 6, 1944—Mission: Berlin, Germany (23/24)

The Perkins' crew pulled the mission to Berlin, again. The target was industrial plants in the suburbs with 424 heavy bombers flying. Ship number 31225, Scheherazade carried 5,000 pounds of GP and incendiary bombs. The crew proceeded with their flight checks, taking off at 0700 hours, soon assembling at 20,000 feet. Myers, the radio man, immediately started picking up German radar, indicating they knew the group was on their way. Soon they were attacked by German fighters and it became a hell of a rough mission over Amsterdam air defenses. It was no surprise, Berlin was the most well-fortified of any target. Bombardier Tom Foley, remarked, "Jeez, this flak is like pea soup!"

Don Collier wrote in his diary, "We knew Hitler was down there in his Reich-bunker, and it was like we were showing up to the party without an invitation. We hoped our bombs would be our calling card to Herr Fuhrer."

The sky was full of bombers for miles in all directions moving toward the same destination. As the minutes passed, Perk's crew saw one B-24 trailing smoke and a B-17 break apart and fall out of the sky in flames. They saw four parachutes from the B-24 and none from the B-17. The formation stayed tight all the way to the IP. Foley took over, keeping the plane level to the target. Every man on board was alert for possible collisions. Finally, the bombs dropped on Berlin, and the planes turned away towards the south. Cameras took photos of the smoke and fires beneath. After that the Luftwaffe were merciless, flying through the formations and their own flak. They followed wounded planes, attacking, even shooting at parachutes. There were so many airmen bailing out of doomed aircraft, it looked like an Allied invasion.

The Perkins crew landed at Rattlesden at 1620 hours and learned that the bomber force lost a total of 53 B-17s and 16 B-24s. They found out an 88mm shell hit Lt. Socolofskys plane,

Dottie Jane, killing their radioman, Alton Moore, who was a good friend of Cliff Myers. Perk's crew wondered how they had been spared. By the grace of God, they hadn't sustained any fatal hits but there were twenty flak holes in their fuselage.

B-17

At a briefing of a room full of seasoned officers of the 447th bomb group, Colonel Harris said, "The Allied invasion of France is expected at any time and the Army is short of qualified pilots and crews." He continued, "There is no question, Hitler's air defenses, aircraft, submarine pens, armament factories and oil production have been weakened by the Allied bombing raids; but they have not been destroyed. The mission to Berlin with the loss of 69 allied aircraft and their crews demonstrates that fact. Those industrial sectors are using slave labor to quickly rebuild and resupply the needs of the Wehrmacht. The USAAF needs to keep hitting those targets over and over until they don't get up again." He reminded his men, "It took over a year to train each airman here; most of you fifteen to eighteen months." He paused and took a deep breath and looked in the eyes of the young officers. "I'm asking you men to volunteer to stay on for a few more missions, to help end this bloody war in Europe." Again, the Colonel took a long, measured look around the room, knowing his brave airmen had seen so many of their friends lost in air combat as they did the day before. "I'm asking you to do more. Because if you don't, those young high school recruits will have to do the job, with much less experience and far more casualties." Perk thought of his younger brothers having to come fight this battle.

While Colonel Harris had their attention, he used a pointer to point to a spot on the map of Italy and he said, "Some Eighth Air Force flight crews are being transferred here, to the Fifteenth Air Force in the Mediterranean Theater, at Foggia, Italy. There are a couple of dozen bases on the east coast near Bari that are running missions in Eastern Europe. They are hitting hard-to-reach targets like Austria, that are too far from England, or those accessible only over the Alps." he pointed to the line of mountains and then to the eastern targets and turned back to the men. "The 15th has also been hitting Hungary, Romania, Yugoslavia and Northern Italy."

At those airfields, the climate is sunny, and better suited to launching raids against the enemy, with less aborted missions." Perk thought, "It was true his crew was frustrated over all the scrubbed and aborted missions flying out of foggy England that had caused the extension of their tours."

The Colonel continued, "The enemy air defenses are less developed than in Western Europe. The benefits are obvious; shut off the oil taps in Romania, take out those distant factories in Hungary and attack the Nazis from the east." He ended his pitch with, "I hope you brave airmen will consider continuing one of the greatest ventures of the Allies around the world: to defeat these fascist sons-a-bitches, once and for all." He looked around, holding the attention of every man in the room, and nodded, "Thank you, gentlemen." He said as he stepped off the stage and left the room.

The Colonel had tried to present a credible case, asking them to extend their tour and do a "few" more missions. Perk and Glenn knew, if experienced crews didn't do it, like theirs, some wet-behind-the-ears boys were going to have to come overseas and do the job. They had seen plenty of those young men who flew a few missions and were shot down, killed-in-action or became prisoners of war.

Perk wasn't sure his crew would want to extend their tour, especially after yesterday's horrific raid. He and Glenn presented it to them that evening, assuring them it was their decision to make. Perk said he understood if some of them wanted to go home and he wouldn't think any less of them. After a short discussion among themselves, Collier spoke for the group, and gave their answer, "Okay, we want to finish the job together."

Of the original crews that arrived in the Eighth Air Force in 1943, only half of them at Rattlesden were still flying. Most of those had achieved membership in the *Lucky Bastards Club:* those that had completed 35 missions. In a few more months the Perkins' crew would be members, too.

7.

Someone Has to Finish the Job

March 7 and 8

There was a thick overcast that day so there were no missions but a couple of bomb groups got their orders they would be going to Italy. They said they hated to leave the Mighty Eighth because it was a great bunch of guys. Perks crew was credited with 24 hazardous or long missions flown at Rattlesden. Their whole crew had volunteered to extend their tour.

Collier and Moore went to Stowmarket to a USO dance and came back saying they heard a swell big band and danced with some pretty WACs and Army nurses.

March 10

Their squadron leader came to their hut and told the Perkins crew they had made their last official mission from England. They were on their way to the MTO or Mediterranean Theater of Operations. Perk's crew were apprehensive of the unknown, but some of them were eager to see new territory and exchange the foggy weather in Great Britain for the sunnier climate of the Mediterranean. Even though they were leaving soon and off the roster, their crew could still be called up as spares with other crews.

March 11

The briefing the next morning at 0630 had the Perkins crew going as spares to the Ruhr Valley. Luckily it was scrubbed because of bad weather.

March 12-14

It was a repeat of March 11th. They were up at four AM to go to Berlin, but they didn't need the crew after all. The false alarms were grating on everyone's nerves. There would be more days of waiting for their orders to ship out to the MTO. The Perkins crew were curious about the 15th Air Force group in Italy in which they soon would be a part.

Transferred to the 15th Army Air Force

Early in the war Hitler had built armament factories and large oil production refineries in Eastern Europe, far from the range of bomber bases in Great Britain. Seven months earlier, in August 1943, 178 bombers took off from allied bases in North Africa, to bomb nine Romanian Nazi oil fields, their storage facilities, transportation routes and shipment points. The Third Reich was ready for them and the allied mission had a disastrous outcome. Fifty-three British and American aircraft were shot down and 660 airmen killed on that single allied raid which would become known as *Black Sunday*. The raid only reduced Hitler's oil production by 46%. The Nazi's were determined and resilient, increasing production back up to the maximum, soon after the attack. Most likely it was in that terrible defeat that Eisenhower knew they needed to establish bases in Italy, closer to the Romanian oil fields.

The 12th Army Air Force had seen their share of combat with the hard-fought Allied victory in North Africa over German Field Marshal Erwin Rommel's troops. The Allies neutralized and took prisoners of nearly 900,000 Italian and German soldiers. The British 8th Army and U.S. 5th Army took Sicily by August 1943, and without losing momentum, continued north, toward Rome, taking Taranto, Foggia, Salerno and Naples by September. As the Allies moved up the Italian Peninsula, bases were established as was the case on the Foggia Plain. It was ideal for air bases because the land was flat, near the Adriatic Sea, and in range of the Nazi oil production and armament factories in Eastern Europe. Eisenhower had achieved his goal.

The Third Reich in Eastern Europe had been out-of-reach to the Eighth Air Force in England. In November of 1943, General Eisenhower asked General James Doolittle to lead the 15th Air Force in Italy. The famous USAAF pilot was known for the successful first bombing of Tokyo a few months after the attack on Pearl Harbor, for which he received the Medal of Honor.

Within six months 27 airfields, in Italy, were operational, with steel mesh runways, Nissen huts, tent cities for personnel, ground crews, mechanics, air crews and air planes. They were successful in taking the air war to those factories and oil refineries in Eastern Europe that supplied the Wehrmacht. Besides closer proximity to the Eastern targets, weather was a deciding factor for the location of the new bases in Italy. Britain and Northern Europe were notorious for their overcast and soggy weather. In sharp contrast, the Mediterranean was usually sunny and clear.

March 15, 1944

The Perkins crew was given a two day layover pass in London on their way to the MTO. The crew left by train from Stowmarket, arriving in the afternoon at the Brighton Hall Hotel. They decided to make a great time of it and they went to Ramona's Bar to "raise the roof an inch or two" according to Collier. They spent the evening playing darts with some fellas from the Great Ashfield Air Base. Perk asked the guys if they knew his buddy, Louie Massari, a radio operator in the 385th bomb group. Unfortunately, they did not.

Hungover and bleary eyed, the next day they caught the morning train to Prestwick, Scotland, and slept most of the way. They were told they had to wait four days to fly on a transport to Italy. Not a group to pass up an opportunity to go wandering, they took a train to Glasgow, Scotland, on a two-day pass. The city was a nice place but they decided they preferred London because there were a lot more things to do. The second day they went up to Bishop's Castle and then to the Horseshoe Pub where they talked to a B-17 gunner who was waiting to go home. He just got out of the hospital after being all shot up during the "Big Week" on the mission to Diepholz, Germany. He had taken flak in the thigh and almost lost his leg. He couldn't walk very well using crutches. The men bought him a whiskey and wished him well going home.

March 17-18

The airmen were still waiting in Scotland to get a transport to Italy. These delays weren't bringing them any closer to home. Collier wrote in his diary, "We were getting damn tired of waiting." Although the Perkins crew had hoped to fly to Italy, they realized it wasn't going to happen. Perk got the news that an alternative, a large troop transport ship was in the organizational stages. There were other aircrews being transferred to Italy as part of the upcoming invasion strategy of the continent. The danger of ships being sunk by German U-boats had been greatly diminished by the employment of the convoy system, use of airborne ASW radar on Liberators and PBY aircraft after 1943. Improved intelligence to decrypt the U-boat codes further diminished the devastating submarine attacks on allied shipping.

Perk's crew got orders to return to Rattlesden by train. They would be taking a transport ship out of Liverpool within ten days. On the subject of their excursion around the British Isles, Marcuse said, "Things could be worse, boys. We could have flak and fighters trying to kill us." They caught an afternoon train back to London and headed to Ramona's Pub, where they met a couple of British nurses who knew of an underground club where they all could go.

March 19

When Perk's crew finally got back to the base at Rattlesden, they took a good ribbing from the guys on their Big Trip to the Mediterranean Theater. Marcuse had a good story to tell about the British nurses and the underground club. There was still no word when the transport ship would actually arrive. In limbo, the men accrued a lot of sack time, wrote letters and did a lot of "hurry up and waiting." They tried to get a pass to go back to London.

March 20

Finally, with a two day London pass in hand, a couple of the crew returned to the Imperial Hotel. In the late afternoon, they walked around Trafalgar and Piccadilly Square, popping in to see a review of British singers and a comedy act. The six non-commissioned officers went for a few beers and while sitting in a wooden booth in a dark pub, they talked in whispered tones about what they had heard about the Mediterranean Theater. Collier said "One of the boys in the 99th BG said it was no picnic. The Germans are still there, only 100 miles northeast in Rome." He told them the military bases are primitive, set up quickly after the Allies occupied the area. He said, "Everyone sleeps in tents with few facilities. The missions often fly over the 15,000 foot Alps." The airmen in the pub thought about Collier's description of their new base and realized Rattlesden was bad, but Foggia could be much worse.

The men were still ready for a change of scenery and they rationalized they might fly more often and finish their tours sooner. Moore told a joke about an Italian tank for sale on the black market. It had five speeds; four were in reverse. Everyone snickered.

Then Marcuse told one about a B-17 bomber going down with four men left on board and only one serviceable parachute. He said, "One guy was from France, another from the US, one was from Scotland and the last from England. As the plane lost altitude, the Frenchmen downed a glass of cognac, and said 'Pour La France!' and jumped without a parachute. The American downed a glass of bourbon, said 'For freedom!' and jumped without a parachute. The Scotsman downed a glass of whiskey, and said "For Scotland!' and threw out the Englishman." The guys had a good laugh. Then they threw a few darts, had another pint or two and for a little while they forgot about the war.

Back at the base Perk, Garrick, Foley and Glenn listened to the radio describing the ongoing eruption of Mount Vesuvius. Ash and rocks had damaged a number of aircraft in the vicinity of Foggia Plain. The fuselage and wings of airplanes were pierced by molten fragments of rock hurled from the volcano. Glenn said, "I can't believe airfields had damage, a hundred miles across the Italian Peninsula from the volcano. Our 5th and 8th armies are battling on the ground to take Rome while Mount Vesuvius is erupting and we are heading right into the middle of it."

The Ship, Capetown Castle

March 27

After waiting weeks their squadron leader told them they were leaving for Italy that night. The evening train departed, allowing the men to get some shut-eye before their five AM arrival in the Port of Liverpool. They grabbed their gear from the train over-head and ran down the causeway where they boarded the ship, *Capetown Castle*. It was a 27,000 ton ship with staterooms and had been used before the war for mail transport in England. The four officers somehow got first class cabins with white sheets and towels. The rest of Perk's crew got pretty nice cabins, too. There seemed to be only a few Yanks on board the all British ship. They felt they were really living in style until they went to the mess hall and decided the meals weren't fit for hogs. Collier said, "The doughy kidney pie wasn't edible and the boiled potatoes were bland." Maybe these Brits can eat this stuff but we can't."

Capetown Castle

There wasn't much to do on board except for daily life-boat drills and sleeping. The men emerged from their cabins at dawn as they joined a big convoy with eight escort destroyers on their way past the Bay of Biscay. It was cold as hell and the men mostly stuck to their comfortable cabins, playing cards and writing letters.

Perk, Glenn, Foley and Garrick attended a briefing on board the ship about the Foggia Airbases. Most of the lecture by Colonel Wright was about the reasons why the Army Air Force had set up the bases for strategic hits on Eastern European targets.

At noon, off the coast of Portugal, the *Capetown Castle* ran into a horrific Atlantic storm which tossed the ship like a canoe. The rough seas continued for a week until they reached warmer waters. A couple of Perk's crew were seasick and stayed close to their bunks. The porpoise began escorting their ship with big dramatic leaps out of the sea in unison like an Esther Williams movie. They had been on board the Castle for ten days and it was hard to tell how much longer before they reached the Strait of Gibraltar.

April 6

That evening, cruising into the Mediterranean, the Perkins crew stood on deck looking for the shore in the distance. It was a clear, balmy night as they sailed through the strait. The narrow 13-kilometers-wide waterway divided the continents of Europe and Africa. Spain and Gibraltar were on the left and Morocco was on the right. The men could see a few tiny lights on the distant shore of Tarifa, Spain. With a deep breath, Perk said, "What a grand sight."

The next day the ship convoy sailed into welcomed sunny skies as they hugged the north shore of Africa. Two more convoys joined the group and there were military ships everywhere. Perk stopped counting at 45 vessels.

Route the Capetown Castle took to Naples, Italy

It had been 18 months since the Allied victory of Operation Torch in 1942, in which General Eisenhower, Patton and British Marshall Montgomery took back Morocco, Algiers and Tunisia from the Nazis and opened up the Strait of Gibraltar to allied ships. The Castle docked at Algiers to take on fuel and provisions.

The two 19-year-old gunners, Warren and Marcuse, were full of energy and wanted to jump off the ship before it docked. The whole crew decided to walk into town from the port, where they stopped at Queenies Bar. The hungry airmen picked up a falafel sandwich and a beer before continuing to look for edible food in Algiers. They found an outdoor market and each bought a couple of bags of food to take on board to supplement the terrible British mess food. They certainly wouldn't starve over the next few days.

April 7-9

Back onboard the Capetown Castle the men played cards, ate their Algerian market food and walked the decks looking out at the beautiful Mediterranean Sea. The convoy moved slowly, still on the lookout for German U-boats that may have slipped past the Allies at Gibraltar. On the morning of the ninth, some of the convoy left them for Allied ports in North Africa and their ship went on with several escorts into the Tyrrhenian Sea between Sardinia and Sicily. Both Islands had been the site of fierce and bloody battles just eight months earlier.

April 10

Perk would always remember where he was on his 23rd birthday as the transport ship cruised into the port of Naples, Italy. He thought, "I won't miss the smell of diesel smoke." The ship's single midship smoke stack seemed to infiltrate his aft cabin and most other areas of the ship. Still the waters of the Mediterranean were beautiful and clear. Growing up in the high desert of California he had not been to the beach and had never learned to swim. If he were to have ditched his plane over the English Channel or in the Mediterranean Sea, he had only his Mae West life vest to save him.

As he stood at the rail of the ship he thought of his 21st birthday celebration with his family, two years ago. His mom had made a chocolate cake with candles. His father had given him the wrist watch he was wearing. That evening he had gone to Pancho's ranch and was surprised by a party with a big banner for him. He had his first beer and a pretty piano player sang, "Oh Danny Boy" to him. That was a lifetime ago; so much had happened since then.

He and Glenn went to a couple of onboard briefings of the war in the Mediterranean Theater, which helped to explain how the Italian dictator, Mussolini, came to be under the thumb of the Third Reich. In the late 1930s Mussolini had designs on acquiring parts of North Africa which were promised to him when he signed the 1939 Non-Aggression pact with Hitler. The two fascist dictators became unequal partners. Italy's weak economy and lack of preparedness for war turned out to be a big disappointment to the Nazi leader. Italy had few suitable raw materials and fewer modern armaments. Weak military leadership resulted in Mussolini's defeats in Sudan, Kenya and at the Battle of Keren in East Arica, partly because of the lack of coordination between Italy's military branches. By the time the US was drawn into the war in 1941, Mussolini had become a weak puppet of the Third Reich with the German Wehrmacht taking over his under-fortified defenses throughout Italy.

After the Allied victories in the North African campaigns, General Eisenhower entrusted General George Patton, alongside British Field Marshal Montgomery to take the large Island of Sic-

Railroad troop transport, Naples to Bari

ily hoping that success would be a gateway to the mainland peninsula of Italy. Ultimately, it was a prudent decision and the Allies pushed up the boot to the Gustav Line where they established a dozen allied bases on the Foggia Plain in late 1943.

The Capetown Castle disembarked at the Port of Naples on the west coast of Italy. They found that the only transportation assigned to them was a crowded box car to Bari, across the peninsula, on the Adriatic east coast.

Home of the 15th Air Force and the 99th Bomb Group

They spent the next two hellish days crammed like cattle on a train with 40 other soldiers. They were given K-rations and buckets in the corners. From Bari they were transported by truck to Foggia airfield. At midnight they were told to report to the base field hospital tent, where they were given bloody stretchers and an Army blanket. Glenn commented to Perk, "This war really is

Foggia tent city in mud

206

hell. It isn't hard to imagine who occupied these cots before us." Regardless, the canvas stretchers offered some insulation from the cold floor.

April 13, 1944—Arrival at Tortorella Air Field

The Airmen awoke to the sound of the heavy rains pounding the tent roof of the infirmary. They were looking forward to their own quarters and anything other than the bloody hospital cots. At Tortorella Air Field they were assigned to the Ninety-Ninth Bomb Group, of the Fifteenth US Air Force. The American base was shared with the 209th Royal Air Force, with their Lancaster Bombers, Vickers and Wellingtons. The crew labored most of the day to put up their own tents in a huge rain soaked tent city and they tried to make their tent livable. In the late afternoon they got GI haircuts, the first since their journey from England to Italy.

By the time Perk and his crew arrived, General James Doolittle had moved on to be the commander of the Eighth Air Force in England and Major General Twining took over the 15th's command in Foggia.

The transplanted airmen attended briefings on why the region was important to the allied victory in Europe. More than one airman looked at the landscape and questioned why anyone would want this God forsaken land. Bloody and hard fought ground battles at Sicily, Taranto, Salerno, and Naples yielded land but not without a terrible cost of thousands of allied soldiers' lives. So far, the Germans were held at the Gustav Line but many of the Allied ground troops had been recently diverted back for the coming invasion at Normandy.

In addition, the 15th Air Force faced geographical realities few Americans had encountered. Its bombers flew northward over

the Alps to Austria and Germany; westward across the Tyrrhenian Sea, Corsica and Sardinia to French targets; eastward over
the Adriatic to the Balkans, Carpathian Mountains, and Greece.
They faced stiff fortifications in the north from the deeply em-
bedded Germans who had sophisticated and effective ground defenses. Every mission had its topographical dangers.

Perks crew became members of the 416th Bombardment
squadron of the 99th Bombardment group of the 15th Air Force.
The airmen found there were significant differences between being
stationed in Rattlesden, England, and flying out of Foggia, Italy.
The Italian Army base had been a battlefield just six months prior.
Everything had to be built in short order because the bombers and
crews were coming. Great Britain had well established airfields in
the mid-1940s. Some had been former airports. They were twice
the size as the Foggia airfields and had barracks, mess halls, field
hospitals and aviation repair facilities. In Foggia the aircrew slept
in muddy tents, ate C-rations and first aid was offered in a tent.
The Foggia base headquarters was in a brick building, three kilo-
meters east of the airfield, in the town of Tavernola. The former
farm pastures were pitted with blast holes. The new airfields had
to be leveled and outfitted with steel mesh runways. The tent cities
and runways were further damaged by unseasonably heavy rains
that winter and spring of 1943-44. Aircraft repair was not done in
hangars but in the open at muddy hardstands.

The six man tents were lined up in rows with a mess hall at
the far end. There was one, dimly lit, light bulb at the center of
each tent and the floor was grass or more commonly, dirt. Ply-
wood was eventually scavenged for flooring, wooden cots were
used for beds and 55-gallon drums were converted into stoves. As
most of these airfields were captured from the Italians and Germans, wrecked enemy aircraft were a common sight, with metal
from their fuselages and wings, glass and other useful parts found
their way into the tent quarters.

There were seven fighter groups, which included the Tuskegee Airmen, the famous black air crews who flew so valiantly. They were part of the 332[nc] Fighter Group of the 99th. There were no provisions for a large armed force personnel which had no mess hall or hospital if the pilots were severely injured. The shower facilities at Foggia consisted of one bathtub in a hut which was fully utilized all day. Even in winter some hearty souls took showers with a bucket out of the cold drinking well. A veteran U.S. pilot formerly transferred from England expressed his feelings about being stationed in Foggia, "If you were an airman, would you rather sip scotch in a London pub or swig vino in a tent in Foggia?" The truth was there were no weekend passes in Foggia because there was nowhere to go.

In briefings, Perk learned the B-17 crews were transferred to Italy, in the spring of 1944 for two major reasons: the weather and its location. For optimum flying weather Foggia usually had 340 sunny days a year compared to only 58 fair weather days in England. Of the hazards to combat planes during World War II, weather, flak or fighters: weather downed the most planes. England's soggy climate scrubbed so many bomber missions that the Germans rejoiced on those overcast days. Sunny Italy was supposed to be a better climate to conduct a continuous strategic air campaign against the Third Reich's war supplies.

That spring as the crews arrived in Italy, there had been an unusual winter of unrelenting foul weather. Five inches of slippery sludge was on the asphalt and steel mesh topped runways. Two months of rain and flooding caused waterlogged airfields and the tent cities were a mess. The weather conditions in April 1944 were so hazardous for aircraft that the 15th Air Force flew 20% fewer missions than the Eighth Air Force in rainy England.

Eighth Air Force bomb runs flown out of England were too far from the important targets in Eastern Europe, including Hitler's Eastern European oil fields and refineries. From Italy heavy bombers were finally in range of targets like Belgrade, Galați and Ploiești. Once the P-51 Mustangs were equipped with Tokyo fuel tanks under their wings they could better protect the bombers to and from the targets.

The bomb groups of the 15th Army Air Force in the Foggia region, were crucial to reach the Romanian oil production of the Axis supply lines. Romania lay an impossible 1,300 miles from Britain, putting the Balkan oil fields beyond the reach of the Mighty Eighth's bombers. The 15th Air Force in Foggia were able to hit the enemy oil fields, ball bearing and battery factories which were less than 600 miles distant.

The effective bombing missions made by the smaller 15th Air Force did not go unnoticed by the Third Reich. A close associate of Hitler's, the German Minister of War Production, Albert Speer, commented, "I could see omens of the war's end as the bombers of the American Fifteenth Air Force crossed the Alps from their Italian bases to attack German Industrial targets."

8.

Mediterranean Theater of Operation

April 17, 1944—Mission: Belgrade A/F (25)

At 03:30 the crew was rousted out of bed with the sergeant's flash light and roll-call of who was going on the mission. It was their first assignment from the Foggia Plain, flying from Tortorella Airfield.

Taking off and landing on Foggia's muddy mesh runway

15th Army Air Force, 99th

They were apprehensive of what they would encounter in that new theater of operations. They heard if there was rain, the brass still sent missions out. The day before, the mud was four inches deep on the pierced steel planking runways. In the predawn hours it was hard to tell if they would get bogged down or not.

The colonel strutted into the room and unceremoniously raised the screen showing the map. The red yarn stretched point-to-point of the mission to Belgrade, Yugoslavia. The target, an airfield northwest of the city, was not too heavily fortified, he said. It seemed like a "milk run" but the men never used those words because they didn't want to jinx it. The colonel was a look-at-the-bigger-picture kinda guy. To make the airmen feel like they were making a difference, Colonel Twining said the 15th was preparing for the invasion of the continent. Everyday now there was more talk of an end to this awful war. They all knew it wasn't going to happen without an invasion.

Two squadrons joined the formation from other bases and they continued northeast over the Adriatic Sea. The gunners tested their guns and settled in to watch for enemy aircraft as they got closer to the IP. Near Belgrade the Germans' use of smoke screens was effective but their plane's radar helped find the target. Their ship, Moonbeam's 5,000 pounds of incendiary bombs were dropped. Foley was sure they hit the objective because he saw black smoke coming up through the layer of smoke screens. It was a good run. They were surprised there was little resistance besides some scattered flak. Back to the home base and a warm meal before a welcomed bed.

April 20, 1944—Mission: Venice, Italy HG (26)

Perk's crew flew to Venice Harbor and they were surprised there was little opposition except for two fighters who did not approach their squadron. There were a few barrage balloons hung low in the port which forced the formation to a higher altitude. Surprisingly, there was no anticipated Luftwaffe. The gunners were ready but no one showed up and the crew returned to Foggia safely.

With the new mission counting system Collier figured this was number 26. They had exceeded the Memphis Belle. The tour number requirement had been extended to 35. Most of the crew didn't think too much about it but followed their orders and flew where they were told. Their good luck had held out so far.

Maurice—1944

The dark cloudy skies previewed the sad day to come. Mail delivery, usually a welcomed surprise, often included love letters, tins of cookies, candy and knitted scarves and sweaters from home. Perk received half a dozen letters, several of which were forwarded on from family members about Maurice, from Rattlesden. With the delayed mail to him, he read a month ago his mom and dad got the telegram that no parent wants to receive. It was from the Secretary of War, telling them his brother Maurice was presumed killed in action. The telegram said, "The Secretary of War desires me to express his deep regret that your son, Seaman Maurice Perkins was killed in action in the Pacific near the Solomon Islands on the 7th of April, 1943. Confirming letter follows."

Perk's mother said they received another letter from Admiral Halsey, Commander of the Pacific Forces. "It is with regret that I am writing to confirm the recent telegram informing you of the death of your son, Maurice Perkins, while fighting valiantly at Guadalcanal, on board the destroyer, USS Aaron Ward. I fully understand your desire to learn as much as possible regarding the circumstances of his death and I wish there was more information available to give you. Unfortunately, reports of this nature contain only the briefest of details as they are prepared under battle conditions and the means of transmission are limited. I know the sorrow this message has brought you and it is my hope that in time the knowledge of his heroic service to his country, even in death, may be of sustaining comfort to you. My deepest sympathies."

Perk stared at the words on the page but he was trying to process that which he had guessed for a few months. There had been no news of his brother for a year. Sometimes silence has a way of gently informing, preparing those for a terrible truth. He knew now his brother was gone. He wiped his tears away and went to bed.

April 21

Perk built up the courage to open a few more letters from friends and family that were heartfelt for his brother's death. There was a letter from Pancho who had talked to her friend, Major Hutchenson, who knew someone at the Pentagon. The information he got was,

Apprentice Seamen Maurice Perkins was killed in Action aboard the USS Aaron Ward, on April 7, 1943. Maurice was awarded, posthumously, a Purple Heart. He was listed on the Memorial at Manila American Cemetery in the Philippines. The USS Aaron Ward was awarded four battle stars for her valiant service in WWII.

It seemed strange to Perk that his brother died a year ago and everyone was just writing about it now. His brother was just a

17-year-old kid and he would remain that age in Perk's mind for the rest of his life. Images flashed through his head of his little brother with his pet coyote. He still couldn't grasp the idea that he would never see Maurice again. Families of sailors lost on the Aaron Ward would be receiving similar confirmation that their boys were gone, too. They would be grieving now as his family was.

Perk got a copy of a letter from his mom from the State Department about more news of the fate of Maurice. It read:

With sad regret, your son, Pvt. Maurice Perkins, has been missing and is presumed dead, as of April 7, 1943. An account of what happened that day is found here in the ship's narrative.

Pvt. Maurice Perkins had been assigned to the crew of the USS Aaron Ward as a deck crew maintaining the four 40 millimeter AA guns. On April 7th the captain of the ship received orders to proceed to Tagoma Point, Guadalcanal.

USS Aaron Ward

Her captain sighted a dogfight over Savo Island. Maurice was at his station when three Japanese planes came at them out of the sun. The attacking Zeros shot a torpedo, which struck the Aaron Ward, tearing a hole in the port side of the ship. Another torpedo struck the engine room and caused the loss of electrical power. A third Japanese airplane shot a surface torpedo which holed her stern. The rudder was destroyed which caused the ship to swing left while another trio of dive bombers shot their load of bombs toward the helpless Aaron Ward. It was reported one of the three exploded close to Pvt. Maurice Perkins.

Of the 208 crew that day twenty men died, 59 were wounded and seven were missing including Maurice Perkins. The remaining crew tried valiantly to save their ship. As the daylight faded, the tugboat *Vireo* and the rescue vessel *Ortolan* evacuated as many of the seamen and wounded as they could. As darkness fell the tug tried to tow the sinking destroyer to beach her on a shoal near Tineye Point. However, the *Vireo* had to cut their tow lines as the Ward's failing hull finally sank stern-first at 2135 hours. Even though there was limited information known about the death of Pvt. Maurice Perkins on the USS Aaron Ward, the Navy could only say, "We extend to you our sincere sympathy on your great loss. Your son died while bravely serving his country."

Perk read the letter a second time and sat on his bunk thinking about what he could have done to stop his 17-year-old brother from going into the Navy. Perk came to the conclusion that nothing would have changed.

Perk's mother sent him a letter written by a friend of Maurice's. It read:

"Dear Mrs. Perkins, I was a good friend of Maurice as we went through bootcamp and were transferred on to the USS Aaron Ward at about the same time together. We both were working on deck artillery on the morning of April 7th when we were hit by a Japanese torpedo from an incoming Zero. I saw it hit near Maurice when I was knocked to the deck. When I regained consciousness I couldn't see Maurice anymore. There was lots of chaos on board the ship. I am so sorry for your loss. He and I used to go on liberty in Honolulu together. He was a good friend to me. Sincerely, Pvt. 1st Class William Shafer."

Lieutenant Perkins had seen this disastrous unforgiving war at 25,000 feet as crews of men in crippled ships were lost. Sons, brothers, fathers, husbands: irretrievable lives lost forever. Losing his brother made the terrible cost so very real to him. Perk decided he wouldn't agree to more combat missions after he had finished his second tour. His family could not handle another son's death. After 50 missions, there was plenty for him to do in the Army stateside.

In a moment of grief, Perk thought to himself, "This war. This awful war. Like a giant black cloud enveloping Europe and Asia: a suffocating, blight of the land obliterating people and their

Perk standing in front of Moonbeam

217

cities. Armies of men on the ground, at sea and in the air, fighting and dying. There were promises of battles making headway or the ever impending Allied invasion of Europe supposed to be coming soon. Words, just words. His men were flesh and bone. Some mother nurtured each kid in his crew. Fathers shook their sons' hands as they sent them off to war." He was angry. He vowed to do everything he could to survive and keep his crew safe during these last missions. Those parents of his crew would not receive a notice from the War Department about their sons.

Perk looked in the mirror and the man that looked back at him was a gaunt sunken face with deep set eyes. His uniform hung on him like it was held up by a coat hanger. He had been in the base hospital, twice for bronchitis. There was the constant stress of each mission. He smoked too many cigarettes. There was a time when the men worried about not returning from a mission and then some of them got defeatist attitudes and even survivor's guilt. Each mission felt like they were playing Russian Roulette. It was hard not to think those negative thoughts but he and his men had a job to finish. They depended on him and he had to stay focused and stay positive.

April 22

There was no mission. He was exhausted but decided to answer some of the letters. He scratched out a few, saying the same thing, "Thank you for your kind words about my brother. Yes, I will be very careful… He lied and assured them his missions weren't too dangerous and where he was stationed the food was good and accommodations were swell."

Finally a much welcomed letter from Dottie that greatly lifted his spirits. She didn't know about his family's final letter about Maurice being killed. He would tell her sometime but not now.

Just reading her letter felt refreshing and normal. He couldn't say in a letter that he had seen planes broken apart and men falling from the sky. He just couldn't say he had received news of his brother's death.

Dottie said she was still working at the base for the colonel. There were newsy things she wrote about her family and friends, their Christmas, and planned summer trip to Colorado. Her brother, Bob, was back from Guam, recovering from malaria. She had received letters from her sister, Lavonne, still stationed in Hawaii. Lavonne was in a beauty contest and got first runner up. Ruth and her Naval-Pilot husband, Bob Hepting, had lived in La Jolla, California, until he left on his second assignment to the Pacific. Dottie's two older brothers were still working for the Army Corp of Engineers. She said she couldn't wait for this war to be over and for all of the boys to come home. Best of all, she said the sweet words, *she missed him.* Perk read the letter four times before putting it back in the envelope. It somehow balanced out the sadness in the other letters he had received.

Missions Preparing for D-Day

April 23, 1944—Mission: Wiener Neustadt, Austria (27/28)

It was sobering to find out at the briefing the BF 109 facility in Wiener Neustadt, Austria, was turning out 250 fighters a month. The US airmen were told to expect heavy flak as well as fighter defenses trying to prevent their formation from reaching their target. At 0500 hours, when they got to their ship, there were two newsreel correspondents accompanying them, taking movies during their mission. At the beginning of the flight the photographers roamed around the ship but settled in the waist gunner windows taking action movies. The war correspondents were courageous to go up in the bombers when the average rate of downed aircraft was five percent. Many journalists died in the war. Every base had a PAO, Public Affairs Officer, who coordinated with the news media and tried to keep up morale and support back home. They took gunnery training and were sometimes thrown into service in emergencies.

Thirty minutes from the target, over Trieste, all Hell broke loose with black clouds of 88 flak shells exploding around them. All they could do in formation was fly straight through it. Foley was throwing out chaff, those aluminum strips used to confuse German radar. Puffs of black flak clouds exploded so near to their ship. A piece of shrapnel burst through the plane's waist and just missed the gunners and correspondents. Collier reported a shell smoldering in his parachute pack a few inches from his foot. He said, "I hope I won't need that." The squadron was plagued by German 109 fighters that were so persistent they flew right through their own exploding flak. One Me109 came at their ship head on, firing straight at them within 50 feet of their wing. The fighter's shells missed their ship and hit the plane behind them which started smoking from two engines as it fell out of formation and slipped from view.

Foley dropped their 5000 pound bomb load just after the lead plane dropped theirs. Perk steered a gentle left and headed for home. A few fighters chased them but turned back over Trieste. Moonbeam made it to the Adriatic and returned to Foggia

B-17G

safely. The film crew emerged from the plane and looked a bit shaken but said they got lots of footage.

On Perk's return he found out one bombardier in their squadron had been killed when a piece of flak hit him in the heart. It was only his fifth mission. Another B-17 had half its wing shot off and as it was going down five chutes were reported leaving the ship. The Perkins crew had a dozen flak holes in their fuselage and tail of their plane. In the evening Perk sewed Eighth and a Fifteenth air force patches on his jacket before hitting the sack.

The Wiener Neustadt plant had been bombed before with the result of 75 percent reduced production. Disappointingly, they were back up and running, churning out the fighters two months later using slave labor. Because of the quick Nazi recovery the 8th and the 15th Air Force implemented the Restrike Policy for repeat raids to Wiener Neustadt, Regensburg, Schweinfurt and Ploesti. In 1944 intelligence and aerial photographs alerted the allies when the factories were repaired and close to production. The Army Air Force would schedule another bomber mission. The Restrike Policy worked well to interrupt the enemy's supply chains.

April 24

Today some men from the squadron went on a re-strike mission to Ploesti, Romania, but the Perkins crew were not scheduled to go. Those who went, came back with frightening stories of thick flak and many fighters near the target. Evidently, the Germans didn't like the Allied Re-strike Policy. They knocked down a fortress from the 416th squadron and some fellows in other planes saw four chutes leave the ship as it went down. In the late afternoon the supply men came to the tent next to Perk's to get the downed pilots' things; those few remnants of men's lives, now gone. The Perkins crew saw they were on the load list for a mission tomorrow.

April 25, 1944—Mission: Padua (scrubbed)

The crew started on a mission to Padua in Northern Italy but ran into bad weather. About 50 minutes from the target the mission was called off and they returned to base.

The B-17 "My Gal Suzie" had gone down yesterday and had a small black dog named Felix, who stayed in the tent with the airmen. It usually slept on Charlie Pembrook's bunk. The poor thing didn't know which way to turn and didn't want to eat or leave the tent when his crew didn't return. Lt. Hendrick's crew finally adopted the quivering mutt and everyone held out hope the lost crew would find their way back to Felix.

April 26

Wiener Neutadt was a restrike mission today and before the bombs were loaded on the planes, it started pouring rain and the mission was scrubbed. The continued rain made the air strips a muddy bog. The airmen wrote letters home and Collier and Warren played poker with a five-cent-limit. Collier won two dollars and forty five cents. In the late afternoon it stopped raining and two crews played baseball in the muddy field. Everyone went to bed early because they were certain there was another mission tomorrow.

April 28, 1944—Mission: Wiener Neustadt, Austria (aborted)

Their crew was rousted at 0300 hours for a briefing of the mission to Wiener Neustadt. In April the crew had hit the same targets; the marshaling yards, Messerschmitt and Junker aircraft factories. The bomber, *Moonbeam*, spiraled steadily upward in a giant, lazy circle waiting for their squadron to assemble for departure. Over three hundred aircraft gathered over the airfield at eight thousand feet. Perk killed time. They watched their wings, below and above for planes that came too close. They reached 25,000 feet on the way to the target and sixty miles out, German flak was loud, heavy and bursting in black plumes of smoke and shrapnel.

Moonbeam's windshield was hit! A golf ball sized piece of the plexiglass flew into the cockpit and hit Lt. Perkins in the forehead, knocking him unconscious. Halverson, the co-pilot, scrambled for the controls as the fierce freezing sub-zero wind blowing through the hole hit them at 150 miles per hour. Glenn yelled to the navigator to see if the rest of the crew was ok. He told them to prepare for bail-out but wait for his orders. Perk was slumped over in his seat with what appeared to be no other injuries. The sound of the deafening engines just in front of the open windshield and the force of air coming in the cockpit caused a fierce shaking of the plane. The crew quickly took a damage report. The ride was bumpy and erratic with no smoke or other damage reported by the crew.

After what seemed to be an eternity but was about two minutes of pandemonium, Perk blinked and regained consciousness. Glenn shook his arm and shouted above the noise, "Hey man you scared me! Are you alright?" Perk nodded and sat upright. Glenn spoke into his throat mic, "The windshield was hit and a piece hit you in the head and knocked you out." They both assessed the damage and with great relief, Perk saw Glenn had the aircraft under control. They both agreed, they would have to return to their base. With the violent shaking of the aircraft he wasn't sure they could plant the bombs on the target anyway. Perk spoke into his throat mic, "We have to return to base. Our windshield has a hole in it." Foley took the pins from his pocket and replaced them in each bomb. He hated to land with a full load on board.

Thankfully, a Mustang followed their ship for protection, while they flew back to Foggia just 500 feet above the waters of the

Adriatic. They approached Tortorella's eastern runway which was covered with four inches of slime from the rains. When they took off in the morning, the plane's wheels slogged through muck on the steel mesh. Already at a disadvantage, Perk was apprehensive about landing in that soup with a full bomb load. Perk shouted to Glenn, calling for flaps. Glenn shouted back, "Negative, they aren't working!" The flaps weren't coming down and it was too late to crank them by hand. It was hard to tell if they were coming in hot on their approach so he feathered the hydraulic brakes trying to slow down, lowering the landing gear. They both were afraid they would hit the gully at the end of the runway. With some hydro-planing over the mud, Moonbeam finally came to a stop. They jumped down and the crew wanted to kiss the ground if it weren't for the mud. Perk went to the medical tent to check his head for a concussion. The medic said he had a welt on his forehead but declared he was fine.

April 29, 1944—Mission: Toulon, France (29)

The weather was supposed to be sunny and the squadron was briefed on a mission to the Mediterranean port of Toulon, France. It was the top aeronautical and naval equipment production center in Nazi occupied France under the Vichy government. Squadrons from the 15th Air Force were sent on the mission to soften targets at the port in case the invasion occurred at Toulon.

The formation cleared the Italian alps crossing diagonally the peninsula of Italy. Six Me109 fighters trailed them and put up a good fight with the Mustangs escorts amid lots of flak. The lead plane passed over the "beachhead" and it was covered by a smoke screen. They used radar to drop their bombs. The eleven hundred mile trip wasn't too bad: just very long.

The sun was low as the formation of silver birds passed over Rome and made it back to base in time for their sixth month anniversary celebration overseas. The men put together a beer bust for the squadron with ice cream, Coca Cola, sandwiches and cake. The Perkins crew had twenty-one more combat missions to fly, if the Army didn't revise the tour minimum again. The men toasted those who hadn't returned from missions and to themselves for their miraculous survival.

April 30, 1944—Mission: Varese A/C Factory (30)

The squadron had been rousted at 0430 and took off from Tortorella at 0630 flying north over the Adriatic Sea to miss Mount Corno's 9550 foot peak. They turned northwest avoiding the Apennine Mountain range and its fickle updrafts as well as enemy defenses in Northern Italy. The mission target was Varese's battery factory complex in Northern Italy, north of Milan, tucked in the foothills of the Italian Alps. Ten German Messerschmitt fighter planes flew around their formation like bees throwing out their stingers at the bigger wasps. The waist gunner, Marcuse's .50 caliber machine gun jammed at the worst possible time. It took a few minutes but he was able to fix it and defend his side of the ship.

The enemy made several passes at their box, flying in the low position and setting one fort on fire. That B-17's number four engine arched a thirty feet long flame as it slowly fell out of formation. Three men bailed out and the ship was still under control and turned south, as it went out of sight. Those observers assumed the rest of the crew bailed out. Another Me 109 zoomed in close and fired but missed the Perkins' Fort. As they reached the target, the flak was thick and they observed three boxes of B-17s drop their bombs. They watched as two 109s went down in flames after a dog fight with Mustangs. Perk made a slow turn west to go home. The crew stared out the ship's starboard windows at the beautiful snowy white Mont Blanc mountain beneath them. The 15,778 foot lofty peak made their airplane's 25,000 foot elevation seem low. After a thousand mile trip, they were so glad to get back to base.

May 1, 1944—Mission: Trieste, Italy (aborted)

The Perkins' crew were called out to bomb Trieste, Northern Italy. They had loaded the bombs, made all the pre-checks and were ready for take off, when the raid was scrubbed due to bad weather over the target. After that drill they were on the alert to go again the next day. After dinner they hit the sack early.

May 2—Mission: Tento, Italy (aborted)

On the mission to Trento, Northern Italy, the crew got called back while over the Adriatic Sea. They had run into a terrific storm and were able to return safely to base.

May 3—Mission: Ploesti, Romania (aborted)

Feelings of apprehension hit the airmen as they sat in the briefing room waiting to view the target of that day. Small talk and wise-cracks cut the tense atmosphere until the colonel walked into the room. "Ten-Hut!" Then, "At ease."

A collective groan came from the men as the curtain was raised to reveal the dreaded Ploesti Oil Fields in Romania. Ten months earlier in August, Operation Tidal Wave was an air raid of "White

Four" the code name for Ploesti, Romanian oil fields. Almost 200 B-24 Liberator bombers and 1,763 airmen took off from an airfield in Benghazi, Libya. Their mission was to bomb Hitler's gas station which produced one-third of Hitler's fuel needs. That mission turned out to be a disaster as Ploesti had been well fortified with defenses.

The crews were apprehensive as they made it out to their ships, but before take-off, the mission was scrubbed due to bad weather over the target. At the base the men played cards and wrote letters and at noon they used the coal stove to boil some eggs and make some coffee. The men were uneasy knowing they would probably be assigned Ploesti the next day.

May 4—Mission: Ploesti, Romania (scrubbed)

The crew was called out at 0400 on the same mission to Ploesti. Two hours after take-off the squadron was called back, again because of bad weather at the target area. In the evening the crew entertained themselves by going to Perk's tent where they drank wine and told jokes while listening to an Italian music station. The anticipation and mission cancellation, day after day, started wearing on the crew.

May 5, 1944—Mission: Ploesti (31-32)

Roosevelt and Churchill's mission to eliminate Hitler's war supply sources and their means of transportation was paramount to their plans. Few knew how close the Allies were to the invasion of France but they could feel the tension mounting in the air.

The 15th Air Force's mission went forward to Ploesti after two scrubbed attempts. With relief, the Perkins crew encountered very few fighter aircraft but the flak was very heavy when they reached the target. There were high winds and turbulence that tossed their 36,000-pound bomber around like a leaf in a storm. Part of the bumpy ride was caused by the brutal prop wash. Glenn and Perk had their hands full just trying to stay on the bomb run. Overton's top turret was hit by flak and it just missed his head by inches. Another piece of four-inch-long flak came through the waist and barely missed the waist gunner, Marcuse, who might have been singing arias in soprano, had it not just missed his testicles. The crew of Moonbeam was fortunate with only seven holes in the ship's body and tail fuselage. All systems were untouched and operated perfectly to get them home safely. When they finally reached the Adriatic Sea, with a sigh of relief, they removed their flak jackets and dropped altitude low enough to take off their oxygen masks. They had gone to Ploesti and survived the mission.

May 7, 1944—Mission: Bucharest, Romania M/Y (33)

The marshaling yard in Romania was the target, and the Perkins crew took off at 0715 hours with clear skies ahead. The flak was surprisingly not too bad but a couple of our P-51s had a nerve racking 45 minute dog fight with several German 109s. The waist gunners shot six-hundred rounds of ammunition, hitting two enemy fighters.

After eight hours of flight the men were tired and dragged themselves back to base. On their smoking stove, they boiled eggs and ate them with goat cheese, a meal as good as those served at the Ritz. The men were relieved they had no mission the next day.

Foggia

May 8-9

Most of the crew spent their time sleeping and recovering from the rigors of the last stressful mission. Their brains needed to repair from the trauma of battle.

A few of the guys rode their bikes into town to see what was there. On the way they saw some small farms and some white washed, red tile roofed buildings, a bombed out church and other damaged structures from the recent battle. The cobblestone streets had muddy pot holes made by heavy use of military tanks and trucks. Evidence of house by house combat showed in the pock marked shell holes on most buildings. The town hadn't yet recovered and Italians looked wearily at American service men walking in their village. A hand out of gum or chocolate by the airmen to the children showed goodwill and one old man even touched his cap and nodded to the Americans as they crossed paths in the ancient square.

Collier had carved a pair of wings out of plexiglass from the old windshield of their ship. He finished half of it and completed

B-17, Foggia, Italy, 1944

the other half the next day. The men repeated their *Lunch at the Ritz*, boiled farmers eggs on their tent stove. The problem was it took over an hour to get the water hot enough to cook the eggs. But when they were done the meal, served with local goat cheese, was a good supplement for their usual K-rations.

May 10, 1944—Mission: Wiener Neustadt, Austria (34)

The Messerschmitt Factory in Austria was still turning out 250 fighters a month even though Perk's crew had done several restrike missions on the aircraft plant. The Germans proved exceedingly resilient. Allied intelligence asked for continued re-strike bomb raids. During the war there were 470 Allied bomber re-strike raids flown by the 15th Air Force to Austria alone, hitting marshaling yards, oil refineries and aircraft factories.

On that morning's ill-fated mission the weather was bad with a thick cloud layer. Perk flew with the formation of thirty-six aircraft, north over the Adriatic Sea at twenty thousand feet. Their B-17 had a heavy payload of 5,000 pounds of bombs. He cleared the mountains of Yugoslavia. High storm clouds made for a very rocky ride and he and his group tried to climb above the cloud layer. Because of that maneuver they found themselves split into two groups of eighteen ships each. They turned right to go around more thick cloud cover, getting further separated from their group. Within twenty minutes of the target in heavy clouds, Perk and Glenn made the decision to turn around knowing it would be a suicide mission to go in alone. On the way back Myers, their radio man, picked up a transmission from the other group saying "SOS! Send fighter escort to secondary target. Greatly outnumbered by enemy fighters!"

While they were crossing the Adriatic on the way back, another message came through from a fortress saying, "Two engines shot out. Landing on the first straight and level field. The lead ship called back and asked him to repeat his message. He started again and when he had finished the word "Two..." The key was held down for about twenty seconds. They later found out they went down in the Adriatic Sea.

While Perk circled the Tortorella tower to land, two more messages came in. "Give me clearance to land, immediately! I have seriously wounded aboard!" Another B-17 said, "Give me clearance to land immediately. My wingtip shot away. Half my elevator on the left side shot away. Seriously wounded onboard." Thankfully, both ships landed without crashing.

May 11

Tortorella, the American Air Force base in Italy had been the home of the 99th Bombardment Group since December 1943. It was one of the few stations that allowed the RAF tenant status. While the 99th maintained squadrons of B-17s and B-24 Liberators on the west side of the field, the British occupied the east side hardstands with Lancasters, Vickers and Spitfires. The Americans flew daylight strategic missions in formations of 36 bombers or more and the RAF largely flew night bombing raids.

Tortorella tower

On this particular orange dawn morning Perk stepped out of his tent and looked up at the sky. He couldn't sleep as the sound of a Lancaster came back from a night raid. The 1000 horsepower Rolls-Royce engine in the distance, had a higher pitch than the low throaty rumble of his ship's four Wright Cyclone R 1820-97—1200 horsepower engines. He could hear B-17s warming up their engines, breaking his concentration on the aircraft landing on the distant east side of the field. Ages had passed from when he was a boy watching a biplane bank near his house as it flew toward Muroc Airfield. He dreamed of flying airplanes then, but he never imagined the missions he would fly in the cockpit of his airplane. He was a naive boy of 17, seated behind Pancho Barnes in the Travel Air 4000, while working to get his civilian pilot's license.

The integral roles aircraft and their crews would eventually play toward victory in the war was not part of his consciousness in 1938. After all his training as a cadet, accepting a brand new

Perkins crew with Moonbeam

B-17 bomber at Harvard, Nebraska, he and his crew flying it across the Atlantic, was a mere six months before. He wasn't a kid anymore. Perk's ideals of piloting an airplane had changed from the fun and adventure at Pancho's ranch. The responsibility of getting his crew to the target, dropping the bombs and returning safely to the base had dampened his dreams of flying. After the war, some airmen talked about a career flying commercial airlines in that developing industry. Some wanted to start their own mail, or crop dusting business. There would be a huge surplus of aircraft and airmen after the war.

As the dawn in Foggia lightened the sky further, Perk knew clearly what he wanted. If he made it home after these last 15 missions he would ask Dottie to marry him and he would go back to college and become a mechanical engineer, as far away from an airfield as possible. It made him sick knowing they lost two crews of ten men, yesterday. Those lost futures, families they would never have. He was determined to live their lives, honorably and well, for all of his fellow airmen who didn't return from this war.

May 12, 1944—Mission: Tarquina A/D (35)
Mission: German HQ, Rome (36)
Two Tactical Missions

Their briefing at 0400 explained the Fifth Army's big push to break through the Gustav Line in Italy, starting this morning. A newsreel correspondent came along on the mission so Perk and Glenn knew something big was happening; the rare event of two missions in one day. The first target; Marshal Kesselring's German staff Headquarters was twenty miles north of Rome. He was the infamous General in charge of holding the Gustav Line, north of Foggia. Their B-17, Scheherazade, was loaded down with 5,000 pounds of incendiary bombs. The weather was clear over the targets and the tactical mission would proceed as planned. At 0700 Perk's crew flew the lower box, reaching 24,000 feet, clearing the peaks of the Apennine mountains. On Italy's west coast they passed over Anzio Beachhead and saw a hell of a battle going on below, with an armada of ships in the bay, multiple amphibious craft, and explosions everywhere. Their formation banked right at the IP, and continued onto Kesselring's Headquarters north of Rome. After Foley dropped the bombs, the crew took odds on whether they took out the general as they flew back over the mountains and returned to their base.

At 1400 hours they were back at their ship, loaded down with another load of 5,000 pounds of bombs. The maintenance crew chief said their ship had a few flak holes from the first run but no damage had been done. They took off traveling the same route back over the Apennines to the Tarquina beachhead to take out several air defense locations. Tired and feeling overworked after the two runs, they returned to the base at 1830 hours. The newsreel man on board got some good pictures of the bombing and the beachhead. The Perkins crew was on the roster to go out again tomorrow so they hit the sack early.

May 13, 1944—Mission: Trento, Italy, Marshaling Yard (37)

The marshaling yard in Trento, Italy was the target. At the briefing the crews were cautioned not to accidentally hit the two cultural sites, the medieval castle or the Trento Cathedral. They took off at 0600 and flew over Venice with very little flak to oppose them. The return flight was mostly over the Adriatic Sea where they didn't have to worry about flak but they watched out for German fighters. They made it safely back to their base where they celebrated their survival with vino and a shot of Rye. They calculated they had 37 missions to date and with a lot of luck their crew might finish up their tour by the middle of June. They knew they weren't going on a mission in the morning and happily, could sleep in.

May 14

Perk, Glenn, Garrick and Foley found an Italian barber shop in Foggia on the Via Duomo. They all got a luxurious haircut and professional shave. Afterwards, they explored the town around the Palazzo Dogana and the Basilica Cathedral. Even though areas were damaged with piles of rubble, they could see the former splendor of the medieval city before the war. The Italians were happy the Yanks were there and seemed friendly enough. The airmen had been warned not to fraternize with the locals, especially in a country that not long before had been part of the Axis. Mussolini was still alive somewhere in the north but there were rumors the US army was very close to taking Rome.

May 15

Perk, Myers, Overton, Foley and Moore flew a "practice mission" which was ferrying some of the brass and some news crews to an undisclosed location. Naples, Italy, was the destination, which was never confirmed or denied.

May 16

Some of the men found a shop in town that painted airplanes and other things on leather jackets. Collier and Moore went back to retrieve their painted jackets with a B-17 Fortress on the back. It cost them fifteen dollars a piece and they were pleased with the results. The men expected a mission the next day and were apprehensive but eager to complete their tour.

Moore and Collier bought a chicken from a farmer and Overton, their engineer, devised a roasting spit over a steel barrel. The delicious bar-b-que smells drew a crowd among the hungry airmen. Eventually, the farmer had to import chickens from other farms to keep up with the demand. There was an interest in clean steel roasting barrels, too.

May 17

Another day without a mission and the Perkins crew was impatient to get their missions in and go home. At the same time they were relieved they weren't flying. Marcuse said, "Sometimes I feel like a condemned prisoner with a stay of execution." Warren and Collier confirmed the same thought. They didn't have to wait long to get on the roster to fly again. The rumor was this next mission was a big one.

May 18, 1944—Mission: Ploesti, Romania (38)

The Perkins crew were assigned to go back to the Ploesti, Romanian oil refineries. The German air defenses were so effective, the Allies always had losses during Ploesti missions. Hopefully, their luck would hold.

The weather was fair when they left at 0530 hours flying northwest just south of the Dalmatian Islands. An hour from the target they encountered high billowing cumulus clouds and they tried a diversionary maneuver to fly around them but in that action they became separated from the larger group. Perk flew back around and got caught in the clouds, losing sight of the rest of their squadron. Garrick found their bearings and they were back on track to the target but they were way behind. The concentration of black puffs of flak increased and quickly became as thick as a mattress as they neared the IP. Time slowed down as minutes passed like hours. Perk tensed and clinched his teeth and white-knuckled the controls. Flak strikes jarred Moonbeam's aluminum skin and the sound was deafening. Perk thought, "This is what hell must be like. Come on, come on," he said to himself. Flak shells were striking all around them. The bomb bay doors opened as with the rest of the squadron's 1000 pounders cascaded down like a hail storm. There was plenty of black smoke over the oil plants and Foley broke the silence, "I sent a little surprise down the refinery's chimney!"

"Let's get the hell out of here," Perk said to Glenn. They headed southwest toward the safe Adriatic Sea. Glenn asked Overton, "Take a quick accounting of the damages." He reported the electrical system got hit and the heat was off. Over the Dalmatian coast they lowered altitude to warm up. They were all a bit frozen when they landed at Tortorella. Home never felt so good. They counted 17 holes in the fuselage. Perk heard our group had lost one fort by flak and another base had lost seven ships. Ploesti had lived up to its reputation.*

May 19, 1944—Mission: Porto Marghera, Italy (39)

Porto Marghera, Italy, was an Italian/German port near Venice on the Adriatic. It had an important aircraft industry with nearby

---

* Between May 1944 to March 1945, 208,000 tons of explosives were dropped on the Wehrmacht's oil production, oil fields, synthetic oil production and storage depots by the USAAF's Eighth and the 15th Air Force, as well as the RAF. They were successful in turning off the oil source to the Third Reich with their Ploesti raids. For that they paid a heavy price, losing 1,850 bombers and 650 fighter planes and nearly 19,000 airmen.

rail and port access. Flying the reliable fort, Moonbeam, the Perkins crew was to take out those factories, marshaling yards and to disrupt the port. Much of that five hour trip was flown over the safety of the Adriatic. The defenses over Axis controlled Venice were surprisingly mild with not much flak and a few fighters who weren't interested in risking the guns of allied squadrons and escorts to challenge them. The formation dropped their bombs and returned the same way they had come.

It had been so long since the crew had received mail, so it was a welcome sight to see packages from the states. Perk got a letter from his mother and one from Dottie, plus a box of cookies she had made. Most had become pulverized in the journey but he still had to hide the box from those who wished to sample it, still sharing it with Glenn, Garrick and Foley in his tent. Dottie's letter talked about news of her family and friends, movies and football games. She told Perk when he got back home there was a beautiful trail she wanted to show him in the Rocky Mountains. She couldn't wait to introduce him to her sister, Ruth's husband, Bob, who knew the mountains well having been a forest ranger. Perk had been so homesick lately and he read and re-read the letters from both Dottie and his mother several times.

May 20

Perk had a small Brownie camera and had taken pictures of his crew, the base, and the town of Foggia. He knew he would have to wait a couple of months to have the photos developed because there were no developing labs close to Tortorella.

May 21

Perk didn't go to church with some of the crew but went instead to town and heard some good music at a cantina. In the afternoon they were supposed to go to an awards assembly but some of the crew hung around in Perk's tent listening to the radio and missed the whole thing. Radio Free Europe sounded like the invasion would be coming soon with optimism high among his men.

May 22

Perk announced a party in his tent with boiled eggs and a roasted chicken and what was left of his cookies. They procured a few bottles of Italian vino which had a bit of sediment in the bottom but still tasted fine to them. Since they were most likely going on a mission the next day they hit the sack at 2100 hours.

May 23, 1944—Mission: Farentino, Italy (40)

News was the Gustav Line was broken 100 miles north of Foggia. The Fifth Army was circling Rome with Nazi soldiers retreating north. Farentino was a town 45 miles south of Florence, Italy. The mission was to take out a railroad bridge at Ficulle and another at Orvieto. The mission was to disrupt the Wehrmacht supply of troops retreating with their equipment toward Mussolini's fascist stronghold. If the allies broke the back of the oil, battery, ball bearing, aircraft, submarine, tank and munitions industry, they could starve the Axis war.

The Perkins crew in Scheherazade along with three other squadrons flew over the Adriatic and cut in over the Gran Sasso Mountains. Near the target there was a dense cloud cover and they were afraid of dropping their bombs on innocent villagers. They made three bomb-runs in heavy flak and still couldn't locate the target. It would have been suicide to go around again so they turned back toward Foggia and the crew took a collective sigh of relief. Unfortunately, they did not get credit for the damn mission. A couple of the crew grumbled the old fat-cat mission-planners were safe in their bunkers drinking coffee while the 20 and 21-year-old crews were out risking their lives on suicide missions. That night after dinner Perk wrote a letter to Dottie and to his mother and hit the sack.

May 24, 1944—Mission: Atzgersdorf, Austria A/F (40-41)

Two weeks ago the crew flew a mission to Wiener Neustadt with a rough outcome. Heavy Flak and fighters downed a couple of planes while all came back with damage. Perk wasn't looking forward to the mission to Atzgersdorf Airfield near Vienna and the Neustadt target. Again, they were told it was well fortified with 88s and fighter defenses. Austria had a special place in Hitler's heart because it was his birthplace. He made sure it was well protected. His infamous Berghof and his Eagles Nest retreat was only 180 miles from their target that day.

Within an hour of the target the flak was heavy with several 109s trailing their group. Garrick called out on the intercom, "Plane 32068 took a direct hit! Going down in flames." Some of the crew watched it off their starboard wing. Two more forts got hit and slowly dropped out of formation. That sight wrenched their guts every time. They dropped their bombs on the target and turned to go home. Their thoughts were with the 30-man crews who wouldn't be coming back to Foggia that evening. Collier said to Moore, "We got away with it again." Perk knew his waist gunner meant they cheated death once more.

May 25

The CAP crew had no mission today and they played baseball in the dry field. They heard some of the fellows went on a mission to Enzerdorf and they got off course and found themselves over the front lines at nine thousand feet. They got the hell shot out of them and lost a few forts and others came limping back.

May 26

The crew expected to fly again but were surprised to have another day off. Glenn, Foley, Garrick and Perk went to see the movie, "A Guy Named Joe," with Spencer Tracy and Irene Dunn. It had lots of scenes of Liberators flying in loops. None of the guys bought into the dead pilot, guardian angel concept of the plot.

B-17 parked at Tortorella

Marcuse saw newspaper head-lines in Italian which he brought back to Perk. It said that 130 miles north of their air base there was a terrific battle by the Allied Armies to break through the Gustav line at Anzio and Monte Cassino. The Germans were well entrenched and put up a fierce fight to defend the Italian capital of Rome. Perk's crew remembered two weeks ago on their mission to Tarquina, they witnessed tanks, smoke and destruction of that raging battle.

Lt. Perkins, 1944

Finally, the Germans were retreating north and the Allies were marching on their heels, right behind them.

May 27, 1944—Mission: Avignon, France (42)

Colonel Twining briefed the airmen on their railroad and bridge targets at their mission to Avignon that day. He said it was an important supply route near the southern French port on the Mediterranean Sea. The harbors of Marseille and Toulon had been targets before, temporarily stopping the supply of war materials to the Nazis through the occupied territories. He said, "This mission is in support of the coming invasion, so do your best, men."

Glenn and Perk had heard rumors the Allies would strike before summer. Perk whispered, "My guess it could be at Calais, Dunkirk or south at Normandy because of its proximity to Berlin. I don't think it will take place on the Mediterranean because it is too far to march north to Berlin." Glenn nodded in agreement. "Eisenhower could throw everything he has at the Nazis including a second front pushing northward from the cities of Marseille, Toulon or Avignon, tightening the noose around Hitler's neck. The Nazi and Vichy ports are well fortified and it makes sense to soften those targets."

Their mission today was eight hours long with not much projected flak and only a few fighters. With clear skies, the squadron successfully got in and got out, hitting industrial buildings, a railway bridge and storage tanks in Avignon, before returning to Foggia. Collier calculated he and Bill Moore needed seven more missions to complete their tour. The exhausted crew debriefed, ate and hit the sack early.

May 28

There was no mission and the crew went to the hardstand and worked on Scheherazade, cleaning all the guns, checking the equipment and doing safety inspections in the afternoon. With seven missions left, there was no room for equipment failure.

The colonel told Perk his crew was supposed to go to a rest camp for a week and the guys were divided on whether to go or just bust through the last missions to complete their tour. Tonight they would discuss it and take a vote.

May 29

There was no mission again today and they were too lazy to go swimming and played ping-pong and pool in the morning. The fellows talked about going to the rest camp and decided against it because, "we all wanted to go home as soon as possible." The Perkins crew was still on operations status but with no mission the following day. In the late afternoon, a few guys got together and went swimming, a bicycle ride from the base. The weather was warm and the lake was clear and marshy around the edges. He and Glenn and Foley sat on the shore for a while throwing rocks in the water. Perk wondered what Dottie was doing and remembered with the time difference she was probably asleep. He studied the white cumulus clouds and saw an elephant shape with a long trunk. He remembered searching for shapes in the billowing cotton clouds when he was 17 years old at Pancho's ranch. Now, at 23, he felt he had aged ten years when he looked at his reflection. He wondered if his parents would recognize him. They had all lost so much weight. Some of his crew were even losing their hair, probably from the stress, he figured.

May 30

With another day of no missions the fellows decided to go swimming again. They borrowed a few more bicycles and eight of the crew took towels and swam in the lake. They grabbed some food at a small market and a jug of wine and enjoyed themselves on their own rest camp.

In the afternoon the colonel told the airmen that eight crews from this squadron would be going on an important mission but no one knew who would go or what it would be. The assignment sounded ominous because most missions labeled "special" often came with a great deal of risk.

May 31

Again there was no mission today but Perk's crew was notified they were on the list to go on the special assignment. As of yet the destination was still unknown. The weather was turning hot and all crews were given cotton uniforms for summer. Perk's heavy long sleeve uniform was not compatible with Foggia's 80-100 degree Mediterranean temperatures.

9.

The Beginning of the End

THE FOUR LIEUTENANTS of the Perkins crew attended a special briefing on their upcoming mission. The colonel tried to clear up some misconceptions about the Soviet Union and its Allies. He told about the Russian double-cross that took place between England, France and Russia in the spring of 1939. He said, "While negotiating to become an Ally of England and France, Stalin signed a secret pact with Hitler, turning his back on Winston Churchill and France's Albert Lebrun. The Russian leader essentially joined the Axis, with an agreement to not interfere with Hitler's plan to invade Poland. Hitler offered a pay-off to Stalin in the form of land concessions, for the USSR after the war. Stalin did not interfere in the Polish invasion, and with the signing of the pact, Churchill and Lebrun were betrayed."

With a sarcastic tone the colonel said, "No surprise, in the middle of June 1941, Hitler broke the agreement with Stalin, by invading the Soviet Union with three million Axis troops along the Polish-Russian border. Stalin had been double-crossed by Hitler, with deadly consequences to the Soviet Union." The colonel unsympathetically said, "Uncle Joe Stalin had backed the wrong horse." The colonel added, "After the Russian leader was betrayed, and his troops decimated, he then wasted no time signing a treaty with the Allies."

In 1942, the German high command strategically moved most of their oil and armament factories to Eastern Europe. They needed them out of the range of long distance Allied heavy bombers, based in England. Stalin did not have a strong enough Russian Air Force to launch attacks on those German installations.

The Allies devised future plans to get their air bases closer to Hitler's oil and armaments in the east. Long range heavy bombers with fighter escorts were needed, but the lack of flight range due to limited fuel, caused limitations. Eisenhower knew the Air Force bases needed to be closer to Eastern Europe. The Foggia, Italy, bases were closer but some Axis factories were still out of reach.

President Roosevelt proposed a secret plan called *Operation Frantic* to Marshal Stalin for shuttle missions from U.S. bases in Italy to hit targets in Eastern Europe. American aircraft would launch their planes from the Italian bases, hit targets in Hungary and Romania at the farthest point, and land on Russian bases nearby to refuel and rearm. It was a brilliant idea to get their heavy bombers and fighters as far into Eastern Europe, stay the night and bomb targets on the return to their Italian bases.

With the Kremlin's agreement, the U.S. built three bases near Kiev, (in the Ukraine) receiving B-24 Liberators, B-17 bombers, fighter escorts, P-51 Mustangs and P-38 Lightnings. Delivered from the U.S. were some 450 personnel and thirty-six thousand pounds of cargo by June 1944. After Stalin betrayed Churchill in 1939, by aligning his country with the Nazis, the British Prime Minister did not trust Stalin and therefore, did not participate in *Operation Frantic*.

June 1

For Perk and his crew there was nothing going on with no missions. The planes were getting a thorough maintenance once-over in preparation for their special assignment. The men attended two more briefings and as some of his NCO crew had already guessed, the location was Poltava, Russia. Tom Garrick, Perk's Navigator, had a staph infection from a nasty cut on his foot and he ended up in the base infirmary field tent with intravenous doses of penicillin. The crew visited Garrick and the medics had his foot elevated in a sling. Lt. Peter Behmen would fill in as the crew's navigator on tomorrow's mission.

June 2, 1944—Shuttle Mission: Debrecen M/Y (43/44) Poltava, Russia

At the early briefing, the aircrews were told they represented the United States Army Air Force as the first shuttle crews landing on Russian soil. On the way, the squadrons would bomb a target in Hungary at Debrecen, hitting the marshaling-yards. The group would fly on to Russia, landing at Poltava. The base would be known as USAAF Station 559 which became headquarters, Eastern Command, headed by General Alfred Kessler. The Tortorella group of eight planes including Moonbeam flown by Perk's crew, joined aircraft from other bases in the Foggia area.

B-17 lands at Poltava, Russia

Operation Frantic, the first collaborative mission of the war to land in the Soviet Union, was flown by 130 B-17s from the Foggia Airfields, led by the Commander-in-Chief, Ira Eaker, of the Mediterranean Army Air Forces, piloting the lead plane. Perk assembled at 0300 hours from Tortorella Field over the Adriatic Sea, taking his place in the top box of the formation. The aircraft included seventy P-51 Mustangs and P-38 Lightnings, escorting the B-17s and Liberators. As they approached the target at Debrecen, Foley sited the target of the marshaling yards. He waited for the lead to drop their bombs. Perk's grateful crew encountered very little flak and ground defenses and saw no German fighters. This was probably because no one expected them in Hungary.

They continued in formation on to Poltava, bouncing through cumulus clouds, and finally emerging in calm skies. Descending to 10,000 feet they looked below and admired the thick forests and

American and Russian airmen at Poltava, Russia

meadows with areas of green and patches of white spring snow. They found the base and circled the bomb cratered airfield with its new steel mesh runway, complements of Uncle Sam. Poltava had taken a beating from the German Army, before Russia's hard fought victory the year before.

Moonbeam was third behind Commander Eaker's B-17, and Perk felt relief as his landing gear touched down safely at the Russian outpost. The tired apprehensive crew emerged from the underbelly hatch, looking around awkwardly when the Russian ground crew cheered and saluted the "Americanyetts." They shook hands with the Americans and treated them like welcomed guests.

Their group was led to a makeshift mess hall, and were given a shot of vodka and a pirozhki bun filled with meat. After seven hours in the air, the crew was starving and the food and drink were very welcome. American to Russian, the men nodded and smiled, unable to understand each other. Perk knew the word for

Russian fighter with B-17 in the background

251

thank you: "spasiba" which the Yanks used often. In the evening the Russians put on a damn good jazz band performance playing a few Glenn Miller and Benny Goodman songs. The friendly guys of the Red Air Force plied the Americans with more vodka at midnight, trading Russian cigarettes for Lucky Strikes. The tough leathery skinned soldiers showed pictures of their grinning wives and children and made a gesture pointing at their photos and at the American's chest asking to see their family photos. Of course, Marcuse opened his wallet to show several beautiful girls, drawing a crowd of Russians looking over his shoulder. One tipsy Russian heartily patted Marcuse on the back, grinning and winking to his friends. The Russians were colorful characters and rowdy partiers and Perk's crew found their homemade alcohol as strong as gasoline. In fact, it probably was gasoline. He and his crew hit the sack feeling no pain in the makeshift Russian tent city.

American tents in Poltava, Russia

June 3-5

The first three days in Poltava were non-operational. Eaker's men of the 99th were taken sightseeing at staged locations such as a farm cooperative and a very clean bomb factory with spit-shined equipment and shiny waxed floors. Stalin was intent on making a good impression.

D-Day Invasion in France

June 6, 1944—Shuttle Mission: Galati, Romania A/D (45) Back to Poltava

Dragging out of their tents at 0400 hours, the men were briefed on another shuttle mission from Poltava to Galati, Romania. On the way to the oil fields they were hit with heavy flak but only a few fighters came after them. Lieutenant Ferguson's Fort on Perk's starboard wing was hit and fell out of formation. One engine was on fire and their rudder appeared to be mangled. Five parachutes could be seen bailing out as the disabled plane dipped below the cloud layer. Lt. Peter Behman, our temporary navigator, confirmed their bombs successfully hit the targets.

As Perk landed his plane back at Poltava they were greeted with civilians lining the runway cheering and saluting their planes. They yelled, "Americanetts!" They learned upon arrival that Allies had invaded the beaches of Normandy, France, starting the march forward toward Berlin. Today was D-Day! The long awaited invasion had begun. The Russians were as happy as the Americans and the prospect of ending the war. Russia had taken the biggest losses in civilian and military casualties during the war. It was a shared moment of hope that this war in Europe might soon come to a victorious end.

The Russians had prepared food for the crews in big iron cauldrons, filled with a hearty soup made of potatoes, cabbage, carrots, beets and onions. They tore off big chunks of dense dark bread and handed it to the men.

In the late afternoon, Commander Eaker met with the men to announce the long-awaited news that the Allied invasion had begun in Normandy, France, that morning. Most of them already knew but they all couldn't help feeling hopeful this was the beginning of the end of the war against Hitler. Eaker gave details of 5000 ships and 150,000 troops landing south of Calais, establishing a beachhead.

In the early evening, Perk and Glenn met up with their Poltava friends, Mikhail and Alexander, who mostly tried to talk to them in sign language. They were very excited, gesturing about the invasion and they chatted in Russian to each other, occasionally speaking to Perk and Glenn louder and more slowly as if they could better understand them. To share information to their Russian friends about the scope of the invasion, Perk took a stick and drew a boat in the dirt near the campfire. Then he wrote 5000. He drew a stick figure man holding a rifle and wrote 150,000 next to it. The Russians reacted with animated gestures and more shots of vodka and slaps on the back.

As the evening progressed around the campfire, they showed the Americans card games and exchanged more Lucky Strikes for brown Russian smokes. Glenn coughed and choked on the first drag into his lungs and said with a constricted voice, "These Russian cigarettes might include other ingredients besides tobacco." Foley joked they tasted like donkey dung. They noted that most Russian soldiers rolled their own cigarettes.

The Perkins crew talked amongst themselves, wondering how this D-Day development would impact them, with only three missions left to complete. They would still be in the Army but flying combat missions would be over and there would be a new assignment somewhere. They believed they wouldn't be sent back to England after their Mediterranean tour. They all hoped to finish up their duties stateside. Glenn stated the dreaded fact that they could be now sent to the Japanese war in the Pacific.[*]

June 7

The Perkins crew had a free day without a mission and they hitched a ride to town in a Russian *Go Devil*, similar to the American *Willy* jeep. The village was bombed to hell by the Germans but most rubble was cleaned up. Within one of the only shops standing, Perk gestured to an old woman about a little carved bear on a shelf. He held out a fifty-cent piece in his hand and the toothless woman grinned, took the coin and wrapped the bear in a newspaper, handing it to him. He wanted to bring something home for his four-year-old sister, Barbara.

Back at the base they played Poker and Rummy with their crew in the evening. Perk, not much of a card player, didn't like gambling his money away. Over the nine months his crew found themselves in numerous games with Collier and Bill Moore who were good poker players and usually came out ahead. The crew were dead tired and hit the sack in their sparse six-man tents.

June 8-10

There were no missions planned and Glenn and Foley went with Perk back into town with Vlad who spoke a little English. The townspeople had been warned not to fraternize with the Americans

---

[*] Ernie Pile wrote from Normandy Beach, France:
  The next day, he observed the wreckage as he walked on Omaha Beach. "Submerged tanks and overturned boats and burned trucks and shell-shattered jeeps and sad little personal belongings were strewn all over those bitter sands," Ernie told his readers. "After it was over it seemed to me a pure miracle that we ever took the beach at all."

but Vlad explained, "These Yanks just want to buy some souvenirs." Perk was able to buy two scarves; one for his mother and one for Dottie. Afterward, on the street, they ran into their friend, Barney, who told them he had flown twenty-four missions. Perks crewmates did not mention they had flown 47 and had just three left before shipping out for home. The crews were told to pack up and they would be leaving Russia the next day with a bombing target to be announced at the briefing in the morning.

June 11, 1944—Shuttle Mission: Foscani A/D (46/47)
Back to Foggia

After ten days at the Poltava base their squadron was called back to Italy. The men said goodbye to Mikhail and Alexander and they shook hands saying, "spaseba." Their shuttle mission target on the way back to Foggia was to bomb the oil fields north of Ploesti at Focsani, Romania. Only this time the Germans were waiting for them. There were a hell of a lot of flak and Me109 fighters that attacked their squadron, some flying brazenly through their formation. Collier, Moore, Warren and Myers got a workout with their .50 caliber machine guns. They thought they hit an IAR 80 Romanian fighter and downed a Messerschmit. Collier radioed that a fort got hit and he saw five parachutes bail out before the plane blew up. Marcuse saw a P-38 pilot bail out over the sea and the gunner hoped he would be rescued by seaplane.

When Moonbeam touched down at Foggia, the battle-worn ship was riddled with 15 holes in the fuselage. It was a miracle that none of the flak hit the crew or vital parts of the airplane during that hellishly tough mission. So far, their good luck had held, once again. As part of the Fifteenth Army Air Force, Perk's crew had bombed the Romanian oil fields four times, helping to slow the oil taps of the Wehrmacht, once again.

June 12—No Mission Today

The men were so happy to be back in Foggia and glad they were home for a while. The men caught up on letter writing and sleep as well as a game of baseball in the now dry field.

June 13, 1944—Mission: Munich, Germany (48/49)

The Perkins crew were a little superstitious about the last missions of their tour. They didn't know whether Foscani would be counted as a single or a double. That morning when they got to the briefing room at 0300 hours, the colonel lifted the screen showing their destination. There was a collective groan from the men because they were headed to Munich, Germany, one of the toughest targets with well-fortified defenses on the ground and in the air. The route to Munich, over the Alps was risky with them carrying 5000 pounds of heavy explosives and incendiary bombs. The target was Oberpfaffenhofen, an aircraft factory and airport southwest of Munich.

At the briefing the colonel explained the purpose and significance of the work the crews were doing to win the war in Europe. "And you, gentlemen, can stop the flow of goods to the enemy on land, by bombing their Axis routes, oil refineries, and armament to cut off Hitler's transportation of supplies. As the German Army is being pushed back through France after D-Day, you will be hitting them inside Germany so they have nowhere to go." His pep talk would motivate the crews through their last two missions. He ended with a quote he heard from General George Patton. My friend, General Patton said, "Now I want you to remember that no bastard ever won a war by dying for his country. You win it by making the other poor dumb bastard die for his country." That got a hearty laugh as the airmen were dismissed.

At 0500 hours, thirty-eight planes assembled at 10,000 feet with the help of yellow flares. They rose to 25,000 feet as the temperature dropped to a freezing 30 degrees below zero. They met up with several other squadrons and made the perilous journey over the Austrian Alps. Perk looked down at the 13,000 foot snow capped peaks and hoped the squadrons could make it over them on the return trip from the target. He flew through heavy flak as their group dropped their bomb loads on the Dornier Turbine Blade Factory and the Oberpfaffenhofen German Aircraft Center. The navigator and bombardier were sure the mission had done significant damage to the two Munich industries.

As they turned to go home, enemy 109s and 190 fighters were all over them. Overton said their number two engine gas line was hit by flak and severed in half. Perk and Glenn saw gasoline flowing from the line, drenching the hot supercharger. Fearing it would explode, they had little choice but to keep it operational to maintain altitude to clear the high peaks of the alps on their return to base. Perk feathered the propeller and Glenn gave the order to jettison everything they could to maintain altitude on their three remaining engines. Overton radioed Perk that both Collier and Moore got pieces of shrapnel in their backside. Perk responded, to apply first aid, if possible.

As their good luck held, the engine did not explode and Moonbeam cleared the Alps and made it to the Adriatic Sea where they flew a few thousand feet above the water. As they neared Foggia, Glenn shot red flares by the control tower to signify wounded on board. After landing Collier and Moore were taken to the base clinic. At debriefing, the visibly shaken crew agreed that it was a damn rough mission. They were given the choice of doing their last mission tomorrow or waiting a few days. Even Collier and Moore made the choice to go because their injuries were not too bad and they wanted to finish their tour with their crew mates.

June 14, 1944—Mission: Shell-Kollas-Fanto, Budapest, Hungary (50/51)

None of the men brought up the fact, this was their last mission, but it was the gorilla in the room at the early morning briefing. They tried not to be superstitious about it but to think of it as just another assignment. As the six by ten foot screen was revealed with red ribbon lines to the target, they saw Budapest, Hungary, at Shell-Kollas-Fanto oil refinery. Their secondary target was a battery factory nearby. At least they weren't flying over the Alps on this mission. Their ship had been inspected, patched, an engine fuel line replaced and the bomb bay was loaded with 5000 pounds of incendiaries when they took off and rose to 10,000 feet over the Adriatic. By the time they reached 25,000 feet, closer to the target they found flak was a menace, but there were fewer enemy fighters than expected. The 109s seemed to back off when they saw their Mustang escorts and the large formation numbers. Garrick was back as navigator after his foot ordeal while his crew was in Russia. He had subbed on a couple of missions and would finish his tour at the same time as his buddies. After dropping their bombs on the oil refinery and looking back to see numerous fires below, they turned and skirted around the Belgrade defenses on the way back to the Adriatic and home. The safe landing at Tortorella Air Base had never been so sweet.

The over-exuberant, wildly happy crew was raucously celebrating their completed double tours of duty. It had been luck and skill that they weren't shot down, killed, injured or taken prisoner. They had beat the odds. With hearty pats on the back, bear hugs and toasts, the men were so grateful to have finished all their missions and survived. With a prayer from their co-pilot, they all thanked God for their safe completion of their tour. Glenn added a prayer for the safe return of all those crewmen seen parachuting from other aircraft the past six months, who might be hiding with partisans or in prisoner-of-war camps. A few words were said about those brave airmen whom they knew had perished and wouldn't be coming home to their families: God rest their souls.

Back in the mess tent, Marcuse produced a couple of bottles of red wine and they toasted all around to their good fortune. The Perkins crew wanted to fly back to the states, together, rather than taking a crowded troop ship across the Atlantic. Whether Perk could procure a plane, taking it out of combat was going to be difficult. Bombers were still needed even with the new shipments of B-17 Gs and B-29s coming in weekly into Foggia. Perk had heard of a few crews who had transported older B-17F back to the U.S. It was a long hazardous flight across the Northern Atlantic, or Southern Atlantic routes to get home in a brand new plane, let alone flying a combat battered aircraft. Going by ship transport had its dangers from German subs. He put in a request for an airplane to fly home.

Waiting to Leave While the War Goes On

June 15

The day after flying his last combat mission, Perk slept in until 0800 and after breakfast wrote a letter to Dottie. Memories of her had helped him get through the 51 missions. They had written to each other through his ten months abroad while their friendship grew into something more. He realized from her letters, which he read multiple times, she felt the same way about him. He looked forward to holding her and seeing her again. His life and survival, which had seemed so uncertain in the early fall of 1943, now had promise and a future. He had put a lot of thought into what he wanted to do with his life and with whom he wanted to share it. He loved Dottie. She was the one whom he saw in his future. Perk didn't know where he would be stationed when he returned to the states, with two years left to serve. It was apparent that victory was possible in Europe, as the news indicated. Germany was losing the war but Hitler hadn't given up yet.

There would be eleven more months of combat with one last big battle at the Belgian Ardennes in December 1944. Known as the Battle of the Bulge, it was the last major Nazi offensive campaign on the Western Front during World War II. After the German defeat, General Eisenhower would need a plan to demobilize four million servicemen and U.S. equipment, back to the United States. Some of the airmen had been in Europe for two years and their tours were complete. The Army devised a point system to determine who would stay in the European countries to occupy them, and which soldiers would be sent home for training for the ongoing Japanese war in the Pacific.

The Perkins crew had received their release orders, disengaging themselves from the 99th Bomb Group. The question was how would they get home? Half the Italian Peninsula was still in German hands. Western forces came from North Africa up the boot of Italy from the south and passed the Gustav line to Rome. The Russians moved quickly into Poland toward Germany on the Eastern Front. The Allied armies pushed forward, liberating France. Northern Europe was controlled by the Axis powers who were now retreating.

The aircrews knew when the war eventually ended, there would be a mass exodus of troops and equipment. Back in Seattle, Washington, in mid 1944 the larger Boeing B-29 had begun to take over the assembly lines used for B-17 production. As the new planes and parts were delivered to Europe, derelict B-17, and B-24 doner planes were sidelined and used for cannibalization of their parts. Shipments of B-17 replacement parts were delayed as B-29 parts became more plentiful. Orders were given that a few of the B-17Fs could be delivered back to the states by returning crews.

June 15, 1944 was referred to as the "Pacific D-Day." An invasion fleet departed Pearl Harbor, to launch *Operation Forager*, the allied invasion of Saipan. The Island was finally taken by July 9th but with a high casualty count of 29,000 enemy soldiers and heavy civilian losses. The victory ended up being one of the most costly battles in the Pacific. Out of 71,000 allied troops who landed, 2,949 were killed and 10,464 were wounded. But with the capture of Saipan, the United States Army Air Force's B-29 bombers were finally within reach of the mainland of Japan. A clear victory but a horrific price to pay.

Perk and his crew hoped they would not have to fight in the Pacific War. That day of reflection on June 15th, ended with his crew joining him in his tent with a couple of 50-cent bottles of Marcuse's Italian wine. They put two chickens on their rotisserie, boiled some eggs and celebrated their safe completion of their missions. Perk had submitted his request to get a B-17 to fly back to the states but he wasn't certain there would be a Flying Fortress for his crew.

June 16

After sleeping until noon, Perk, Glenn, Garrick and Foley went to a movie at the base theater and saw *Air Force* with John Garfield and Gig Young. There were lots of scenes of B-17s fighting in the South Pacific just after the attack at Pearl Harbor. The four thought the action scenes were pretty realistic.

The rest of the crew went to the small town of Foggia, got some drinks and Marcuse and Collier ended up in a fight with some wise guys from another base. Collier said that he ruined a new set of khakis and he complained of a few sore places on his chest and forehead. The guys found out Collier was fighting a guy who was an amateur boxer. When the dust had settled, Don boasted the other guy had two shiners and a busted nose. The rest of the crew teased Collier relentlessly, "It was lucky the boxer was taller than you because his boxing punches went over your head, and your hits were leveled at his nose and below." Marcuse teased, "That guy was definitely myopic." When the gunners returned to base and told Perk, he realized his NCOs had too much time on their hands. It was time to go home.

June 17

After laying about, playing a few games of baseball and writing a couple of letters, Perk went again to the base theater to see another movie, Knickerbocker Holiday with Nelson Eddy and a pretty Constance Dowling. None of the men thought it was very good. It was a musical that took place in 1650 New Amsterdam. Garrick was the only guy from New York and he tried to convince his buddies the movie was historical. Most of the men weren't buying it and Marcuse mimicked Constance Dowling singing in a frilly bonnet.

June 18-25

The Perkins crew waited anxiously for their orders to fly home. They spent their days in afternoon baseball games, playing poker for pennies and writing letters. Perk and Glenn often rode their bicycles and peddled around the Italian countryside. They happened on a family's small winemaking enterprise and were invited to see how they made the wine from the grape picking, crushing in a big vat, fermentation, and filling the bottles. The family was very nice and liked the Americans, inviting Perk and Glenn to lunch with fish from the Adriatic and their homemade wine.

Perk got a few letters from home. A long letter came from Dottie and he read it slowly to make it last longer. "I spent my last week's vacation at our Peaceful Valley cabin with the family," he read. There were descriptions of horseback riding, fishing with her mom and hiking up to Brainard Lake with her brothers, Dick and Bob. She said, "Ruth found out she is going to have a baby and everyone was so excited. She had come back home while Bob was on his second tour in the South Pacific." Ruth was volunteering for the Red Cross in Hastings.

Perk wrote a letter to his mom saying he thought he would see her soon, letting her know he was coming home. To Dottie he said the same but also told her how much he missed seeing her pretty face.

Poltava Bombed

June 26

The men heard the reports that the base at Poltava, Russia, in which they had been stationed just three weeks before, was bombed by the Germans on June 22nd. The attack by 150 German bombers lasted for two hours and destroyed forty-five B-17s. Besides the American fighter planes, they destroyed all the Russian aircraft as well. Most of the 450,000 gallons of high-octane fuel brought in by the Allies had been hit, causing massive fires. The munitions storage facilities were also hit: a devastating loss.

In the Russian-American agreement, the United states had built and paid for the base and the Russians were to set up land and air defenses to protect it. Clearly after the attack, they could see Stalin had made no provisions to fortify and defend the base at Poltava. At the time of the German attack, the Russians even refused to give clearance to the US fighters to take off in order to defend the base. Some officials even thought it was Russian sabotage to reduce American influence in the region. After the devastating attack, there were other shuttle missions but the trust between the two nations was broken. There was further Soviet hostility and non-cooperation that started with the Americans unable to get permission to support the Warsaw Uprising or to repatriate American POWS from Soviet territory, a further betrayal.

Operation Frantic set the greater historical importance for disagreement foreshadowing the coming of the Cold War. Relations between remaining Americans at the three Soviet airfields became extremely cold and tense. Churchill had declined to take part in Operation Frantic and had previously warned Roosevelt not to trust the Russian President. His advice turned out to be prophetic.

Orders to Go Home

June 27-30

The Perkins crew waited to hear how they would return to the states, playing football, watching movies, playing cards and writing letters home.

July 1

Finally after two weeks of waiting, Lieutenant Perkins received orders that he would be part of a group of five B-17s to return to the United States by way of the South Atlantic route. All five B-17s were from the Foggia Complex. He was also assigned a wounded airman who needed advanced medical treatment in the states as well as another officer, Major John Hansen, who would also be accompanying them on the flight. He was glad there were five planes flying in formation looking out for each other on the long journey home. He should be assigned his aircraft any day.

He immediately went looking for his crew and found them on the makeshift baseball field. The long awaited orders of them going home initiated cheers and hearty back slaps from his men and they all looked to Perk as the man that would fly them safely across the Atlantic and back to the states. Collier said, "Thank goodness we won't be on a slow, crowded troop ship." The heavy burden hit Perk when he thought of his responsibility for the lives of 12 people. Had they returned to the states on a troop ship, his responsibility would have been much less. He told himself it was going to be a "milk run," similar to the Northern Atlantic route they took from Nebraska to England. At that time, he was flying a new aircraft straight off the assembly line, but these ships were flown rough and patched to fly another mission. Mechanical issues crossing the Atlantic might be a big problem and even though they were flying in numbers, he wasn't sure exactly what he could do if he or one of the other forts had to ditch in the ocean. At least they weren't facing flak or fighters threatening them.

July 2

Perk felt he had to write a letter to his mother telling her about Dottie. He described her sense of humor, her intelligence, red hair and that she was pretty. He added that she worked as a secretary for a colonel at Harvard Air Force Base in Nebraska. He described how they met and said he thought she was a wonderful girl. He said that he had been writing to her while he was overseas and he loved her very much. Perk didn't want to blind side his family when he showed up with Dottie.

The last letter from Dottie said that she couldn't wait to see him and there were many things she had to tell him. He didn't have much experience in writing affectionate letters but he wrote back to her and told her she was never far from his thoughts while on base or in battle. He explained he would be coming back within the month and he couldn't wait to see her. Those amorous letters mirrored what was happening as thousands of lonely soldiers came back to the states. Many had seen their buddies die. Perk and his crew had drawn lucky numbers and had been among those guys that had survived. If the war had taught them anything, it was how short life could be.

July 3

Lt. Perkins crew's combat missions were complete but they watched as many of their buddies left for the Ploesti Oil Fields. The several times Perk's crew had flown to Romania it was really rough. On that July day two aircraft did not return with two others shot up pretty badly with injuries aboard. Poor guys.

July 4

July 4 invoice for a B-17 transport back to the US

Perk went to the supply tent on the American Independence Day and Sgt. Mike Kane gave him an invoice for a fortress that Perk hadn't seen before; B-17F # 41-24542, *Dream Gal.* He quickly signed for it, fearing they might change their mind. He filled out a couple more forms and walked out of the supply depot with the invoice for his ride home. The sergeant said he thought the aircraft came from Amendola Airfield but he wasn't sure. It had a pin-up girl painted on its nose, sleeping on a half moon crest. Perk wondered how many missions it had been on and what damage it had sustained, but he put those questions out of his mind and counted himself lucky to have that invoice in his hand.

The Perkins' crew was issued their exit orders three weeks after their last bomb raid to Budapest, Hungary. As the crew's families back in the states were celebrating with fireworks and picnics, Perk's crew was preparing their ship for their last trip home. A bag of mail was shoved into the bomb bay area.

There was a briefing that morning on the South Atlantic route the flight path the five planes would take home. The anticipation amongst the airmen was palatable.

On that 4th of July, Perk and his crew celebrated their own Independence Day with two chickens from a local farmer. The guys roasted them on Charlie's roasting spit. They boiled eggs and bought two bottles of homemade red wine: all which constituted a feast.

Perk's mind was with those airmen with whom he had flown on missions in formations who would never come home. He lifted his cup for a toast on this last celebration, "To those airmen who were lost over Europe." He cleared his throat as it cracked before continuing, "Idealistic men, taken before they had their futures. To them we salute." His crew was silent as they raised their cups.

At 2200 hours Perk walked back to his tent pitched in tight rows. He paused and looked around, "I won't be sorry to leave here," he thought. The base was barebones with few comforts. Without the combat stress, he also looked forward to getting back to the states where he had a bed inside a building, with an indoor toilet and a bath. None of those amenities were available at Tortorella.*

---

* Ernie Pyle had been there once and wrote, "Few of us can ever conjure up any truly fond memories of the Italian campaign. The enemy had been hard, and so had the elements. There was little solace for those who had suffered, and none at all for those who had died, in trying to rationalize why things had happened as they did."—Ernie Pyle

10.

Going Home

The last morning at Tortorella Airfield, the crew were awakened at 0430 and sent to their final briefing with all their gear to go home. The familiar setting felt like a mission but without the armaments and enemy targets. Perk, Glenn, Foley and Garrick were briefed along with the officers from the five other aircraft: two from Amendola, one from Celone and one from Lucera Air Fields. Perk was the lead plane with radar and Tom Garrick as navigator. The Southern Atlantic route was displayed by the intelligence officer on the map. The assemblage of pilots, co-pilots, navigators and bombardiers of the five B-17s saw the first destination was Tunis, Tunisia. Their one night refueling and layover was short. The next day when they flew to Casablanca they had a longer layover. Depending on the airfield, the weather conditions and the performance of the aircraft enroute, they got a 72-hour pass in Morocco. From there they would leave for Mallard Field in Dakar, Senegal on July 9th. The briefing room map showed a stop in Liberia before leaving the African continent and crossing the Atlantic with one fuel stop on Ascension Island before landing in South America. The group would hopscotch up the east coast of Brazil making fuel stops at Belem and on the Island of Trinidad in the Caribbean before the final push to Florida.

Perk remembered the North Atlantic route, Goose Bay, Labrador to Wales and on to England. At least this time they weren't dealing with the freezing November temperatures on the ground and in the air. He thought, "This mission is doable with mostly short hops and two long runs. He felt confident as long as there were no unforeseen problems with aircraft or weather. They were told that all five aircraft originated with the 15th Bombardment group, delivered in 1943. Perk checked to see that *Dream Gal* had some previous fuselage damage and two of its engines had been replaced. He thought she was as flight ready as she would ever be.

His crew's gear was loaded on the plane. He met Major John Hansen who was hitching a ride to Florida. Perk met his one evacuation patient, a gunner who had been pretty shot up by flak over Austria. He was gingerly lifted on the aircraft and helped onto a bench provided in the waist of the ship. Sergeant Hank Barker grinned at the crew and said he was just happy to be going home. Perk made sure there was a first aid kit, water and parachutes and Mae Wests for everyone and the two extra passengers. The crew chief made an adjustment, installing extra rheostats so Hansen and Barker could plug in their heated suits and get oxygen. They were ready to go at 0630 after their pre-flight checks.

At 0640 Perk was told one of the aircraft, *Miss Liberty,* had an engine that wouldn't start. That must have been an awful disappointment for its crew, who would have to wait perhaps weeks for other aircraft to make the crossing in tandem. He took a deep breath, grateful that his aircraft had passed all of its pre-flight checks. He and the three other B-17s moved toward the main runway. Collier commented to Moore what a tough break it was for the crew of *Miss Liberty,* who must have watched sadly while the other four aircraft left for home.

One by one, the four B-17 bombers took off and cleared the trees as the sun was coming up in the cloudless skies over the Foggia Plain. The airplanes banked right over the Adriatic Sea and headed southwest. At an altitude of 20,000 feet the group flew over the southern Apennine Mountains, which rose up 6500 feet. Mt. Vesuvius, which had erupted in March, had a big gaping hole crater at its peak with black smooth, sides from the ash and lava that had cascaded down from its rim. Glenn said he had read the eruption cost the 340th bomb group 25 million dollars in the loss of 80 B-25s at Pompeii Airfield. Their tails and fuselages were melted from the hot ash and were a total loss.

Perk looked beyond the Apennine range and could see the aqua waters of the Mediterranean Sea. On their starboard side rising majestically skyward was Sicily's Mount Etna which had wisp of smoke coming from its peak. The four B-17s headed toward Africa and left the continent of Europe behind.

The 460 air miles between Tortorella and Oudna Airfield, Tunisia, took a little over three hours. "Just a milk run," Perk thought. His landing gear touched down on the runway mid-morning and the four aircraft taxied to individual hardstands for maintenance and refueling. The crews were picked up by jeeps and taken to the operation building. The temperature was intensely hot at Oudna Airfield with the heat rising from the steel mesh runway and causing the crew to drip sweat in their insulated flight suits. They were directed to their quarters where they gladly changed into summer tan uniforms before heading to the chow hall. The base had a few more amenities than Tortorella with a well equipped mess hall, canteen and hot showers, constructed after victories in North Africa.

Collier and Moore were on their second beer when Perk and Garrick joined them at the canteen. "It is so hot you can fry an egg on the pavement." Collier said. It cooled down into the 80s by evening when all the crews met up and exchanged stories of their tours. 1st Lt. Jenkins' crew had been transferred from the 12th to the

15th bomb group and had flown 35 missions. Frank from the crew of *Royal Flush* sat at the old wooden upright piano and played a pretty accomplished ragtime. It reminded Perk of the piano at the Wednesday night soirees Pancho put on at the Happy Bottom Riding Club. As he closed his eyes, he was back there surrounded by the Muroc Airfield boys and Pancho's barnstormer friends, laughing and telling colorful stories. After a couple of beers, Perk and his crew decided to take showers and hit the sack because of their early flight time on tomorrow's leg to Anfa Air Field.

July 6, 1944—Casablanca, Morocco

The crews met at 0500 hours at the hardstands to get an early start on the challenging non-stop 1370 mile flight over North Africa. They would be flying over mountains, high plateaus and deserts. Perk was hoping there wouldn't be any mechanical problems with any of the four aircraft in his group. He worried about flight crews with unfamiliar aircraft, heat and dust storms effect on the old B-17s. "So far so good" Perk thought as he was briefed about USAAF bases at Algiers and Oran, for emergency landings. After the severe abuse he knew most B-17s endured during missions, he still had confidence in the old birds. The ground crew at Oudna Airfield had replaced a worn tire on *Flyin' Ginny* that went unnoticed by the Tortorella ground crew. Off they went before dawn's light, bumping over the mesh runway, congregating at eleven thousand feet before flying west toward the Atlantic Ocean. Air turbulence continued over the Saharan Atlas Mountains, causing a bumpy ride. To escape the updrafts Perk ascended to 21,000 feet where everyone had to use oxygen and their heated suits. The ride was smoother and their cruising speed of 160 miles per hour might get them to Casablanca sooner. Every fifteen minutes Glenn checked with the crew, and

Anfa AirField, Casablanca

passengers, Major Hansen and Sgt. Barker, to see if their oxygen was OK. He didn't want to lose anyone to hypoxemia when no one noticed. Collier and Warren had taken the responsibility of making Sgt. Barker was comfortable during the trip. Perk hugged the coast line to avoid the updrafts of the Atlas mountains in Algeria and Morocco. By 1430 hours, *Dream Gal* approached Anfa Air Field and touched down with no problems as did the rest of the three aircraft. They were home for a few days, given a 48 hour pass to explore the historic city of Casablanca.

This would be the first time Perk and his crew were on the Atlantic Ocean since April when they took the Capetown Castle from Rattlesden to Naples, Italy. He and some of the men got a bus ride into the city center to the Hotel Excelsior on Rue El Brahim, known to be one of the nicer lodgings in the city.

Appointed like a Sultan's palace, every room had plush red velvet chairs and intricately designed tile work. There were beautiful fountains, a pool and a great restaurant and bar. Various Hollywood movie stars had stayed there and rumor had it that FDR and Churchill had a secret war meeting at the hotel in early 1943. Foley

Bazaar, Casablanca

wondered, "Do you think Hedy Lamar stayed in this room, or Ingrid Bergman?" After a luxurious dinner the officers spent some time in the bar. An orchestra played while a couple of guys danced with pretty WAC nurses. The music was Glenn Miller and it made the boys feel like they were back home in the states.

Perk, Glenn, Garrick and Foley shared a big corner fourth story room with a balcony that looked out on the street and beyond to the busy harbor. Perk looked at the striking skyline of buildings with a mosque-tower just at the moment the *salah* sang out for afternoon Islamic prayer. A few of the devout could be seen kneeling on prayer rugs while life on the wide boulevard continued around them. Men laughed and argued at a cafe below as others sat smoking hookah pipes in an alleyway across the street. An old peasant directed a donkey with a switch, tapping his leg, while the over-laden beast carried twice his weight in parcels on his back. A small boy grabbed an orange off a vendor's fruit cart and escaped through the stalls, while the owner shouted and gestured after the little thief.

Perk had read about exotic Casablanca in books and he was eager to explore the interesting old city. He put his wallet inside his buttoned shirt, having been warned about multifarious pickpockets. The four young airmen left the security of the hotel and walked down Rue El Brahim turning right toward the harbor. Passing various whitewashed buildings they crossed under a tiled arched alleyway and followed pictorial signs leading to the open air market. Their wandering path led into the large square, bustling with hucksters, beggars, hundreds of covered stalls, and roving rickety carts. It had to be the fabled Medina. Perk and his group walked close together. Two in front with two behind, like the tight aircraft formations they had flown on missions. They stopped and stood back to back for a moment. They were enthralled in the noisy crowd, hypnotized by the exotic scenes of vendors selling olives, cured meats, spices, dyed cloth, metal pots, and woven carpets.

A few characters eyed them opportunistically. The four young officers stood out in their identical crisply ironed khaki uniforms with their garrison caps on top of their buzzed haircuts. Perk said nervously, "Let's get going." The formation of officers moved forward through the crowd and clumsily side-stepped two black cobras with flared hoods, giving a wide berth to them as they coiled and reared up on a rug. A small crowd gathered around the spectacle as the snake charmer played a lilting song on his flute. The airmen watched as a long hook was used to lift and lower the snakes back into a large covered basket. They nodded and smiled at two water carriers, wearing large brimmed red fringed hats with tin cups clanging on their waist belts. Men in caftans, and women in veils rushed by with their parcels. A turbaned vendor displayed a pile of human teeth on a table, offering to fit the client's mouth with dentures. *As You Wait,* the sign said in English and Arabic. There were kiosks of leather goods, jewelry, potions and decorated daggers. Fresh vegetables and falafel counters tempted the men's palate as they walked. The alluring and colorful Medina fascinated the airmen as they continued through the center of the marketplace. At a small kiosk, Perk stopped and bought a white carved necklace of bone for Dottie and one for his mother before walking on.

In Morocco there were images of the raw and ugly side of war. Emaciated immigrants, with their gaunt, hollow-eyed children, were escaping persecution from German occupied territories. They were slouched in the shade against the wall with their hands out. Perk bought two bags of oranges to give to child beggars on the street and the bags were empty in minutes. Afterward, he handed another child a few coins which were accepted with a bow, but a gaggle of children came running towards them, spotting the give-away and the four empty-handed officers ran, escaping down an alley and into a tavern.

The men were grateful to get something to quench their thirst, escaping the 115 degree heat outside. The bar had overhead wicker fans, moving on a mechanical pulley system, which

A street in Casablanca

Perk found interesting. There were a few British officers sitting at tables in the canteen and they had seen Brits out on the street walking in groups. Garrick remembered the British saying, "Only mad dogs and Englishmen go out in the midday sun." The Americans in Perk's crew ordered falafel, a meat-like sandwich with a couple Coca Colas each. Afterward, in the late afternoon they walked to the harbor and saw an ornately carved mosque before walking back to their hotel.

July 7

Abdellah, the portly man in a red fez hat, standing behind the hotel desk, recommended the beach at Mohammedia to the young airmen. They had asked him what there was to do in Casablanca in the mid-summer heat. The men grabbed their swim trunks and found a taxi big enough to fit the four of them. As the tightly packed cab drove north along the dusty dirt roads of the

Postcard, Hotel Excelsior, Casablanca

coast, there were fascinating scenes out the window of lumbering camels carrying huge loads of papyrus fronds, a donkey with a mother and three children on its back, and women walking in groups, covered in blue burqas with only their eyes showing.

The young Lieutenants weren't surprised at the ever present military and the war remnants of the fierce invasion from eighteen months previous. Passing the beaches on the coastal road, they saw a half-sunk landing ship at the surfline. There were ruins of bunkers and barbed wire barricades all along the beachhead. Foley said, "Jeez, this ain't Miami." When they reached Mohammedia there were few people and they decided swimming where a battle had recently taken place might not be too safe. They enjoyed sitting under a grass umbrella, on the beach for a while before walking to the little village for a cold drink at a seaside cafe. Then as the afternoon sun got closer to the horizon they found a taxi to take them back to the Excelsior Hotel where they ate steak and potatoes in its fine restaurant, Terrazza Bosquet. In the evening they wrote letters to family members that Abdellah promised would reach the United States. Perk inserted a postcard of Casablanca in his letter to Dottie and said he hoped he would see her soon, signing it, "Love Perk."

July 8

The men slept in late and ordered bacon, eggs and strong coffee, to be sent to their room from the hotel kitchen. Perk thought he had better check on the rest of his crew down the hall, not having seen them in a couple of days. Collier, Marcuse and Myers were still in bed, while Warren and Moore were getting dressed to go into town. He was relieved they had kept out of trouble. Perk had warned the flight crews of the four ships, they could be left behind on the Allied base had they found themselves in the brig or arrested by the local police. Moore stood at the door. "They have been little choir boys," he said, smiling at Perk.

On their last afternoon in Casablanca the four crews and their passenger, Major Hansen, congregated at a colorful French cantina with white-washed Moorish arches. There was a trio of musicians and a piano player providing back up, for a beautiful dark eyed female singer. She sounded just like Margaret Whiting, singing "That Old Black Magic," and "Don't Sit Under the Apple Tree." The boys hadn't heard American songs performed live since London and they clapped and whistled along with the other American servicemen. Perk suggested they walk back to their hotel together as a group, because of the late hour and the nefarious looking characters that were roaming the dark streets.

July 9, 1944—Dakar, Senegal

Forty-five minutes before take-off, at 0730 hours the crews met at their aircraft to do flight checks before leaving for Senegal. Garrick, roughly calculated they could fly the 1424 miles in just over nine hours. Their southern route across French West Africa charted a course to Mallard Field in Dakar. Most of the crews had never even heard of Dakar before the war. They were unaware of the fierce battle that took place there between the British Navy and the French Vichy government in 1940.

Perk and the three other crews needed to stay the night for refueling and servicing of their planes by the ground crew. Lt. Davidson's number four engine had been sluggish that morning but performed OK on the journey to Mallard Field but still needed checking. Their flight was uneventful and a bit tedious but they were globetrotting their way home and that is all that mattered to the men. The group of aircraft flew over the port and were given clearance to land on the main runway.

Mallard Field, Dakar

After landing they looked around and found the base to have huge storage facilities from shipping and air transport for the war. There were HQ buildings attached to the control tower. They were assigned their quarters for the night in tin roofed huts. Housing forty-two men was not always an easy task. Perk and his crew were exhausted and hungry from the long flight and after eating in the mess hall they found their sparse quarters for the night and hit the sack early.

July 10, 1944—Monrovia, Liberia

The ground crew had worked on Lt. Davidson's number four engine, cleaning the spark plugs and checking the wiring. On the final test the engine came through with flying colors and all planes were cleared for take-off by 0800 hours. The crews were ready to make the five hour trip to Monrovia, Liberia, their last

Postcard from Monrovia, Liberia

stop in French West Africa, before heading out over the Atlantic. The four ships reached Roberts Field by 1315 hours and each B-17 made flawless landings given turbulence caused by a dust storm. Sand and dust in airplane engines did not mix.

At the mess hall, Perk talked to one of the Army servicemen stationed at the base. He explained how Liberia had a contract with Firestone Tires in the United States to supply them with rubber during the war. He told Perk there were coal and fruit plantations which were an important source of imports to America. He had no idea that Liberia was so important to the war effort. Walking around the area, Perk saw a lot of churches and he concluded the Liberians must be a very religious people.

July 11

The officers of *Dream Gal* had a marginally good night's sleep in one of the base huts. Each of their canvas cots had mosquito nets to protect them from malaria infected insects. Perk was frequently aware of their high pitch buzzing a few inches from him on the outside of the net. Dottie's brother, Bob, had caught the parasite, spread by infected mosquitoes. While serving in the South Pacific he spent a month in the base hospital with a high fever.

Perk woke his enlisted crew in their Nissen Hut and he and his three officers walked across the field to the mess hall and found themselves the only ones dining. They stood at the counter in front of this enormous portly and friendly Liberian cook. "Ya Hello-o. What'll ya have?" he asked cheerfully.

Perk answered, "What have ya got?"

The man grinned with snow white teeth and replied, "Jefferson, fix you the very best breakfast in Liberia, my man."

"Well, alright! Thank you, Jefferson." said Perk. Four plates were piled high with fresh scrambled eggs, brown rice and corn bread with honey. He poured four cups of strong black coffee. After devouring their meal, Perk returned his tray, and utensils to Jefferson and complimented the man, saying, "That was the best breakfast I've had in a year."

The friendly cook grinned back at him saying, "Blessings to you, Lieutenant," and he added looking toward the sky, "And God be with you up thah."

July 12, 1944—Ascension Island, United Kingdom

The next morning the crew mustered at the canteen for another of Jefferson's "best breakfast in Liberia." At 0600 hours they met at their ships for their pre-flight checks. Major Hansen helped load Sgt. Barker into the hatch. Flight checks for the entourage of aircraft, was a go-ahead for the 1000 mile journey from Liberia to Ascension Island. The four B-17s lumbered down the mesh runway, turning southwest out to sea. Just under three hours flight time they crossed the Equator. It was a beautiful cloudless sky with no wind as they flew over the silvery blue Atlantic Ocean. Fifteen thousand feet below they saw a convoy of merchant ships and a couple of cruisers on their way to West Africa. Perk thought of Richard, his younger brother, in the Merchant Marines. The six and a half hour flight passed quickly and Glenn alerted the navigator to be on the lookout for the little island. Using his throat mic he called the navigator, "See anything, Garrick?"

His reply was, "Just a bunch of water, sir. We are looking for latitude 7.9467° South, by Longitude 14.3559° West. It's practically sitting on the Equator, sir." Ascension Island had recently acquired the new High-Frequency Direction-Finding or *huff-duff* as Garrick called it. Lucky for the Perkins group it was a type of high frequency radio direction finder for communication over long distances. It was an instrument the Brits were using to listen in on transmitted enemy U-boat radios. In this case it picked up Cliff Myers radio signals, Perk's radio man, and precisely guided the four B-17s into the island.

Wideawake Army Airfield was named after the colony of sooty tern birds nesting nearby. He alerted his crew and the three other aircraft to watch out for flocks of birds near the base. They could mean disaster if sucked into the engines of planes landing or taking off.

Their landing flight plan called for tracking a course on the eastern side of the island and entering the runway from the south, heading on a north by northwest approach. Perk flew around the inactive volcano toward the south, turning northwest to land. Even though Perk had landed on many short mesh runways during the war, it was always a relief when his wheels touched down without a hitch like they did that day. Perk commented to Glenn, "Well that was like hitting a bullseye on a dart board, floating in a bathtub." The eight-mile-wide island was a British colony where they spoke English and used the British pound. Glenn had commented, they would be right at home after Rattlesden. The other Forts followed and came in, proceeding to their hardstands. Perk and his men jumped out of *Dream Gal* onto the hot black volcanic composite runway.

In the stifling humid July heat, Perk felt the oppressive temperatures as they finally were picked up by jeeps. Standing there waiting on the tarmac he was sweating buckets inside his flight suit and gear. Being so close to the Equator, he encouraged his crew to drink plenty of water. After the shuttle, they checked in at HQ and secured beds for the night. First on their minds was a cold beer but they found the base pub had only warm beer like the English pubs. Perk and Glenn opted for a cold Coca Cola with ice, a couple sandwiches and some chocolate cake. They hit the sack early but it was still sultry hot and they again slept under mosquito nets in their skivvies.

July 13, 1944—Natal, Brazil

On Thursday at 0530 hours, *Dream Gal* and the other B-17s took off from Ascension Island, flying due west toward the eastern coast of Brazil. Their destination was Natal's Parnamirim Field, the biggest US air base outside the US in the western hemisphere. The group was on schedule at 0915 hours, when Glenn spotted some formations of cumulus clouds ahead. As they got closer to the clouds, the roller coaster turbulence was fierce and to avoid collisions, the four aircraft spread apart. Perk ascended to 29 thousand feet to rise above the clouds. Somewhat apprehensively, Glenn asked Garrick, the navigator if this could be a hurricane.

Garrick said, "We might be in the tail end of a cyclone or in a tropical storm. "This close to the Equator, hurricanes are unusual and form much further north or south because of the cold air from the poles." He guessed this was a tropical storm. Perk looked ahead and saw big dense cumulus clouds that billowed high above their altitude. All he could do was fly through them. It was a pretty rough two hour ride until they came out of the storm into clearer skies. Garrick said they had flown a bit off course but eventually the four aircraft reunited and Perk's navigator kept a close watch charting the remainder of the route to Brazil.

After ten long hours they made radio contact with Parnamirim AirField in Natal and Perk was cleared for landing on the main runway. On his approach a red light went on his instrument panel for number three engine and not long after started to sputter. Coincidentally, Lt. Shepard on *Flyin' Ginny* said one of his engines had been acting up, too. Thankfully, all the Forts

Natal, Brazil, Parnamirim Field

made textbook safe landings. They were damn glad to be on the ground after that eventful ten hour flight.

The ground crew at Parnamirim checked out both *Flyin' Ginny's* number four and *Dream Gal's* number three engines and found they were just low on fuel. They were given assurances they were good to go on tomorrow's leg to Belem, Brazil.

After dinner in the mess hall, the crews hit the canteen for a cold beer and met several air crews ferrying B-29s across to North Africa and England. The excitement among the four homeward bound crews was palatable because they were finally on the continent of the Americas. There were no more oceans to cross, no raging wars on the ground beneath and they were closer to their homes. They had successfully made it across the Southern Atlantic. Although no one expressed anxiety before the ocean crossing, his crew, who had St. Christophers and lucky charms, brought them out over the vast expanse of water.

That Damn Number Three Engine!

July 14, 1944—Belem, Brazil

Lt. Thomas Garrick was one of the best and most capable navigators Perk had ever met. He respected and admired his skills, studying charts, maps, weather patterns, tables and conferring with Sgt. Clifford Myers, their radio man who was proficient in radar and signals. Without both of those men's expertise, Perk's crew may not have been so fortunate during their 51 missions. One or two degrees deviation can mean an error of hundreds of miles. Perk and his crew were lucky to have them.

Perk didn't want to admit he was tired. The responsibility of his crew and as lead ship was wearing on him. He thought of a poem by Robert Frost that ended with, "… But I have promises to keep, and miles to go before I sleep, and miles to go before I sleep."

The gaggle of aircraft took off at 0600 hours heading northeast toward Brazil's Belem Airfield. It was a seven hour flight, and he imagined having the afternoon to see one of the famous Brazilian beaches. He had seen a movie in the base theater in Foggia with Carmen Miranda singing, "Ai, Yi Yi Yi." All airmen on the way to Belem imagined Miranda and Betty Grable walking down a beautiful tropical beach in Brazil.

At 1135 hours a red light flashed on Perk's instrument panel. "That damn number three engine!" Glenn swore. Garrick checked his map and said they were 120 miles from Belem. Perk monitored the light for ten minutes and then switched to the auxiliary fuel tank with no improvement. He could see oil and then dark smoke from the engine and he worried about a fire. The prop coughed and sputtered and he feathered the engine and dropped his speed to 130 mph. Glenn alerted the crew although they already knew something was wrong. The other forts saw *Dream Gal* drop down in speed and out of formation as her number three engine stopped. Garrick spoke to Perk about an emergency landing at Sao Luis Airfield which they had already passed. They had a better chance of landing and getting repairs at Belem. Perk and Glenn made the decision to shoot for their original destination, Belem Air Field. Perk used the rudder and flaps to balance the aircraft to keep her level. Glenn advised two of their sister ships to go ahead to Belem. He asked Lt. Frank, on *Royal Flush,* if he would be his escort for the last 125 miles to the airfield. Perk knew this was dicey but he had flown on three engines before, but with 88s and Messerschmitts shooting at him he could do this.

Lt. Shepard on *Flyin' Ginny* led the way and he and *Cincinnati Queen* pulled ahead and eventually disappeared in the distance. It took Perk's total concentration to keep his plane level and his shoulders and upper arms ached. Glenn could take over but Perk decided to fly and land the plane himself, lowering in altitude to 10,000 feet.

The minutes passed slowly as the crew looked down at fishing boats and a few cruisers below. They had limped back to base on past missions and had jettisoned weight, dumping bombs and equipment in farmers' fields or the North Sea. There was nothing extra to throw out on *Dream Gal.* Collier broke the tension speaking into his throat mic, "Maybe we should toss out Bill Moore's lazy lard ass just to stay airborne." It got an obscene response from Moore but broke the stressful atmosphere in the waist. All the crew wore their parachutes and Mae Wests, but none of the men had ever practiced parachuting before. The good news was they weren't over enemy territory. Perk hugged the coastline knowing jumping over land, even if it was a Brazilian jungle, had a better chance of survival than jumping over water.

Within a few miles of Belem Airfield, Perk got clearance to land on the main runway. Reassuringly, a couple of ambulance and fire trucks were waiting, reminding Perk of the delicate off balanced job he had to do to set the bird down gingerly. At that moment he heard Pancho's voice in his head, "You can do it, Red." As all three wheels touched down on the steel mesh runway, the crew cheered. Last minute communication to the tower and they made their way to the nose hangar. Perk thanked Lt. Frank for having his back and promised him a cold beer.

As Perk's crew swung out of the hatch onto the tarmac, the heat and humidity took their breath away. Belem was also close to the Equator and the heat was oppressive. The boys hoisted their gear onto the transport trucks and jumped aboard. It was nice to be traveling on the ground, Perk thought. They were driven to HQ for a debriefing and for sleeping quarters assignments. The heat and humidity zapped Perk's energy and he wondered how the US service men worked all day in this heat. They met up with the crews of *Flyin' Ginny* and *Cincinnati Queen* who had arrived earlier.

They were raring to go to Love Beach and had found a bus that would take them that afternoon. "We're in," said Collier, Moore and Marcuse. At 23, Perk worried about his plane's engine since it was their ride back to the states. The ground crew wouldn't know anything for 24 hours with several other ships in the hangar. He realized he was starving as he jumped in the back seat of the jeep on the way to the mess hall.

This was the first base that had swamp coolers in the officer's canteen. Perk, Glenn, Garrick and Foley talked about the precarious journey from Natal and how they were white-knuckling the last miles to Belem. "I thought those guys at Natel had done a thorough check on the number three engine." Perk said. The CO had told him that Belem had the best U.S. ground crews and an ample parts supply.

With a lot more grumbling and a few sandwiches and cold drinks, the four guys decided to hit the beach with the other crews. Perk hesitated until Garrick badgered him into going along, "When are ya ever gonna be in Brazil again, Perkins?"

In the late afternoon the airmen caught the standing-room-only bus to Love Beach to the north of town. The sultry temperatures had cooled down a bit and an English speaking boy, on the bus, standing near Glenn pointed to their stop for the beach. The airmen jumped off the bus and walked past shacks and curio huts toward the shore. Feeling the cool breeze and smelling the salt air, they arrived at a gorgeous white sand coastline with short cliffs, palm trees and emerald water. It was the most beautiful beach Perk had ever seen. Foley, Garrick and Glenn had their swim trunks on and they left their shirts on the beach and raced into the lapping waves, splashing each other. They hooted and hollered in the surf like children. Then they floated on their backs in the marvelous refreshing water. They had been men fighting a hideous war and now they were boys again.

Perk went in the water for a while but he wasn't a good swimmer, plus he sunburned easily. He grabbed his shirt and walked down the beach and up a grassy cliff where he found the shade of two palm trees where he laid down and fell asleep. After a while Garrick woke him to say they needed to catch the bus back to the base. He had been dreaming about home and Dottie.

After dinner Perk and Glenn went to the nose hangar to see if their ship was fixed and ready for tomorrow's flight. Sgt. Patterson, the head engine mechanic, asked Perk, "Do you want the good news or the bad news first?" Perk said, "Give me the bad news." Patterson replied, "Your engine block on #3 is cracked and two of the cylinder heads are shot. There was oil all over the place. You were lucky it didn't catch fire." He was a plain speaker and chewed on an unlit cigar as he spoke. The engine was on the ground and he pointed at it, "This was an original engine from 1942, and has seen a lot of war. He pointed out the cracked block

Brazil's Belem Airfield

and damage to the cylinder heads. I found pieces of shrapnel inside the housing. You're gonna need a new engine and I can't get one for a week. Mostly now, they are sending parts for B-29s, not B-17s."

Perk said, "If that's the bad news, what's the good news?" Patterson said, chewing his cigar, "Well, the rest of the ship checks out fine and you and your crew get a week to lay on the beach in Brazil."

All of the boys wanted to get back to the states, but they were still in the Army and would be back to work on some Army base or possibly sent to duty in the Pacific War soon enough. Patterson was right. The good news wasn't so bad. It was an all-expense, one week, paid vacation in Brazil.

Perk needed to talk with Lieutenants Frank, Snow, Hansen and Shepard for a consensus of what to do. As far as the Army was concerned their orders were to deliver four B-17 aircraft from

Belem's nose hangars

Foggia, Italy, to Morrison Field, Florida. If some of the airmen wanted to leave tomorrow and not wait for the repairs of one ship, they could leave but they should travel in pairs in case of more mechanical problems. The pilots, co-pilots and Lt. Hansen met in the mess hall that evening. "Which ship will stay the week with us and which two want to leave?" Perk asked.

Lt. Shepard said he was getting married at the end of this month and he was anxious to get back to Harvard Airbase. Sgt. Barker was hoping to get some medical treatment on his legs at Walter Reed and Hansen and Snow just wanted to get back to the states as soon as possible. It was finally agreed that Shepard would take Hansen and Lt. Snow would take Sgt. Barker, leaving tomorrow for Trinidad. Both pilots had room on their planes because neither had a bombardier, giving them space for one man. They should be the ones to go and they got final permission from the base commander to leave the next day. While Perk's crew and that of Lt. Frank waited for plane parts they would be spending time enjoying the tropics. The officers and enlisted crews staying, felt they had pulled the longer straws. There were worse military assignments than swimming the beautiful beaches of Belem in the daytime and enjoying the exuberant nightlife of Brazil at night.

July 15

By 0630 hours *Flyin' Ginny* and *Cincinnati Queen* taxied down the runway on their way to Trinidad, Puerto Rico, and on to Florida while the other two crews slept in, at the barracks. With their week's pass, Perk and his crew decided to get off base and stay in a hotel in town. The old but elegant Palace Hotel in the Para district appealed to the men for its central location, nice rooms, a bar and a good restaurant. Lt. Frank's crew joined them sharing four to a room so the expense was not prohibitive. They met in the Copacabana Lounge in the evening and drank tropical rum drinks with a pineapple garnish. There was a ten piece orchestra and a beautiful Latin singer who sang lyrical songs, some in English and some in Portuguese. They enjoyed watching serious and accomplished dancers do the Samba, Rumba and Tango dressed in colorful costumes. They were on leave for a week and they planned to make the most of every day.

Both Lt. Perkins and Lt. Frank warned their crews about fraternizing with local women or getting into trouble in this Latin country. Ending up in prison in Brazil or worse, in a knife fight would not end well. The men promised to be on their best behavior and to stick together in groups of at least four, especially at night. "Stay out of trouble." Perk and Frank warned. In the Palace Hotel with its white sheets and monogrammed towels, Perk hit the sack just after midnight and was asleep as his head hit the pressed pillow cases.

July 16

After a breakfast of bacon, eggs, biscuits, pineapple, and black coffee, Perk, Garrick, Foley and Glenn were off to explore the city on foot. Since they were free on a pass they didn't have to wear their uniforms and the men changed into white linen shirts, shorts, cheap panama hats and sandals bought in the open marketplace. They passed a couple of their crew members on the street who hardly recognized them. Their friends stopped, turned around and hooted at the three guys' appearance. "Why, Lt. Perkins, I never realized you had such white knees!" Perk had swung around to say something but his crew had turned the corner and disappeared.

The four officers walked to Guajara Bay to the riverfront district and old town. The charming colonial architecture, churches and colorful tile houses had such old world grace. Colorful flower boxes and laundry hung out second story windows and the aroma of Brazilian cooking filled the narrow streets. They finally came upon the three-hundred-year-old Forte do Presepio, an old fortress, and they walked the ramparts and looked out to sea. There were big iron cannons, remnants used to defend against invasion. Perk thought of how far they had come in war armaments with aircraft and jet fueled unmanned rockets.

July 17-20

For the next few days the airmen slept in late, ate like kings, walked all over the old city and spent lots of time at the beach. In the evening they went to the elegant Copacabana Lounge where they enjoyed the Latin dancing and music of Brazil. It would be hard to leave when their airplane was repaired.

Perk had gotten badly sunburned on the first two days and stayed pretty covered up while Gattick, Foley and Glenn continued to get substantial Brazilian tans. Perk made the comment, "You guys look like you have gone native, where I just look like a red lobster." Through those days on leave, Lieutenants Perkins and Frank continued to play den mother to their crews, checking to see if all men were accounted for each morning. Only once there was some concern about Marcuse, Warren and Myers who were drinking at a beach bonfire and they fell asleep and woke up at dawn still on the beach. Marcuse also had lost his wallet with $30 in it and he had to get a new ID at the base headquarters. His most egregious loss was his prized collection of pretty pin up girl photos which he said were irreplaceable.

July 21

Dream Gal's replacement Pratt and Whitney R-1690 engine had arrived the night before on a Gooney Bird C-47 cargo plane. The ground crew already had the old number three engine out and the new one on the hoist platform ready to be lifted into place. By the next day Sgt. Patterson said she'd be test flown, refueled and ready to go tomorrow at 0730 hours. Patterson was a talker and he told Perk about a Para restaurant located in a neighborhood not far from the open marketplace. He raved about the authentic Brazilian food and Perk said he would check it out.

That last night Perk and his fellow officers invited the rest of their enlisted crew to dine with them at *Brazilia Paraense,* the home restaurant that Patterson recommended. The seafood was outstanding, cooked with Amazonian tribe recipes using different spices. They ate Filhote, a fish from the Amazon river, cooked with tomatoes, onions and Jambu, a type of watercress served over rice. Melena, the matriarch, brought the men delicious Caipirinha, lime and soda drinks with Cachaca, a type of rum, of which they each had several. For dessert the family served the airmen paraense fruits and local chocolate from Combu Island. It was a warm and delightful celebration of their last day in Brazil. Before the flyboys left the para restaurant, the family hugged all the men. Perk would not forget the colorful Afro-Latin dance, music and food of beautiful Brazil.

July 22, 1944—Trinidad, British Crown Colony

At 0630 hours the men's gear was loaded onto the two aircraft and Perkins and Frank took off east over the Atlantic and banked northwest toward Trinidad's Waller Field, 1370 miles away. The two forts hoped to be there in eight or nine hours given the air currents and wind conditions. Perk had confidence in Patterson's assurance that both ships were in tip top shape for their trip to Florida. To play it safe Perk opted for a refueling stop in Puerto Rico at Borinquen Field to be on the safe side. It was between Waller and Homestead in Florida. Before he left Belem, the commanding officer told Perk that both Lt. Shepard and Snow had successfully reached Morrison AirField on July 18th, a great relief to Perk.

Garrick navigated both planes, pinpointing them onto the main runway at Waller Field. *Dream Gal* and *Royal Flush* had performed like champs. The air base was congested with aircraft and reminded Perk of Rattlesden. This little known base had become the most trafficked destination in the South Atlantic Route to Africa and Europe. After a quick meal at the mess hall the airmen hit the sack early. Perk stayed up to write a quick letter to Dottie about their Latin adventures.

July 23, 1944—Puerto Rico, U.S. Territory

At 0900 hours the two B-17s took off for Puerto Rico. Garrick reported the destination latitude as 18.5026° N above the Equator, by 67.1409° west of the Prime Meridian. Borinquen Army Airfield was in the upper eastern corner of the island. Perk had loved reading Robert Louis Stevenson's *Treasure Island* as a boy, a book about pirates and buried treasure in the Caribbean. In fact, Black Beard had been in the Caribbean in Puerto Rico, Antigua, St Vincent and Santa Lucia islands.

After the wonderful week they spent in Brazil, Perk, Glenn and Garrick had talked about exploring both Trinidad and Puerto Rico. Unfortunately, their stays on those islands would be too short to see much, other than the US bases. The crews were getting anxious to get back to the states and they had been expected at Morrison Airfield a week ago.

Back in the USA

July 24, 1944—Tampa, Florida

That morning, Perk and his crew made the eight hour flight from Puerto Rico to Tampa, Florida. It was supposed to be their last stop in their Southern Atlantic route to deliver their aircraft to Morrison AirField. He landed *Dream Gal* without any hitches and *Royal Flush* followed behind him successfully landing, ending their adventurous flight home to America. It was a journey that was supposed to take 11 days, but because of the engine replacement in Brazil, took three weeks. His crew had become close in the ten months, sharing the task of staying alive while doing a job the Army had assigned them.

That evening Perk used a personnel phone to call his mother. He was allowed five minutes and he called when he thought she and the family would be home finishing up with dinner. His mom answered and he said, "Hi Mom, it's Clarence."

"Oh my heavens!" she shouted. "Fred. Come quick. It's Clarence!"

Perk then said, "Mom I only have four minutes. Do you have a pencil and paper? Take this address down." He spoke in short clear calming sentences because he could hear his mother's voice shaking. "I am stationed at Fort Worth Army AirField, Fort Worth, Texas, RTU, 300 West Lancaster Ave, Fort Worth, TX. Did you get all that?" She said she did, and she read it back to him. Perk had only time to say he was fine and he was going to Nebraska to see Dottie next week. He hoped to be home soon and he would call them back later. They both said they loved each other and the line went dead.

July 25, 1944—Tucson, Arizona

Lieutenants Perkins and Frank were assigned orders at Tucson to deliver the B-17s *Dream Gal* and *Royal Flush* to Davis-Monthan Air Force Base in Tucson, Arizona. Both aircraft took off at 0700 and flew 1720 miles to the 309th Maintenance and Regeneration Group's airfield. They were directed to park their aircraft among acres of other stationary aircraft. There were B-17s, Liberators, Stearman, P-47s and some aircraft Perk couldn't identify. He even saw an old Travel Air 4000 like Pancho's. The hundreds of aircraft couldn't be all waiting for the scrap bin? Perhaps they were to be assigned to the conflict in the South Pacific or sold for civilian use. Perk had heard about sales to countries building their military air force or domestic sales for use in mail and passenger transport. Davis-Monthan acted as a parts warehouse to resupply aircraft from combat bases around the world. Perhaps Perk's last engine replacement received in Belem, Brazil, came from Davis-Monthan.

He and Glenn looked out at the other old B-17Fs parked wing to wing and he realized just how many of the thousands of aircraft produced for the war might end up here or at other bases they were now calling boneyards. The name made it sound like a graveyard for aircraft; those shiny machines that had been meticulously constructed by thousands of workers in factories across the country. These airships had served their noble purpose of helping to win a war, but now there was no more honorable job for them than delivering mail in a banana republic where aircraft repair parts were scarce? It was a demoralizing end for those Fortresses that had carried airmen on missions and to a probable victory in Europe.

At one time he would have given his eye teeth for a crack at owning one of those planes. He recalled his original plan of owning a small airplane and working as an engineer to support it.

That had changed. Had he gotten air flight out of his system? He had seen how fast lives end in an airplane. He was a practical guy. At this point, Perk hoped the Army would assign him something with his feet on solid ground.

Perk and Glenn stood looking up at the fuselage of *Dream Gal* in its final destination. Perk said, "She has been a trustworthy friend, delivering us from the Mediterranean Theater of Operations." They had flown across the Atlantic to South America, landing in the Caribbean and flying north to Florida. Now he and Glenn were standing in an Arizona boneyard, looking at the fortress that had brought them home. What an inglorious end he thought.

He didn't remember every ship he had flown on missions but certain B-17s stood out in his mind during his tour in England and Italy. Perk said to Glenn, "The fort we took possession of at Harvard Air Force Base, *Dead Man's Hand,* was a brand new ship. What a beautiful aircraft she was. Other ships I remembered us flying, were *Scheherazade, Moonbeam, Big Stoop,* and then *Dream Gal.* Those were ships that had all been dependable aircraft." He said, nodding his head. "We flew several of them multiple times and they served us well under the most dangerous circumstances. He said, "I wondered how many of them were still in service."

Perk didn't articulate it then, and he dared to think about it now but during most of his missions he felt like a duck at a duck hunt. While he flew in formation, the Nazis 88mm flak air defensive shells exploded all around him while German 109s and 190 fighters were shooting at their ship. At the end of each mission he felt like his number just hadn't come up yet. Perk felt damn lucky to have survived an incredible 51 combat missions. That was something to celebrate.

Whether his luck was due to a series of circumstances; his two years experience of training for his civil pilots license, before the war, might have somehow benefited his high number of successful missions. Perk and Glenn talked about their training in 1943 and flying their first mission in January 1944. "That was a few months after those horrific air battles at Ploesti, Romania, in August and at Schweinfurt in October, where 114 aircraft had been shot down and all those crews lost." Glenn lamented.

Perk said, "In those later years of the war, after 1942, there were improvements in aircraft and protective equipment. Hap Arnold's design of tighter formation structure, with escorts protecting the formations to the target and back, probably improved our odds of success. That began with our first mission. The new PFF radar system and Norden Bomb Site made it easier to find the targets in overcast weather and gave us a higher rate of success on missions. "We were really lucky to have flown when we did."

Still out of 51 combat missions, he could recall six terrifying raids where he wondered how they made it back to the base. Perk remembered, "We took a terrible beating on several occasions and tried to return to the base without the security of the formation. On a couple of those harrowing missions we were so badly shot up and were fortunate to have one or two P-51 fighter escorts join us just in the nick of time." Perk remembered, "On one return, the Mustangs were engaged in a 45 minute dog fight with four German Messerschmitts. Man oh man!"

Glenn reminded him, "What about the time flak hit the windshield and sent a chunk into your face and knocked you out cold. The wind was coming in so fast through the hole in the cockpit, I almost called for a bail out. But you came to, and we were able to get the ship back under control and return to base."

Glenn put his boot on the inside tire of the landing gear. He remembered February 10th, their mission to Braunschweig, Germany, where they came under heavy attack by German fighters. "Remember, we lost an engine, had an electrical fire in the waist, and our oxygen and all hydraulics were shot out. Losing altitude and low on fuel, we realized we couldn't make it back to

Rattlesden. And, as if nothing else could go wrong, we flew into a snowstorm over the English Channel. Garrick had found the closest Allied runway and cleared the Cliffs of Dover. We waited until the very last minute to lower the manual landing gear, only to find, they were jammed."

Oh God, "I remember." Perk said, "I had no choice but to belly-land the ship. We came in hot, sliding sideways into a snow field at the end of the runway. Oh man! That was dicey. The silence of being stopped after the clatter and roar of a crash landing. The astonished look on each of the crew's faces was incredible. And none of us had a scratch on that mission or landing." He shook his head and chuckled. Glenn kicked the tire with his boot. "The durability of these B-17s and the tenacity of our crew, saved their lives." He and Glenn hopped on an air transport back to Tampa Florida and got back by midnight.

Standing in Florida after returning from overseas, none of his crew expected much fanfare. Those guys on the Memphis Belle with their 25 combat missions were welcomed home at a ticker-tape parade in New York. Perk's crew was like hundreds of other airmen who had done their jobs and returned quietly to the states. Their reward was survival because many airmen had not survived. But the war wasn't over yet. Hitler wasn't defeated although every day brought more favorable reports that the Allied armies were getting closer to Berlin.

Perk had been assigned to his crew, just ten months prior, in October 1943. Glenn Halverson, his co-pilot, had saved his behind many times in the air. Tom Garrick had navigated them through most of their missions with expert skills knowing one wrong calculation could get them killed. He never saw him make a mistake. Foley, his bombardier, mostly hit his mark and was headed to flight training for Mustang Fighters. Overton was not just our guardian angel, offering first aid to the crew but he had kept the Jerrys off the roof in his top turret. Myers was a radio hound, providing contact with bases and finding radar signals on the North and South Atlantic crossings. Marcuse was a darn good waist gunner. Bill Moore made up in courage and bravery for his short stature, picked specifically for the most dangerous job on the plane, a crack shot as their tail gunner. Warren and Don Collier claimed many kills as gunners and had many fine leadership skills on their missions. It was unusual for a single crew to remain together for as long as the Perkins crew. After those frenzied bombing missions in England and Italy, his crew had become like brothers.

Perk and Glenn smiled about those liberty passes to London and Bournemouth. "They were like an education abroad, for those 18-23 year old guys. Most of us had never been away from home before the war, like me," Perk laughed. "And on the way back to the states, the week-long stop in Brazil was a highlight he would not soon forget."

Goodbyes and New Assignments

July 26, 1944

After working together as a team for almost a year, they were going their separate ways. Perk hoped they would keep in touch but he couldn't be sure they would. He had become good friends with Glenn, a classmate in pilot training and with Tom Garrick. He liked them both a lot. Glenn's family lived but a four hour drive from Perk's family home and they were the most likely crew members to keep in touch.

On that last day before the Perkins crew set off to their separate assignments, the men exchanged addresses of their parents' houses, knowing they could be found there. Most of them said they hoped to get together with the crew again, after the war was over. They all marveled at the unusual fact the crew stayed intact and no one was badly injured on missions other than catching some shrapnel or frostbite.

Perk came up to each of his crew, men he highly respected. There was no question they owed each other their lives. He looked each one in the eyes and gave them a firm handshake. He said a few words to each man, nodding and pursing his lips so as not to show the emotion he felt. Each man was leaving for different parts of the country with new orders. Fighting in those hellish skies over Europe, they all had earned his admiration and Perk certainly had theirs. Don shared the sentiments of the whole crew when he saluted Perk and said, "It has been an honor to serve with you, sir."

After that, each NCO was given a week's pass to go home, see their family or sweetheart before starting their new assignment with the Army. Officers were given two weeks. Some were hitching rides with transports, some boys bought Greyhound bus tickets and others had family picking them up. Most of Perk's crew would never see each other again.

July 27

Perk was assigned to Fort Worth Army AirField, at Fort Worth, Texas. He was able to get on a transport airplane, a short hop from Florida. Mostly, what he was thinking was how short it was to Colorado where Dottie was working. He was assigned to a RTU or Replacement Training Unit in Texas. It was a B-29 heavy bomber school used for the transition of pilots, copilots and flight engineers. B-17s and B-24s were being phased out as B-29s were being delivered and progression in the aerial war in Europe needed replacements.

The B-29 Superfortress was twice the size of the B-17 and could fly faster and longer. It had an analog computer-controlled system that allowed an operator to direct four remote machine gun turrets. The 28-cylinder Pratt and Whitney 3500 horsepower engine was 60% more powerful than the B-17 engines. Although the new B-29s had fires and overheating, common because of the double stack cylinder configuration, leading to temperatures as high as 300 degrees. This had led to 20 crashes due to non-combat mechanical errors. They found it hard to do maintenance on parts, too. Perk was impatient with the delays in delivery of the B-29s which further impeded its training program.

B-17s and B-24s had flight engineers but the Boeing B-29 Superfortress needed a flight engineer with his own control panel stationed right behind the pilot. The panel contained all operating instruments except those the pilot used to control the altitude and direction of the B-29. The flight engineer computed the aircraft's engine performance, weight and balance and fuel consumption from the control panel, relaying it to the pilot. The pressurized and heated cabin made a big difference to the crew because they no longer needed oxygen masks or heated suits. Those essential features, if present in the B-17 bomber, would have saved countless lives as men passed out at 30,000 feet, silently dying from oxygen deprivation or freezing at 60 degrees below zero. Simple features that didn't exist in the Eighth Armies aerial combat equipment in 1942.

Flying B-29s and B-17s in February 1945, the U.S. bombing campaign reached a high point with a 1,000 bomber raid on Berlin escorted by 400 fighter planes. The Dresden raid had 1300 Royal Air Force Lancasters, which caused a devastating fire storm that destroyed the city. Advancing 82nd and 101st Airborne allied troops liberated concentration camps, Dachau and Auschwitz, which made the extent of the Holocaust clearer to the Allies. The Pacific war was a different story. Triumph over the Japanese had a long way to go before there was a clear road to victory. An invasion of the islands of Japan was expected but the extended Pacific war in the Dutch East Indies (Indonesia), Malaya and China could go on for years at the cost of many more Allied lives. Still there were favorable reports in the news about the Japanese being routed from Burma and Saipan, with a strong offensive going on in the Philippines.

FDR and Churchill made it a point to meet on several occasions, during the course of the war, to plan their strategy of victory. Between 1941-1944 they met at least four times at FDR's Hyde Park home. In August 1943 they agreed to collaborate on the scientific research of the British Tube Alloy project with the U.S. Manhattan Project to develop an atomic bomb. Both men agreed it would be kept secret, especially from the Russians. They discussed the intelligence information, that German scientists were already developing an atomic weapon, themselves. The U.S. / British shared agreement included the possibility of using the atomic bomb against both the Germans and the Japanese.

11.

Beginnings and Endings

July 28

In the mess hall Perk ran into a friend, Roger Halburn from Basic Training in Santa Ana. Perk had gone on to air cadet training and his friend had gone to mechanics school at Kirtland Air Force base in New Mexico and had been stationed at Fort Worth for servicing and replacing engines of B-17s, B-24s and B-29s. Perk had done a favor for Roger in Basic Training that he never forgot. Roger went out on a bender and was AWOL (absent without leave) and Perk got Roger back in his barracks with no one the wiser.

As the two men left the mess hall, Roger climbed into a black 1938 Ford Sedan and Perk was impressed and asked Roger how he ranked on his pay driving such a nice car. He explained he bought it from his father to get to and from Los Angeles where his family lived. His father had a few contracts with the Army and had bought another car. Mechanical issues with the old Ford were never an issue because Roger was a good mechanic. The gas rationing stickers imposed at the beginning of the war made it difficult for him to get too far each month, but he had his ways to acquire gasoline.

"I hate to ask, Roger, but could I borrow your car? I need to get to Hastings, Nebraska, to ask my girl, Dottie, to marry me," said Perk. He had been thinking about asking her for months. In Fort Worth, Texas, he was the closest to Dottie in Nebraska. The closest he had been in over a year and he didn't want to lose his chance to see her.

Roger said, "Well, I am stuck on duty for two weeks and you are welcome to borrow my car. The problem will be getting gasoline." Roger said he might be able to help with that, too. Perk had a total of 20 gallons of gas ration cards, not enough to drive to Nebraska and back. Roger worked on B-29s at the Fort Worth Airbase and he found the aircraft engines would sweat off fuel when they first were started. Roger collected the few droplets of avgas in pans and carefully transferred them to barrels. Technically the gas was used to start the engines and the drips would have ended up on the ground anyway. Roger kept the gas in drums in the trunk of his car. There was only one problem. The military added red dye to their aviation fuel, checking cars for the pink gas as they left the base, in order to keep theft down.

Perk asked if he could get arrested for this and Roger said, "They check the gas tanks but never the locked trunk of my car because they know me and my car." He told Perk to first buy five gallons of regular gas on his ration card for his tank to get off the base. The fifty gallons should get him to Nebraska to see Dottie. How he got gas to drive back to Fort Worth, was his problem. Perk had a couple of gas rationing cards for his way back.

Perk was a little nervous about exiting the base with what could be construed as contraband gas, but there was no problem especially at 0600 hours. The guards were a little sleepy and didn't ask to check the tank. He drove north toward Oklahoma City and after a hundred miles he pulled off on a country road and closed his eyes for a bit when he found himself nodding at the wheel. When he woke after half an hour he checked the gas level with a dipstick and filled the Ford's gas tank with a siphoning hose from the trunk's avgas stores. He breezed through Oklahoma City and when he got to Wichita, he stopped for food and coffee and a phone call to Captain Floyd McComas, a buddy who lived in Harvard Air Force base housing. Floyd lived with his wife and baby and he invited Perk to his house for a shower and a sandwich.

Then he called Dottie's parents' house and learned she was working at the base and got off at 5:30. He got the number for the colonel's office and called Dottie. He recognized her voice when she said, "Colonel Shay's office."

"Hi, Dottie. It's me, Perk."

"Oh, my gosh Perk is that really you?! I can't believe it. Where are you? When did you get back?" she asked.

"It took us three weeks to fly back from Italy by way of South America, with a delay because of a busted engine. I got back to Fort Worth, Texas, two days ago and I couldn't wait to see you. Can you have dinner with me tonight?" Perk said hopefully.

"Oh my! You are here. Yes, my girlfriend, Lorene Mans and I were just going to a movie with a group of girls from the secretarial pool but I much rather see you."

"Ok, I'll pick you up at 5:30, when you get off work. Is that OK?" Perk asked. His heart was racing. He had secured a date but now what? He had been thinking for a year, just what he would say to Dottie the first time he saw her. "I've missed you. I have not stopped thinking about you. What are you doing for the rest of your life?" None of it seemed right. Hopefully, it would come to him when he saw her. He hadn't been this nervous when he met her parents for the first time. "I can do this." he reassured himself.

It was a hot day in Hastings as Perk stood leaning against the Ford sedan in his tan uniform waiting for Dottie to walk out the door of her work. It had been almost a year since he had seen her and he was nervous. After a few minutes she emerged and walked toward him smiling. She was wearing a white print dress and black and white shoes. He stood up straight looking at her. He thought how pretty she was with her red curly shoulder length hair backlit in the late afternoon sun. She had turned twenty-one the day after his twenty-third birthday in April. She seemed more a woman and less a girl now. She smiled even more broadly at him. "Welcome back, Perky." she said, as she walked up to him and gave him a big hug. "I can't believe you're here."

They looked into each other's faces and he kissed her. It was something he had thought about for so long. The kiss lasted longer than expected and they both were a little embarrassed. He let go and cleared his throat. "Umm, how about dinner?" he said as he opened the passenger door for her.

"Wow Perk, where did you get the car?"

"I borrowed it from Roger, a friend at the base in Fort Worth. It's a long story. Get in and I'll explain." he continued, "Let's go to the Clarke Hotel?" He said, "It is the only place with an elegant dining room with an orchestra."

The time flew by that night and Dottie and Perk talked about what they had been doing in the eleven months since he had been gone. Perk didn't want to talk about his missions flying B-17s. He told her a little about Brazil and flying back to the states. He wanted to hear all about what she had been doing, what had happened in the U.S. and what her family was doing. At the end of the evening, she asked him to go with her family to Peaceful Valley for the weekend and he accepted.

It was a warm clear day in early August for a picnic and a hike up to Emerald Lake, near the cabin. Ann had packed a sack lunch of sandwiches, fruit and cookies in a backpack. Perk and Dottie stopped on the edge of the lake and sat on a massive rock eating their picnic lunch. Perk said, "I've had a lot of time to think about you while I was overseas and I decided that anything I want to do in my life, I want you to be by his side. I fell in love with you before I went overseas but didn't feel I could tell you in case I didn't come home."

Dottie said, "I feel the same way about you, Perk. I love you, too."

By Emerald Lake that day, while she sat on a big boulder, he got down on one knee and asked her to marry him. Dottie said, "Yes, I'll marry you." She put her arms around his neck and kissed him.

Perk stood up, addressed the echoing peaks surrounding the lake, and shouted, "Dottie Bouricius is going to marry me!" They giggled their way down the trail past streams on the way back to the cabin.

Perk had to get back to Fort Worth Air Force Base to return the car to Roger and pick up his orders. Before the couple left Peaceful Valley, Guy and Ann gave them a prenuptial dinner with eight friends. They were

E. SATURDAY, AUG. 19, 1944

Mrs. Clarence A. Perkins was Miss Dorothy I. Bouricius, daughter of Mr. and Mrs. G. Bouricius of Hastings, before her marriage on August 11 to First Lieutenant Perkins of Los Angeles, Calif.

Dorothy Bouricius Weds Lieutenant C. A. Perkins

Mr. and Mrs. G. Bouricius of Hastings announce the marriage of their daughter Dorothy I. to First Lieutenant Clarence A. Perkins, son of Mr. and Mrs. John A. Perkins of Los Angeles, Calif. The wedding took place at Smith Center, Kan., on Friday, August 11.

The couple was attended by Miss Lorena Mains of Hastings and Captain Floyd G. McComas Jr., of the Harvard air field.

The bride wore a white silk street-length dress and a corsage of red roses. She also wore a white hand-carved necklace which the bridegroom brought to her from Africa.

Miss Mains chose a lavender linen dress and her corsage was of white carnations.

Mrs. Perkins graduated from Hastings high school and attended Hastings College for two years where she was affiliated with Chi Omega Psi society. She was also a member of the Order of Job's

from Palmdale high school in California and attended Antelope Valley Junior College for two years before entering the army. He was stationed at the Harvard air field in the summer of 1943 and left in November for overseas duty. He completed 51 missions in England and Italy as pilot of a B-17 bomber and received the Air Medal with four oak leaf clusters. He returned to the United States the first part of this month.

A prenuptial dinner was held for the bride Thursday evening preceding her marriage. It was held at the Carter Hotel with eight guests attending. The evening was spent quietly.

Sunday evening the couple was honored at an informal reception and dinner at the Harvard air field Officers Club. Twenty-five close friends of the couple were guests. Lieutenant Louis Ziff was in charge of the arrangements for the affair.

Lieutenant and Mrs. Perkins

Mrs. and Lt. Perkins

given 40 gallons in gas ration cards and with what was left in the trunk tanks of the Ford sedan, they would make it back to Fort Worth.

Perk and Dottie didn't have much time for preparation. At 1100 hours Dottie walked down the aisle in her white silk dress wearing a corsage of red roses and the carved necklace Perk had bought for her in Africa. She looked beautiful walking toward Perk who stood at the altar in his immaculate uniform. The wedding took place at Smith Center, Kansas, on August 11th, 1944. The rest of the ceremony was a blur until the pastor said, "By the powers vested in me I now pronounce you, Mrs. and Lieutenant Perkins." Their friends, Lorene and Floyd acted as witnesses and grinned as Perk and Dottie walked back down the aisle as a married couple.

Following the Justice of the Peace ceremony they had a dinner at the Harvard Officers Club with Lorene, Floyd and 16 other friends in attendance. Perk had finished his training at Fort Worth in a couple of days and was assigned to the Examining Board Training for Recruitment in Los Angeles. The couple took a bus to L.A. calling it their honeymoon even though Perk would be working.

Ruth and Bob Hepting—February, 1945

After his first tour of 52 missions flying Black Cat PB4Y's, in the South Pacific, Bob had returned to California for training in the new PB4y2 model seaplanes. Bob reported to North Island Naval Station, San Diego. He and Ruth, his wife of two years, lived a few miles north in a small cottage by the coast in La Jolla. Their little white rental house was in a courtyard of small bungalows that faced each other in a "U" shape. The Heptings were introduced to the other tenants on the courtyard and were soon invited to a Friday night barbeque by one of the Naval officers also renting there.

They got to know the other residents and enjoyed sitting and talking on their front step during the evenings. Early spring was a wonderful time for Ruth and Bob as they appreciated the perfect climate and beautiful sunsets. Those four months passed quickly as Bob finished his training. The time had been the happiest for them as they spent weekends walking on the beach and renting bikes in the beautiful small village of La Jolla. At the end of May, Bob got orders to return to the South Pacific on the same day Ruth found out she was pregnant.

"What shall we name the baby?" Ruth asked. "How about Frank or Harry if it's a boy," she suggested.

Grinning at her, Bob said, "And if it's a girl, how about Nancy after my favorite song."

As Bob packed up to leave, she made him promise to return to her. Ruth went home to her parents in Peaceful Valley to await the birth of her baby and Bob took a flight to Honolulu on his way to Tinian Island, where he was stationed. He hung a pair of baby booties in his airplane while on missions.

The war in the Pacific continued, as the Allies had victories at the battles of Iwo Jima, The Philippines and Okinawa. Bob and his crew were given a mission flying from Tinian on reconnaissance, inside Cam Ranh Bay in French Indochina.

Four months into her pregnancy, Ruth was staying at her parents' house in Hastings and she received a telegram from the war department. "We regret to inform you that your husband, Lt. J. G. Robert E. Hepting, is missing in action." She sank to the floor with the telegram in her hand, hardly able to catch her breath. There had to be some mistake. He had promised to come back safe to her. There was little information on Bob and she resigned herself to wait and hope that news was wrong and he would return.

Ruth felt the baby growing in her, but grief and worry were such overpowering emotions. Most of the time she felt paralyzed with fear that he wouldn't come home. She fantasized Bob was on an island, somewhere in the Pacific, trying to get back to her.*

The Death of Roosevelt, Mussolini and Hitler

It was significant that before the end of April 1945, three of the leaders of the Axis and Allied powers would be dead and Germany's surrender would soon follow. Franklin D. Roosevelt died of a heart attack in office on April 12, 1945, at Warm Springs, Georgia, and the nation went into mourning. Winston Churchill wrote, "It is cruel that he will not see the Victory which he did so much to achieve. In FDR there died the greatest American friend we have ever known." Sixteen days later on April 28, Mussolini and his girlfriend were shot by partisans while escaping to Switzerland. On April 30, Hitler took his own life in his bunker in Berlin. Eight days after that, on May 8th, Victory over Europe was declared.

After President Roosevelt's death in office and his Vice President took over the office of the Presidency, The American people were tired of war and felt that they had already given too much of their young men. President Truman looked at the high casualty counts of allied soldiers, Americans were still dying in those

---

* The war correspondent, Ernie Pyle wrote, "That is our war, and we will carry it with us as we go on from one battleground to another until it is all over, leaving some of us behind on every beach, in every field... I don't know whether it was their good fortune or their misfortune to get out of it so early in the game. I guess it doesn't make any difference, once a man has gone. Medals and speeches and victories are nothing to them anymore. They died and others lived and nobody knows why it is so. They died and thereby the rest of us can go on and on." Ernie Pyle was killed on April 18, 1945, by enemy fire on the island of Shima.

places like The Philippines, Iwo Jima and Okinawa. Men were coming home after the victories in Europe, and were preparing to go fight in the Pacific war.

The Nuclear Bomb

July 1945

The Greyhound bus sped south down Highway 1, passing the small New Mexico town of Truth or Consequences. "That's a quirky name for a town out in the middle of nowhere," Dottie whispered to her infant in her lap. It had been a long tiring eleven hour ride from Denver, Colorado. She and her three month old son, Gary, were on their way to meet her husband, Perk, stationed at the Las Cruces Air Force Station. She tried to quiet her baby, as his whimpers turned into wails. In those pre-dawn hours, on July 16th, everyone had been asleep on the darkened bus. She threw a blanket over her shoulder and began nursing her baby which satisfied and calmed him. The lady who had occupied the seat next to her was kind enough to move to another empty seat to give the young mother more room. "Finally, he's asleep." Dottie muttered. She looked wearily at the luminescent watch Perk had given her for her birthday. It read 5:07 in the morning. Fatigue and monotony overcame her and she closed her eyes. The rhythm of the wheels on the road made her eyes heavy and her limbs felt like lead weights.

After a time, Dottie was awakened by a commotion and loud talking in the back of the bus. She squinted at a bright light out her window toward the east. Illuminating the landscape was an enormously big fireball that moved up from the ground on a stem, increasing in height and volume. She wasn't certain what she was seeing but within the loud conversations she heard someone say, *"explosion."* In the distance the big yellow mushroom rose higher from the desert floor, sucking up energy from its tree trunk, increasing in size and billowing up higher into the dawn sky. She stared at the eerie scene, mesmerized, as people on the bus stood up and leaned over the seats on her side of the aisle to get a better look.

One man had a camera and snapped a picture. "It might be some kind of munitions explosion from the Army base," he said.

Two elderly ladies sitting two rows up from Dottie, discussed it, "I said to Ralph the other day, having so many POWs living near us was trouble. Jane, you don't think they might have sabotaged…"

Dottie stopped listening. Gary was still asleep on the seat next to her, but in the distance, the billowing cloud of light rose miles up, elongating at the stem as the bus continued south.

First atomic bomb test, July 16, 1945 at Alamogordo
bombing range, New Mexico

The war in Europe had ended in May, with the unconditional surrender of Germany. Perk and his crew had returned home to the U.S. and had been given other Army assignments. The protracted war with Japan had gone on for almost four years with no end in sight. Dottie had six people in her family, in the armed services. Her sister, Lavonne, and brother, Bob, had been stationed in the Pacific. Bart and Willard were working for the Army Corp of Engineers stationed at Alamogordo, New Mexico. Ruth's husband, Bob Hepting, was missing-in-action somewhere in the Pacific, while they were expecting a baby in December.

Perk's brother, Maurice, had been killed at Guadalcanal and his brother, Richard, had joined the Merchant Marines, stationed on a ship, somewhere in the Pacific. Dottie's husband had been assigned to recruit young airmen for the Air Force cadet program.

Disheartened, she thought, "I am so ready for the whole rotten war to be over." She glanced nervously back at the big cloud of violet smoke in the distance. "What *WAS* that thing?" she muttered. Her question remained unanswered as the Greyhound passengers settled back into their seats. The engine of the bus hummed and the coach gently rocked its way down the road as they moved further away from the tall fireball.

Dottie stepped down from the bus holding her son and a diaper bag over her shoulder. They had finally arrived in Las Cruces and a kind porter helped with her two suitcases. She was glad to call Mesilla Park home, at least for a few months while Perk was stationed nearby.

August 1945

As the world rejoiced about Germany's unconditional surrender on May 7th, 1945, the war continued in the Pacific. It had been two weeks since the Army Corps of Engineers at Los Alamos had successfully tested the first atomic bomb in the desert at White Sands, New Mexico. On August 6th, the top-secret mission of a B-29 Superfortress, named Enola Gay, took off from Tinian Island, in the Marianas, bound for Hiroshima, Japan. The pilot, Colonel Paul Tibbets had been briefed on the target and payload bomb, weighing 9,700 pounds. The Manhattan Project scientists ironically called their creation, *Little Boy*.

Flying at an altitude of 31,000 feet, Tibbets arrived at the target and released the bomb at precisely 8:15 AM. He immediately dove his aircraft away to avoid the coming shock wave. It took 53 seconds for *Little Boy* to fall to the predetermined detonation height of 1,968 feet above the target city of Hiroshima. Although Tibbets had already flown 12 miles away, the Enola Gay was violently rocked by the horrendous blast. The crew strained to look back at Hiroshima. "The city was hidden by the cloud boiling up, mushrooming, terrible and incredibly tall," Tibbets recalled. The Enola Gay successfully returned to Tinian Island along with her two escort B-29s.

The terrible destruction and fire enveloping the city of Hiroshima caused a firestorm over a five-mile radius reducing the city to ash. A piece of Hindu scripture was quoted by Oppenheimer, the father of the atomic bomb: "Now I am become Death, the destroyer of worlds."

Emperor Hirohito did not acknowledge the destruction of Hiroshima. President Truman and his military advisors waited three days for some response from Japan, expecting a surrender. None came. They had no choice but to authorize a second atomic bomb to be dropped on the Japanese city of Kokura. A more powerful plutonium bomb, *Fat Man*, weighing 10,800 pounds was loaded on another B-29 named *Bockscar* and piloted by Major Charles Sweeny. Again, the heavy aircraft took off from Tinian Island, on its way to the target. Bad weather necessitated a change from the city of Kokura to the secondary target of Nagasaki. Nestled in a narrow valley between mountains, Sweeny delivered his device to its destination. The contained valley-like topography of the city of Nagasaki, reduced the bomb's effect, limiting the destruction to two and a half mile radius with no firestorm that followed. The message finally got to Japanese Prime Minister Tojo and Emperor Hirohito. Their government finally agreed to a full and unconditional surrender.

By July, 1945 Japan controlled over 463 million people, or 20% of the world's population in occupied regions and territories of the Pacific and China. With the dropping of the two atomic bombs on Japan, the death toll on Hiroshima was 140,000 people while 64,000 had died at Nagasaki. The rationalization of the decision to drop the bombs on Japan was to save more lives with a quicker end to the war. The possible years of battle required to retake the Japanese conquered lands would have certainly cost considerably more lives on both sides.

September

The war was over for the fighting men in the Pacific and in Europe and for the Perkins and Bouricius families, who had spent the years waiting and supporting their sons and daughters in the military. It was over for those who had given their lives and for those who survived the terrible odds. On September 2, 1945 the official *Japanese Instrument of Surrender*, took place aboard the ship, the USS Missouri in Tokyo Bay which effectively ended World War II.

Six weeks after Ruth received the telegram from the war department that Bob Hepting was missing in action, the Bouricius family went to a celebration in Estes Park, Colorado, and watched townspeople join in the exuberant celebration of the end of the war. They beat on dishpans and screamed excitedly and hugged each other with the words, "The war is over!" Ruth touched her right side of her stomach as her baby kicked in her womb. She also felt the telegram in her left pocket reading, "We regret to inform you that your husband, Lt J. G. Robert E. Hepting, is missing in action."

The agonizing news of her husband's fate came not long after the end of the war. A letter arrived from one of her husband's three crew members who had survived the plane crash of their PBY Catalina SeaPlane. Taken back to the Philippine Islands, one of Bob Hepting's crew, Hank Mathews, took time to write a letter to Ruth.

"As Lt. Hepting was flying our Black Cat, low on a reconnaissance night mission in French IndoChina, our aircraft took a direct hit by Japanese land artillery. Our engine was shot out and Bob courageously landed the burning aircraft on the water in Cam Ranh Bay. The plane made a hard landing and flipped over. Lieutenant Bob Hepting was killed on impact. Three of our crew were able to get out of the sinking plane and swim to shore. Two of us had major injuries. The seaplane sank in two minutes, engine first in forty feet of water. Those of us who survived the crash were immediately taken prisoner. After three months in captivity in a prisoner of war camp, Japan surrendered to the Americans and our Black Cat airmen were liberated by the U.S. Marines. None of us survivors would have made it without Bob's quick handling of the aircraft." Hank said, "We are so sorry for your loss and we hoped you can find some solace in knowing that Bob did everything he could to help save the lives of his crew." He added, "We all loved Bob like a brother."

Ruth's husband, Lt. Bob Hepting was shot down on July 1, 1945, just five weeks before the bombs were dropped on Hiroshima and Nagasaki, which ended the war. Bob and Ruth's daughter, Nancy Ruth Hepting was born December 13, 1945.

Perk's 17-year-old brother, Seaman 1st Class Maurice Perkins was officially listed as killed in action on April 7, 1944. He was on board the USS Aaron Ward, which sank during the battle of Guadalcanal on April 7 1943. As with Lillian and Fred Perkins, thinking of their son, Maurice, the last image they remember of him was as he waited at the bus to go to San Francisco.

> "It is rather for us to be here dedicated to the great task remaining before us that from these honored dead, to that cause for which they gave the last full measure of devotion, that we here highly resolve that these dead shall not have died in vain."
>
> —Abraham Lincoln

Both families mourned their sons, the children they would never meet, the marriages they would never know and the lives they would never have. Although Ruth remarried nine years after Bob Hepting's death, she never stopped loving Bob. When Ruth was 92, at the end of her life, she still had his picture on her dresser. His absence passed over Ruth and Nancy like a fog, never quite fulfilled with what could have been.

Both families joined those other American families who mourned the 416,800 U.S. military servicemen and women who had lost their lives.

Epilogue

THE BOURICIUS AND PERKINS families welcomed their remaining daughters and sons home after the war. Lavonne Bouricius was a WAVE, and her brother Bob Bouricius had been in the Army. Both were in the South Pacific and came home to marry and raise families. Dottie's two brothers, Bart and Willard Bouricius, worked on the top secret Manhattan Project at the University of Chicago and at Los Alamos, New Mexico. They returned from the war and married and had three children each. Willard stayed on working into the 1950s at the Nuclear Science Lab, at Los Alamos at what would eventually become the U.S. Department of Energy. Bart came home and worked for the seismological lab in Golden, Colorado, and built a cabin near the Bouricius cabin for his family. Perk's best friend, Louis Messari, came home to raise a family and start an insurance business.

After Perk had flown 51 combat missions in Europe, he continued his service, recruiting airmen for the Army until the war ended. Perk never piloted an aircraft again. Dottie and Perk had two children, Gary and Holly. After finishing college, at University of California, Perk became a Mechanical Engineer. He spent his 35-year-career at North American Rockwell and Rockwell International, both affiliated with Boeing Aircraft Corporation, the very company who built the B-17 bomber. He worked in the ever expanding rocket division as the Cold War got underway in 1945 between the United States and the Soviet Union. Perk helped design the guidance systems for the Minuteman Nuclear Rocket Program, pushing man's inventions to the far reaches of outer space and guiding them back to Earth.

It has been 78 years since the end of World War II and most of the boys that flew those B-17s are gone. Perk died at age 82 in 2003 and Dottie passed away in 2005. Their families remember those men and women who fought bravely, even giving the "last full measure of devotion," as Maurice Perkins and Bob Hepting did, for peace after that unimaginable war.*

---

* Estimates put the death toll of WWII in those 30 countries involved in the war in Europe and the South Pacific at 78 million people including 24 million Russians. Shockingly, sixty percent of all Jews were killed in Europe and not long after the war, many survivors immigrated to the new nation of Palestine.

Author's Research, Bibliography of Resources and Articles

The primary research sources used in writing this book were interviews with family members: Gary Perkins, Danny Keef, Barbara Orloff, Nancy Hepting Claycomb, Ruth Bouricius Nippe, Dottie Perkins and Clarence "Perk" Perkins, Holly Perkins Smirl, John G. Massari's, Louis' son, family history logs, diaries of the Bouricius family. Red Collier, Don Collier's son, who supplied a brief log of the Perkins 51 missions.

Books

Crocker, Mel, *Black Cats and Dumbos: WWII's Fighting PBYs.* Crocker Media Expression, 2020.

Kessler, Lauren, *The Happy Bottom Riding Club: The Life and Times of Pancho Barnes.* Random House LLC, 2000.

Miller, Donald L., *Masters of the Air: America's Bomber Boys Who Fought the Air War Against Nazi Germany.* Simon & Schuster, 2007.

Minker, Ralph L. Sandra O'Connel, and Harry Butowsky, *An American Family in World War II.* Word Association Publisher, 2005.

Pappalardo, Joe, *Inferno*. St. Martin's Press, New York, 2020.

Parkin, Robert Sinclair, *Blood on the Sea: American Destroyers Lost in WWII*. SA Capo Press, 2001.

Snyder, Steve, *Shot Down: The true story of pilot Howard Snyder and the crew of the B-17 Susan Ruth*. Sea Breeze Publishing LLC, 2015.

Stevens, Charles N., *An Innocent at Polebrook—A Memoir of an 8th Air Force Bombardier.* 1st Books, 2004.

MacArthur, Robert Crawford, wrote the song in the 1939 "U.S. Air Force" song, also known as "Off We Go into the Wild Blue Yonder."

Articles

Stevenson, James Perry, "Arrogant U.S. Generals Made the P-51 Mustang a Necessity." Sea Breeze Publishing LLC.

U.S. War Department army website of the Eighth Air Force and the 99th Bomb Group, 15th Air Force.

U.S. Naval Historical Society—Maurice Perkins Seaman 2nd Class and on Lieutenant Robert Hepting.

The Eighth Army Air Force Museum and the 15th Foundation, 1306 Dahlgren Avenue, SE, Washington Navy Yard, DC 20374, Mailing Address: P.O. Box 15304, Washington, DC 2003.

National Aviation Heritage Area, 26 S. Williams St, Dayton, OH 45402.

Pyle, Ernie, "Here is Your War." New York: World Publishing Company, 1943.

Pyle, Ernie, "Last Chapter." New York: Henry Holt and Company, 1946.

Acknowledgments

I am grateful to all the people who provided me with valuable information in one form or another via email, phone interviews and in person. The primary research sources used in writing this book were interviews with family members: family history logs, diaries of the Bouricius family. Red Collier (Don Collier's son), who supplied a brief log of the Perkins 51 missions. Special acknowledgment to Gary Perkins, who followed Perk's war years and created scrapbooks and accounts of B-17 bomber pilots, conversed with Perk's former crew members and their families and shared all of his information and insight with me in order for me to write this book.

Thank you to Red Collier, who shared an account of his father's log of the Perkins combat missions.

My special appreciation to Louie Massari's son, John Massari, who shared a website and his father's information, before and during the war.

To Danny Keef for his account of Perk's story as he told it, on his way home with Perk, from Alaska, during the last year of his life.

To Dottie Perkins and Ruth Hepting who told us their stories verbally and through their diaries and letters.

To Nancy Claycomb who shared her father, Robert Hepting's story, as well as that of her mother, Ruth Hepting.

To Barbara Orloff, the only sibling left of Clarence Perkins' family, who shared information about Perk and her brothers, Richard and Maurice.

Thank you to Bob Smirl, Melena Smirl, Heather Wiebe and Lena Kane who read and edited this book, *Above and Beyond*.

Lastly, a special thanks to my father, Lt. "Perk" Perkins who, with his humble silence about the bravery of he and his crew on those 51 missions, inspired me to write this story.